T0106097

Outgrowing
FEAR

Cease Drinking from the Well

HIGHGEE

iUniverse, Inc.
New York   Bloomington

Outgrowing Fear
Cease Drinking from the Well

iUniverse books may be ordered through booksellers or by contacting:

*iUniverse
1663 Liberty Drive
Bloomington, IN 47403
www.iuniverse.com
1-800-Authors (1-800-288-4677)*

*Because of the dynamic nature of the Internet, any Web addresses or
links contained in this book may have changed since publication and
may no longer be valid. The views expressed in this work are solely those
of the author and do not necessarily reflect the views of the publisher,
and the publisher hereby disclaims any responsibility for them.*

*ISBN: 978-1-4502-4696-5 (sc)
ISBN: 978-1-4502-4697-2 (dj)
ISBN: 978-1-4502-4698-9 (ebook)*

Library of Congress Control Number: 2010932919

Printed in the United States of America

iUniverse rev. date: 02/10/2011

To my mother, who I can't express enough of my eternal love for and, my aunt-*sister mi*, who I loved equally as a mother, and my grandma, who in a subtle way taught me how to look at life.

CONTENTS

*'Wonderful' mind lives happy
in the confine of what they
define for it as reality;
it cherishes it,
lives by it,
dies by it.
On the other hand,
a free mind looks
deeper than the surface meaning.
Which one are you?*
Bob

*"It's not enough to know you are sure,
you have to know why you are sure."*
Ruth

The Search Begins

He sat in his favorite chair, out in the open as always, gazing at the stars that adorned the sky, wondering how the clouds broke and then merged into another. Sometimes a small patch of cloud would break away from the mother cloud and float, seemingly without direction on its own, maybe it was trying to find itself and its place in this vast universe, detaching from the collective consciousness. Also, he could form a picture of anything in the clouds and his thoughts and imagination would take to the heavens and beyond, developing wings and flying off, to where? Your guess would be as good as his. But one thing was certain, his thoughts were limitless. 'How did we get here? What is my purpose here? Is everything or anything real? Is there a beginning and will there be an end? What does it mean to be alive? What does it mean to die?'

Sometimes these questions pounded his brain--his mind, like waves hitting the shore, relentlessly and endlessly, and sometimes frighteningly. Few times things made partial sense, but most of the times they were totally nonsense. But deep inside him somewhere he knew he might not just have all the answers – maybe that was the way it was meant to be. But then, by whom and why? Why the mysteries?

Regardless of everything that went on in this man, he loved to celebrate life. Marveled at how the different and colorful species interacted with one another. The eternal conflict in nature –either to eat or be eaten; life depending on life for continued existence, the balance of a ball in space, the stars, and the people that used the stars to foretell the future of man, the ever nurturing part of Mother Nature and the ugly side, a world of opposites; yin and yang. But nevertheless, a beautiful place, and he cherished it with all the dangers, fears or what have you that went along with it. One of Louis Armstrong songs, *what a wonderful world,* popped up in his head and he smiled. So, wherever his thoughts took him, he was glad to be part of this world; glad to be part of the love and the pain. But the nagging question never went away. 'How did I get here?' He didn't have a clue! What could he have been other than a man, to contemplate nonexistence would be scary.

To that question it seemed everybody was willing to provide him a sure answer. He should look no further. But who was he going to believe and based on what? There were countless answers to one question!

Suddenly his thought was interrupted again. "Honey, honey," cried a woman's voice. "They've started another senseless fight, and the children, the elderly and the weak are going to pay the price, not forgetting raping the women – it comes with the package." She was pretty upset at the things man did to man in the name of one thing or another.

He ran to her and put his arm around her shoulders. "Everything will be all right." He said without believing a word of it himself. She was no dunce, either. It was just the right thing to say at the moment.

One of his thoughts sped back into his consciousness like a bullet train. Since time immemorial man had been at man's throat. Sometimes it could be perplexing trying to understand man. He was like a universe within a universe. Nature and the vastness of space could be mission impossible, but man, maybe he could dissect him, knock some sense into that thick skull, or rather, see how this well-oiled-machine worked. And no thanks to all the professors of theology trying to rationalize religion and man…and all the brain-scanning-scientists, too.

"Honey, just change the channel," he said, reaching for the remote. "Don't let it ruin our evening again." Choosing his words calmly and at the same time reaching even closer to her body.

Changing the channel was not changing the situation on the ground. What if this could be happening where he lived? What if? What if? But, whatever what if? Tonight he would brush that aside for later.

He held his wife closer and kissed her passionately on every part of her body. He could sense the frustration dissipating and gradually being replaced by something warm and cozy. Sweet sensation was flowing like an electric current from him to her and vice versa. "I'd like to rip your gown off right now, right here and make love to you like never before," he said in a soft and deep sexy voice. She always loved a little naughty talk.

"Hmm…what's stopping you?" She replied eagerly, already weakening at the knees. She started shedding her night gown, revealing her smooth olive skin, at the same time tilting her head back while removing the pin that held her long, jet black hair so it cascaded on her shoulders. She gave a faint sound and stared at him with her brown eyes as if she didn't know what would come next. She wrapped one of her long legs (a weakness for him) around him like a rescued girl holding on for dear life. She was only a couple of inches shorter, anyway. No one would have guessed she was in her late twenties. She still had her slim and well proportioned figure, probably because she ate right most of the time and was active in sports, just like she did in college, or it could be that nature was kind to her body.

They made love again and again, on the floor, on the dresser, every conceivable and inconvenient place in the room, however. The chemistry was still hot after eight years.

"Good night," he said, still holding her from the back as they tried to fall asleep together. "Sweet dreams, honey…Oh, what time do you want me to wake you up tomorrow? Remember your big project tomorrow, huh?" She asked in a tired but satisfied voice.

"I thought I just did it." He smiled, kissing the nape of her neck.

"Ah…yes dear, wake me up at six-ish. Thanks."

He let go of her and turned to his side of the bed. He couldn't sleep holding anyone, even with the most beautiful woman by his side. He didn't know why, he just couldn't, no matter how hard he tried and he did try. He would like to believe he still made passionate love as he did when he first discovered the beauty of making love, now that he was in his mid thirties. Whoever said sex would slow down after a while didn't know what he was saying. His favorite food still tasted the same, yummy. Why not sex, with the love of your life.

In his mind he had traveled to every part of the world and the universe, tasted every food, cherished everywoman, and argued every point or discussion, whatever you would like to call it. He had seen the ugliest side of man and the amazing spirit of oneness that couldn't be matched by the crudest nature of man. With all his food tasting and contesting every single point and the adoration of all women, he never gained any weight or physically fought to defend his points or womanized in reality. He believed strongly in one man, one woman. But the question of soul mate was still hanging in the air.

And the imaginary life mirrored the actual one everyone knew about. Right down through his lineage it seemed every race had contributed one chromosome or another to usher him into what constituted as life on this planet. The final product stretched on the bed at 5'9 with a curly black, low cut hair and a round face with pointed nose. Women jokingly teased him that he looked like them. He took it as a compliment. Like his wife, he was not that muscular. He did not even dream of it, but was athletic. Maybe his birth had prepared him to question things or it could be his curiosity to know things himself that propelled him on this difficult and thankless mission. He was one of many. This was not the virgin miracle. This was man transcending barriers to love one another physically and emotionally, disregarding the norms of the society.

The questions raged on; his gender, tribe, race, culture, nationality, politics, eternity, and the number one on his list that seemed to tie everything together for him. 'Why do I have to believe in God?' He understood why he had to be good and why not to be bad, why to love and not to hate, the God-thing just smelt like a rotten broccoli. But by all accounts, he perfectly understood that religion was not the only ill that plagued man; it had many equally toxic institutions that rivaled it. It was just a fertile land to man's mind and heart; a nice place to start the incision.

"Sleep tight, honey." He forced the words out of his mouth. With his light skin barely showing under the covers he drifted off to sleep.

The alarm went off at Seven o'clock for some unexplainable reason. He didn't remember setting the alarm. His alarm had always been his wife, the ever so dependable when you needed to make an appointment in time. Thank goodness for light sleepers. He got up reluctantly, still half asleep, his eyes still half closed. He reached for Ruth on the other side of the bed. As he was still scrambling around the room a note fell from the dresser.

"Ruth…honey," he called her but there was no answer. She had forgotten to wake him up. This was unusual. She was the timekeeper of the house. There was no need to worry about that now.

He rushed to the bathroom, turned on the faucet to wash his face. The cold water woke every cell in his body and he started humming a tune in his head as he brushed his teeth. One of the things this guy could be proud of was his quick dressing. He ran downstairs throwing his jacket on as he was going. It matched the shirt and pants. He was never a dandy dresser, just something simple, but he never wore a tie. He always wondered whether that made man smarter or incomplete. He was a simple man. And he would like to keep it that way.

He got into his old, light blue BMW and zoomed off. As he was about to turn right he caught a glimpse of the two-story-building he called home in his rear mirror, wondering whether he locked the gate. His stomach was growling. He wasn't that hungry but would find something to eat after meeting with his boss. He glanced at his briefcase; every document he brought home was in there. Luckily for him there wasn't that much traffic. Still he got to his office a little bit late.

He now had to find all the remaining paper work left in his desk drawers to take to Frank's office. He was still scrambling when the door opened.

Frank stepped into his office and shouted his name. "Bob, you're late! Anyway, there's this new project that I need you to work on now. That can wait...Overseas Construction can wait. Maybe I'll find someone to continue where you left off."

Bob was completely lost by now. He had already prepared for this job for months and now he had to shelve it.

"But sir," he protested.

"No, but sir, this takes precedence over that and you are just the man for this job." Frank said spreading the new plan on the table.

He stood up to register his complaint, yet he ended up looking up at his boss's face literally at 6'5, and a huge body to match, with a goatee that seemed out of place. Taking him down was out of the question. A martial art expert would think twice, too. Sometimes he wished he could stare him down with the kind of decisions he made. He knew of a short-man-syndrome, but how would the psychologists explain this towering one. This guy was no Napoleon. But he didn't have to stand on a stool to level the gaze, he only had to learn to say no and that would do it; damning the consequences. But...but this time he would do as commanded.

"A new complex must be built within nine months." He continued without that much care about his objection. "This project is important; you know I wouldn't do that to you, right? It's from above. And besides, you have always wanted something done to the massive land that surrounds this building. I can recall you saying, 'this land can house a small city,' huh." He said pointedly.

"Let's take a walk. I'll introduce you to your team. And...whatever you think of them, don't worry they are professionals. Overlook the outward appearance, okay." Frank cautioned.

Bob was scratching his head, a look of what was this guy saying was stamped all over his face. 'I know he drinks, but it's only seven-thirty or so in the morning. Well, you never know sometimes.' He thought.

They both walked out of his office and headed to the conference room that was big enough to host twenty people. And the faces that greeted them explained Frank's warning when they opened the door.

Bob looked at the group and was speechless; he couldn't find the words to describe them. 'Something is wrong, something is really wrong.' He kept repeating it in his head. 'This isn't normal.'

"Here is the man to coordinate the whole project. His name is Bob. He will be back to get to know you guys." Frank said as if in a hurry. Actually, he just wanted Bob to have some time to himself before really knowing them. He knew him too well.

After they had their brief introduction and parted. Bob shut the door behind them and both headed to Frank's office. He wasn't known to stammer but not on this occasion.

"I...I...I...can't work with these people. They will tear themselves apart. We will never get any work done. Is this some kind of a joke?"

Frank pushed his small glasses to the edge of his nose and stared down at him. He spoke in a deadpan manner. "Bob, I hate to play on words right now, but have faith." Still he couldn't help laughing quietly. "They will work with you and anyone that doesn't will be fired." He pushed the folder to him and left.

Minutes later Bob stood there, his heart racing, his hands trembled a bit. He thought briefly about how to approach the situation. Nothing was coming to him. Maybe it would be better to let the chips fall wherever. Holding his breath, he decided to take a walk to clear his mind. But whatever, he needed to gather his strength before facing his crew. This wasn't just him alone trying to figure out why this world was like this in his head. And his head always stayed attached after every argument with himself, but with this group he had to tread cautiously.

✶✶✶✶✶ ✶✶✶✶✶ ✶✶✶✶✶

They were all waiting in the conference room expecting a briefing on the assigned job; what needed to be done and how. They sat in their seats like a regular breed of workers. Each one was in a world of his own. An outsider would automatically see the scene as a cultural exchange program, but in this case there was an embedded and a highly explosive time bomb. This wasn't an avenue for exchanging ideas; everyone maintaining an uncompromising stance.

The door swung open and a man who seemed like he didn't belong to the group walked in. He was wearing a pair of jeans and a white shirt with black shoes. He appeared to be in his early twenties, but a closer look showed he had aged much more than that. Even his clear blue eyes were beginning to fade. His thick eyebrows and bushy moustache didn't help to make him look his age, either. Coupled with all that he walked with a slight limp not caused by an accident but probably by strutting to impress the girls in his teen years. He had tried so many times to change it, but it had become second nature. He took the first empty seat available. He sat heavily and heaved a sigh of relief.

"I'm so glad I got this job." Den said.

All attention was now shifted to him. But he was oblivious of the faces staring at him. He just continued thinking out loud.

"I'm so glad I got this job. I was at the end of my rope. My life was becoming unbearable and that's an understatement. I lost a dear friend. He committed suicide. A good man, but so unfortunate. He was in debt and didn't know how to get out of it. Credit cards were piling up to rival Mount Kilimanjaro. And on top of that he lost his wife to cancer." He said with a bittersweet emotion.

"All he needed for strength was Jesus, in fact, everybody – poor soul. He had committed a grave offence in the face of God. Was he a Christian?" Fred asked in a preachy tone. The question was left unanswered. Den couldn't understand why anyone would say what had just been said. But before he could gather his thoughts for a reply another man was giving his sermon on the same topic.

"In Islam, I'm sorry to say, Allah will punish him gravely in hell." Ahmed added his unsolicited answer, too.

Den couldn't believe his ears. Had he died and gone to hell himself. His eyebrows came together in a frown making him look like he only had one eyebrow. He hated doing that to his face that needed all the help it could get. But whenever he lost his cool he didn't care. Then he took a careful look at the room. What he saw shocked him; he had to be in the wrong building or room or something, any place but this place. As he got up to leave he heard another voice.

"He'll just have to come back and do it all over again." Richard said without any serious concern, looking directly at Den. And the man that sat next to him just nodded in agreement with Richard. As Den took another step towards the exit, backing away slowly from all these zombies he sensed someone was blocking him at the door.

Bob came back, fully prepared, into the room to familiarize himself with his heavenly team. As expected he knew the war of words had started. He stepped in and there was a complete silence. He looked around the room and saw Den standing by the door about to leave.

"You must be Den, right, the new guy?' Den couldn't believe his ears again. 'Am I supposed to be with this group of people?' He thought.

"Have a seat." Bob said.

Den slowly sat down at the end of the room. His heart was beating fast. With all his rational thoughts he still couldn't fathom why he found himself in the midst of this group. But one thing was for sure, if dining with the devil to secure a steady pay check was all it would take, then he was ready. That would be a panacea for the hell ride he was about to take. He had to learn to use a very long spoon.

Bob pulled a chair and sat down, too. "Please, continue to have whatever conversation you guys were having. This is not official and besides I'm not very official, as long as we get the work done, I'm happy. You can discuss about the rain, the moon, why, how, when, what...that's fine by me. So feel free." That was a subtle metaphor in his mind. He was trying not to offend anyone, at least this early; calm before the storm.

By now Jack was fuming with anger. He had wanted to reply to this bunch of self-righteous clowns earlier. But given the go ahead by the boss, he blew open the Pandora's Box. The box would never be closed or patched together again.

"Somebody was telling a heartfelt story of his life and all you guys could talk about was how his friend was going to hell or coming back. Where's your humanity? Where's your sympathy? Where is your compassion? Where is the love you guys shout about every day and night? Give this guy something even if you don't mean it, for crying out loud!" There was a chorus of sorry but he wasn't finished with them yet.

"I'm really losing my patience with you guys." Jack continued. "You guys do nothing but argue about your religion and how we all should follow you like sheep. Who the hell started all this nonsense?"

He was looking at all of them dead in their faces. He prided himself to stare down the devil. He went with no rules and abided by none. According to him, there was only one constant: "If it's not right now, it wasn't right then." He put down a copy of the plan of the complex he was looking at and wiped his forehead with the back of his hand, and then took a sip of the cold coke in the other.

Den did a double take on Jack. He had missed him when he scanned the room. Starring back at him was a stocky, bald headed man in his late thirties. The way he was sitting down his height couldn't be more than 5'6, but he packed a lot of muscle. Iron man he nicknamed him, already. His verbal outburst matched his strength, totally.

"Hey, someone should be my guest and answer that." Jack said in anger. "Ahmed." He blurted. "I hear one Mohammed started your religion." It was more of a statement than a question, looking for an answer from anybody. This guy had made them uncomfortable with his blunt look at things.

"Well," replied with confidence written all over his face. Obviously this guy didn't know the facts. "You're wrong." Ahmed said assertively. He wanted to stand up to give them a lecture but decided to remain seated. He was a couple of feet taller than Jack. He had just cut his long hair so he could wear his small hat so that it would fit neatly on his head, looking the part he was meant to and, his beard just started growing fully to his delight. He was a slim man with piercing, hazel eyes, eyes that could say a thousand words without the help of the mouth. His skin was perfectly tanned. Sun worshippers would die for it.

"Mohammed (May the blessings of Allah be on him) didn't start Islam or the religion," he continued, picking his words painstakingly.

"The Arabs have always worshipped the same God of the Jewish people, but the problem with them was that they also worshipped hundreds of gods which went contrary to Allah's law. Mohammed was chosen by The God to go remind the people to come back, so to speak, to him – Allah. Because…," He said it in a way to show this group of infidels how wrong they were. "The Jews and the Christians had corrupted the words of God and, Mohammed was to warn all people concerning this issue."

"So, he didn't come to condemn the Torah and the Bible?" Fred interjected with a hint of suspicion.

Ahmed glanced at the chubby face of Fred and was tempted to say shut up, fat and ugly, but restrained himself. He stretched his left palm out suggesting he would answer his question in time.

"Of course not, he came to correct the words of Allah, and also being the last prophet of God to mankind; everyman." He said emphatically.

> *Surah 25:48*
> *It was he who created man from water.*
> *In six days he created the heavens and the earth*
>
> *Surah 61:1*
> *Jesus son of Mary, who said to the Israelites:*
> *"I Am sent forth to you from God to confirm the Torah*
> *And to give news of an apostle that will come after me*
> *whose name Is Ahmad.*

"And if anyone of you fails to listen to him, then you are condemned to eternal torture in hell."

If there was a difference between the Christians and the Muslims it was typified by the slender looking and tall Ahmed and the robust and short Fred. There was no need to wonder whether Fred had the Napoleonic trait; it was written all over his demeanor.

But before he could continue to lecture them, Rajiv interrupted.

"I agree with you to an extent." Acting like a teacher who told his student, you were right to this point, but? But Ahmed completely ignored this Indian looking man who had stayed too long in the sun according to him. In terms of body structure you could hardly tell them apart, but their skin tones were sharply different. Rajiv stopped interrupting for a minute. He obviously was waiting for his chance to speak. Bob wondered what Rajiv would add to Ahmed's words or omit from it.

Ahmed continued with a stern look on his face, but the frown didn't stop Fred from quickly putting a word in, again.

"Why would God want to write another holy book?"

This time Ahmed looked straight at him. "Because you Christians and the Jews corrupted his words, so he sent Mohammed, the last prophet, to correct it. These are God's words dictated to him by angel Gabriel. Weren't you listening?" He let out a big sigh.

"Well, if you can be patient." Rajiv said making a face at Ahmed.

"Just let me finish." Ahmed shot back.

Right then Rajiv took over the conversation with a steady and determined tone not to be cut off, again.

"Anyway, what I wanted to say was that Mohammed couldn't have been the last prophet because Mirza Husayn Ali was made the prophet of our time by God." Rajiv said vehemently.

The beginning of the confusion had started. How would anyone make sense of it now? Their outward appearances were matching the inner ones; hard to ignore. How would anyone be able to separate the man from his shadow? It would be a daunting task.

"Who was he?" Ahmed asked in disbelieve.

"Hey, hey," Rajiv was trying to make himself clear to Ahmed. "I'm not saying the Koran is not the words of God. And if I may say also, the Torah and the New Testament, all are words of God, but what we are saying doesn't contradict all these holy books. It's just that the holy book revealed to Prophet Ali supersedes all others."

Baha'i Holy Book
Having created the world and all that liveth and moveth
therein, he chose to confer upon man the unique distinction
Baha'I faith upholds the unity of God, recognizes the unity
of his prophets, and inculcates the principle of the oneness
and wholeness of the entire human race.

Ahmed had heard enough. Who the hell was Mirza, calling himself a prophet and what kind of religion was Baha'i, anyway? He got up and stomped out of the room.

"I can't stand here and be insulted by infidels. We shall see during judgment day. I will see what will save you all; you unbelievers." He said in annoyance as he walked out.

There was a brief silence. Then Rajiv said, "Can I continue now since the intolerant man has left?" He got the green light from the group.

"You see, the revelation that God gave Ali was for the unity of all people and all religions. We are all one now, there are no more divisions."

"That sounds like a good idea. I don't believe what you said but anything that brings unity I'm for it." Bob joined in the conversation, feeling a bit relaxed. Jack nodded in agreement.

"But tell me, what happened to this guy?" Jack would like to know more.

"What do you mean 'this guy'? Rajiv quickly corrected him. "He was a mighty prophet – the one to unite all."

"Okay, I'm sorry." Jack offered his apology. "So what happened to Prophet Ali?"

"Unfortunately there was hostility from the Muslims and it resulted in carnage and destructions of properties just because they didn't want to hear the truth. The prophet died in 1892, but before he died, he appointed his son to continue to interpret the holy book to anyone that would listen." Rajiv stopped.

This was new information to most people in the room, especially Fred.

"So where did all this happen?" Fred inquired. Since this guy was giving them a history lesson, who remembered dates when talking about general stuff. He never thought that anyone could confront the Muslims in the Middle East. They never taught him this in school. He grew up knowing about the Jews and Jesus, and the other religion as he used to refer to it – Islam. Now he would add Baha'i faith to the list of all the fake religions in the world.

"Oh, it took place in the Persian area, the present day Iran. But now our headquarters is in Haifa, Israel." Rajiv answered.

"Oh gee." Jack exclaimed. "Talk about the Middle East sitting on a religious time bomb."

"It seems there's a pattern here." Richard said thoughtfully. He continued to make small designs on the blank sheet of paper on the table. He definitely was the oldest in the group, pushing 50, but you would never have guessed because he looked like he was in his thirties. His grey hair would be the only thing that would show otherwise. He was in great shape.

"But before I go into that, I think man has always wanted to find answers to the meaning of life, but the man that finally helped the world to see clearly was Siddhartha Gautama, popularly known as Buddha. And it wasn't out of suffering that he went searching for the truth, rather, he had all the material comfort any man in any age could have, yet within him something was missing." He paused.

"Yeah...what was missing was Jesus." Fred said with enough conviction for the entire Christendom. But he would be lectured for putting his foot in his mouth.

"My friend, Jesus wasn't even conceived then." Richard replied as a matter of fact. Hopefully, that would make Fred to think before rushing to condemn everything in sight.

"How did he make his money?" Jack asked.

"He was the heir to a small kingdom; a prince...like I was saying." Richard continued with the same soft voice as if no one had interrupted him boorishly. "He left everything behind, the family, and all the material comfort in search of Nirvana."

Jack made a nice gesture to speak. Richard acknowledged it. "What's Nirvana?"

"I'll get to that soon," replied Richard gently and he went on from where he left off.

"He followed the Hindu ways of ascetic living in order to be close to God but discovered that didn't give him what he was seeking. So he abandoned that method and decided to continue to meditate for days and days under a tree called Bohi. There he sat in meditation until he found or reached Nirvana, which means enlightenment. He founded the Four Noble Truths and Eight Principles.

Four Noble Truths
1.   Suffering exists

2. There's a reason for why suffering exists.
3. And there's a way to end suffering.
4. The only way is through what he called the Eight Principles.

The Eight Principles are
1. Having the right View – Knowing and understanding the Four Noble Truths.
2. Having the right Thought –That is letting go of wants and desires and acting with kindness to avoid hurting anyone.
3. Having the right Speech – That is telling the truth, speaking kindly and wisely.
4. Having right Action – That is not to steal or cheat.
5. Having right Livelihood – That is earning a living that doesn't cause bloodshed or harm others.
6. Having the right effort – That is encouraging and developing positive thoughts in order to keep the path.
7. Having the mindfulness –Again, that is being aware of thoughts and actions that affect the world now and in the future.
8. And lastly, having the right Concentration – This is the end result of a peaceful state of mind that arises through the 8th fold path.

"And he started teaching anyone that wanted to know. He was of the mind that all the deities worshipped in the Hindu religion were themselves in a state of evolution. Of course, he didn't disagree with the Hindu religion completely, he acknowledged Karma and Reincarnation." Richard stopped.

He looked at them with a gesture that they could ask all their questions. Fred jumped to the opportunity. Maybe he would ask an informed question after he had been schooled that Jesus wasn't the first to advocate acting towards others with kindness in recorded history. Love thy neighbor was thought of hundreds of years before his messiah surfaced. Whoa!

"You didn't mention God. Did he find God under the tree?" Fred asked cautiously.

Richard couldn't help laughing this time. "Heh, heh, no, my friend, for some reason he found Nirvana – a state of total bliss and never having to reincarnate into this world, which according to him was the goal of every man or soul, and the notion that God was in some place of existence wasn't true. According to him, nothing could exist outside anything. There's no Supreme Being."

"Interesting…very interesting," Bob couldn't stop himself – "everybody was busy creating their idea of what God was, but he took the opposite direction."

"That's what they tell you," Thomas said sarcastically, a Westerner who had gone to India on a relief project when he was only twenty-one. And decided to stay there and got converted to Hindu religion to the dismay of his parents and friends. Asked him why and he always gladly gave his answer, 'it fulfils me.' How could anyone doubt that? It had been fulfilling him for the past eleven years now. He had always felt he was born in the wrong place. He favored the Indian skin to his white one, unlike Jack who was indifferent.

"If Richard could detect a pattern when you guys were talking about the founders or the beginning of your faiths, then maybe the joke is on him. They took my faith and made some of it their own." Thomas said without looking at Richard. "You can call Buddhism a breakaway religion?" He added as a matter of fact, too.

"There's no God in Hinduism, too?" Fred asked. He was finding it really easy to ask questions about other faiths. After all, no other religion made sense apart from Christianity. All others had to be questioned and condemned.

"No, no, in Hindu there's a Supreme Being. In the Hindu religion God takes many forms; one of the forms is as Vishnu – the preserver of life, then as Brahma – the creator, and then as Shiva – the destroyer. To run the world affairs, Brahma – the creator, created demi-gods like Inra – the rain god, Surya – the sun god and Agni – the fire god. So, to the Hindu worshippers, the Supreme Being has limitless forms. And with everything he created, they were created in pairs. God, Vishnu, is accompanied by Goddess Lakshimi and they display the full power of God the Supreme, god Brahma is assisted by Sarasvati but they demonstrate only partial powers of the Supreme Being.

"And then the animals and humans, also in pairs – male and female. But in the spirit realm all of us live beyond the dual nature of the material world, and exist there as perfect beings in full freedom, knowledge and bliss. It's only in the material world that suffering exists…like birth, sickness, old age and dying.

"The interesting thing is that Vishnu enters the world as an avatar; meaning the one that has come down from up there to help humans find truths and unravel the illusion of materialism. Once he took the form of Krishna, and then also as Ram. And our holy book is the Bhagavad-Gita, which means song of the lord and in there; there are stories of how man interacts with God and God with man." Thomas said proudly.

It was as if he had put a spell on everybody to be quiet. After all, Hindu religion was considered to be the first religion of man, debatable though.

"I've always thought that every Hindu worshipper had a separate God. Now I understand the many forms the Supreme Being takes to appear to the worshippers of this ancient religion." Bob broke the spell of silence.

"Oh, I didn't tell you one important thing concerning my religion, and that is we believe in Karma and Reincarnation. People try to have good karma in order not to keep coming back to this material world so they can go back and be one with the Supreme Being." Thomas added.

"But why are all these religions concentrated in Asia and Middle East?" Bob asked curiously. "What about Australia before the advent of the white man and South America and Africa? They had no God or someone with a holy revelation in those parts of the world?" Everyone was looking at one another like those places didn't matter, boss.

But John made a gesture that he would fill in the blanks on that. For some uncanny explanation he appeared to have answers to the questions at hand; about man and his thousands of Gods.

But for some reason it seemed it was Fred's turn to explain or rather to tell his own story of creation. He was tilting towards being labeled fat; one more slice of pizza and it would be official. He was the shortest man in the group, but he compensated that with the way he charged and harassed others with his questions. He could be that size but he wouldn't be ignored. His white skin seemed to glow when making a point. Age wise, he was a couple of years older than Den. He sensed it and said "I don't have to explain anything. It's the most widespread story, because it's true, unlike everything I've been listening to so far."

Den, who had kept quiet all along and had accepted his fate to work with this lot of people, replied him. "But mister, I only hear bits and pieces of the story of how the Christian God created the world."

"All right, I'll tell you." Fred accepted reluctantly.

> *Genesis Chapter 1 Verses 1-26*
> *In the beginning God created the heaven and the earth.*
> *And the earth was without form and void, and darkness was upon the face of the deep.*
> *And the spirit of God moved upon the face of the waters.*
> *And God saw the light that it was good, and God divided the light from the darkness.*
> *And God called he light – Day and the darkness he called Night. And the evening and the morning were the first day.*
> *And God said let the earth bring forth the living creature after his kind cattle and creeping things and the beast of the earth after his kind, and it was so…*
> *And God said, let us make man in our image, after our likeness: and let them have dominion over the fish of the sea, and over the fowl of the air, and over the cattle, and over all the earth.*

"God created all this in six days and on the seventh day, he rested." Fred conceitedly said. "Does that hold true for you, Isaac?" Jack wondered.

"So far, so good, if there's anything missing in our story I'll surely help my Christian brother." Isaac said authoritatively, putting his stamp on it as a Jew; the rightful owner.

"I find it fascinating that you guys are opening up and discussing your faiths this way without throwing punches. It's quite commendable." John was full of praise. He had kept very quiet and seemed not to be visible among the group other than the occasional references here and there.

Everyone turned to Yusuf, as if to say, your turn.

This man could be lost in a crowd of three. Everything about him screamed little; even his long beard looked small with a few strands starting to turn grey, giving him a rather distinguished look. He had to speak at the top of his voice which drained him of energy. He had learned to conserve his strength and only spoke when absolutely necessary. He was closer in age to Richard but really dark skinned. As he was about to start talking Ahmed came back in. It was as if he never left. Nobody paid any attention to him. He had decided not to let the infidels ruin his chance of a good job.

"Guru Nanak was the founder of my religion." Yusuf started. "He was a man endowed with wisdom and unparalleled abilities. He studied with the best out there and was always in contemplation. He was one of a kind, a man of God.

"He went to the river as he always did, but on one particular day he never returned and they thought that he had drowned. They didn't see him for three days, only his clothes were found at the shore.

"After three days he resurfaced and declared that God neither belonged to Hindu nor Islam, and the only thing that everyone should do was to follow God, of course the Muslims were enraged and this led to bloodshed just because of the revelation that God showered on him."

Yusuf stole a peek at Ahmed, who simply ignored him at this time. He already decided not to get angry at them. Judgment day would come soon.

"And yes, we do believe in reincarnation and karma. To us heaven is when you finally rejoin God and hell is to be reborn on earth." Yusuf concluded.

"What is the name of your religion?" Den asked. He was beginning to lose count of all these prophets and their revelations, apparently coming from the same God!

"Sorry, the name of my religion is Sikhism. And the word 'Sikh' means follower, once you see a turban, you see a Sikh." He tapped his head gear proudly and his beard seemed to shake. His eyes and nose looked tiny having been overshadowed by the beard and the turban.

Yusuf looked to John for some kind of approval. Did he miss anything out? John nodded in agreement like a master and followed with a knowing smile. But Thomas shook his head and said with satisfaction. "Yet another breakaway."

Just as everyone was looking for more history of a religion the door opened suddenly. Bob's boss stepped in. He looked around the room and the faces that stared back were curious to know what to come next.

"Well, seems everybody's having a good time. We are experiencing a slight delay with certain supplies. But in no time we'll fix that, and once that's done, we'll have a little respite because we've got to lay the foundation of the complex and there will be no more sitting around while you're being paid. Okay, guys." Frank said it like a boss losing money, shut the door and left.

No one had to tell him the topic going on in there, he just knew. You gathered a group of politicians or sports fans of opposing sides together and, you would have a recipe for volatile argument. No crystal ball was needed to unravel this mystery.

"It's a good thing the company pays anyway." Fred said.

"It's a contract. They have to pay." Den replied.

"I sure need the money." Ahmed agreed after a long silence.

Everybody seemed to be in agreement with Den.

"This is one area no one disagrees with." Bob murmured, laughing. And everyone joined in the laughter.

"Who doesn't want his pocket filled with green? Money is God." The laughter suddenly stopped and all eyes turned to Jack and he was quick to offer his apology.

"I'm sorry guys, really sorry."

Before they could descend on him further, John came to his rescue.

"Hey, back to the subject of man and God." John's voice boomed. The anger in the room appeared to lessen a little. Everyone respected John's historical knowledge of events, which was beyond an average man's. He exuded an aura of all that could be known and that also came with the respect and sometimes, fear and hatred, too. How people knew this was a mystery in itself. Maybe they had heard him speak of something that was profound.

He grew up in a wealthy family in Ethiopia. One of the fortunate ones, but he put the money to use by traveling around the world and studying with all major religions or cults out there. The rest of the family saw him as weird. He took that in good faith. He was as curious as a cat, but curiosity wouldn't kill this one.

All his thirty-two years he was on a quest, he always told himself, to find out things and to experience them, too, first hand. Indeed he had been privileged to have some unique experiences but would only share certain ones due to the level of consciousness a particular person or group he engaged. He learned that the hard way. Nothing was out of his scope of interest, science, religion, nature, love and so on, except the mundane stuff which he cared very little about. He kept his moustache trimmed, not to make a statement, he just kept it. His hair was short and a little bit curly but not that black which went well with his light, brown skin. He never bothered about peoples' personal stories, always wondered what that would do to his personal life. He always kept to topical issues. He only talked about others if they told him their stories; nevertheless, he still drew the line. He would do well in the social scene but shunned it. He could shake it well on the dance floor with the best of them standing at 5'9.

"We'll be doing a great deal of injustice to many other people's Gods or how they thought God created the world or how the world came to be." John began. He was obviously willing to share his wealth of knowledge on the issue. And like good students, they appeared ready to absorb new insight about other people's ways of reasoning, though they might be seen by them as falling short of their accepted religions.

"Has anyone heard of the Aztecs?" He inquired. Only Jack nodded.

"Okay, the story goes something like this. According to the Aztecs, Ometecuhiti and his wife, Omelchihuati, created the world. Ometecuhiti - the Supreme Being also created the lesser gods to help him run the various departments in the world. And he put man as the head of all animals. The people pretty much worshipped all these nature based gods; like the god of the sea, god of the land, and what have you. But the interesting thing is that the Jews share the claim of being the chosen with the Aztecs in the world." John glanced at Isaac for his reaction. True to form, Isaac was shocked to hear that but he hid it well.

"Were they also the Mayans, I get it confused sometimes." Jack wanted clarification.

"No, the Mayans were different and, I actually find their story of creation even more fascinating. Most creation stories say God used clay or sand to create man, but the Mayan Gods created man out of corn materials. They had two Gods called Tepeu and Gucumatz, and whatever these Gods thought about materialized. They thought of a tree and a tree appeared." John replied.

"But if they could do that, how come they had to create man from corn?" Bob cut into the story.

"Remember boss, this is religion, and religion and logic don't go hand in hand. Wonder why any God would take other peoples' land for his chosen?" John queried.

"It wasn't as if clay wasn't used at first." John went on, "but the Gods discovered that when it rained the clay dissolved. So they appealed to the mountain lions and the coyotes to find materials to create man. This was after wood was tried and that proved problematic, too. The animals eventually came up with the idea of using corn, and bingo, man was created."

Everyone was looking at one another as if to say, how could I be made of corn? John knew their thoughts and he would let them have it later.

"Oh, I failed to mention that they worshipped all these nature gods too; god of the sun, and surely, god of corn." John added.

Fred was beside himself with laughter. His chubby cheeks started to glow. "You have just described a classic pagan worship. It's our job to show the world the light." He said condescendingly.

"I disagree with you on that completely." John pointed out. "The word, Pagan, back in those early times was used for a group of people that practiced non-popular religion, and most of the times they moved to less populated areas to practice their faith in peace. (Funny, most of these religions got their Creators' names from them i.e. EL--Jewish God) And that's what you can term a peaceful religion, avoiding useless fighting and confrontation. That's why the Christians call anyone that doesn't believe in their own religion pagan worshipper." Fred looked away from John shamefacedly.

"Most of you cringed when you heard corn material was used to make man. But what we don't understand or fail to see is if our own chosen or given religion…way back when we were young told us that leaves were used to make man, it would make sense to us. It's our unfair nature at work here, not good judgment." John scolded them.

They all looked shocked at the way he reprimanded them, but he wasn't finished yet.

"With their corn god they developed one of the most amazing

civilizations ever known to man. We are not talking of mud houses here, but brick buildings with a city larger than NYC, and landscape that would blow your minds. They developed astronomy that people still refer to in this century. And they also created writing and a thriving culture and commerce, not forgetting arts and science. This was when the Western civilization was nowhere to be found; in the dark ages. They even built their civilization on eco-friendly atmosphere, what we are trying to do now.

"There are numerous cases of different people with their own cultures coming up with their unique way of finding out how to explain this mysterious world, and you can't discount any group's view or truth as they claim it with your own explanation, no matter how inconceivable or ridiculous it may sound to you. Proof is the only leverage here, period." John cautioned.

The door mysteriously swung open and in came a burst of fresh air, and it seemed to blow a little bit of tolerance into the group.

"Maybe you all would be glad to know that the Yoruba people of Nigeria say clay was used in making man." John smiled. "To them, the Supreme Being is called Oludumare, (neither female nor male) meaning the Ruler of heaven and earth. Oludumare also created about seven demi gods to run things down below. They have Sango – god of thunder and lightning, Ogun – god of iron, Iyemuja – goddess of the sea and so on. And people pray and sacrifice to them for favors or to fight their enemies.

One day God told Oduduwa, the first man created to go to earth which was full of water. He was to take some sand and a rooster with him and on getting there, after being lowered down by a chain, (by the way, they claim to still have the chain) to sprinkle the sand on the water and the rooster scattered it with its legs, that was how land came to be. From thereon man populated the world." He stopped to see whether they were paying any attention. They looked genuinely interested or maybe they were pretending to have an open mind.

"Obatala was in charge of fashioning man out of clay, amongst other functions as a demi-god and God would breathe life into them and they would come alive. Obatala was curious to know exactly how God performed this exclusive duty, so he pretended to fall asleep after preparing the clay forms, but God knew what he was up to, and God made him to really fall asleep. I guess that is where the mystery of life remained hidden in their story. When he woke up the clay forms had lives. He was disappointed."

John took a sip of water he always carried and then continued. He could talk for hours on topics like this and at times he would not say a word. A man of extreme opposites someone remarked a long time ago. But before he could go on, Fred posed a question.

"Do the Yoruba people believe in hell, because you just mentioned heaven?"

"No, they don't, since they believe in reincarnation and, judgment day and reincarnation don't go together as you Christians believe. Also you can see traces of rebirth in some of their names." He answered.

John had the floor now. Since most people only knew of their own story of religion or creation, he was ready to furnish them with other people's stories. He had become the unsolicited spokesman for the once upon a time religions.

"These religions might not be popular anymore, but people still practice them or they now have a dual religion, just like dual nationalism." John continued.

"Oh, back to the question of heaven and hell, I think I know why you asked, Fred. Christianity in recorded history wasn't the first to talk of good and evil, angels and demons, and heaven and hell. The Zoroastrian religion was the first to do so. And it even predated Judaism. Zoroastrian religion was the state religion in the present day Iran until Islam came, and now replaced it. I'm sure you can still find people practicing the religion to this day, few in number, though. By the way, the religion also has a virgin birth and of a messiah saving mankind someday. And if something predates something, how is the thing that it predates now comes before it?" John questioned.

Ahmed couldn't believe his ears. He was raised a Muslim, never had been in the midst of people like this. He knew about the Jews and the Christians from the Koran and what his Imams told him. He was standing on a shaky ground. Maybe the decision to come back wasn't a good one.

"Don't forget the Greeks." John jolted Ahmed back from his inner thoughts.

"They gave the world Zeus and many other gods; like Aphrodite – the goddess of love, Atremis – the goddess of hunting, and Zeus who was the God of gods, having a son on earth called Hercules – half

23

God, half man, like Jesus, fighting for justice. And don't forget in a hurry all the Egyptian Gods like Ra, Osiris, although they didn't do so well against the God of the Jews as we have been told to believe." He glanced at Isaac.

"Then in Japan, we have the Shinto religion, worshipping all kinds of spirits. Also, there is Taoism which means the way. Some aspect of this religion is making a comeback, especially in the Western world because of Feng Shui – the art of arranging your surroundings to allow the flow of spirits so that things work smoothly for the believers. But the interesting thing is that these religions – Buddhism, Shintoism and Taoism have an interlocking relationship. Buddhism influenced the Japanese religion, same way as Taoism." John added.

"Hey, hey, my head is spinning with all these religions." Den said helplessly.

"Look man, there are thousands of religions out there. Some borrowing from one another, some radically different; nevertheless, all are trying to explain life. There are old ones and there will be new ones. Religion is forever evolving, just like everything else." John replied sharply and added. "Don't forget the Rastafarians. Thanks to Bob Marley and the Wailers. I am sure you enjoy dancing or listening to him sing about Jah. They use the Christian bible and prefer to address God as Jah. It kind of started because of the oppression of the black people by their white masters. They have their hero in Hesalasi of Ethiopia with their distinguished colors of red, green and yellow. And they believe that the much awaited Jesus was Hesalasi, and Zion is in Ethiopia."

"Okay, okay…what about Scientology?" Jack asked.

"They are just teaching man how to use his mental power (mind over matter) to control his destiny. There's no talk of God here or heaven and hell." John explained as if that didn't matter much to the topic.

"Some people say the whites don't have a God of their own?" Jack asked again.

"That would be wrong. Remember famous Zeus in Greece and all those Roman Gods. But more importantly, most Europeans worshipped Danu, the Goddess, and the way of worship changed as the religion went from one culture to another, but basically the same Danu. It is just another nature-based-worship where you pay homage to what you believe brings you sustenance." John said clearly. "The Hare-

Krishnas on the other hand use the Bhagavad-Gita as their holy book but they separate themselves from Hinduism and Buddhism, just like the Rastafarians with the bible." John clarified.

He took a long sip of the bottled water. It was still a little bit cold and then went on.

"We can go on and on talking about all these religions forever, because from what I know, every language or culture comes with a religion, like a side dish at KFC. It is just the nature of man to question and find his own answers to the mystery of life." He said.

But, as best as he was trying to clarify issues, he found out they still looked confused and surprised like children trying to figure out how the magician performed his tricks.

"Look people," he boomed, "this is really simple to understand unless you think you are superior in any way to your fellow humans when it comes to god or no god. Every corner of the world man creates his own beliefs with his understanding of what is the creator, to give him some kind of spiritual comfort, just like he makes his own culture to determine his fate. But one thing is certain, when all people come together they discover that the universe is a house of many gods and there lies the clash of fates, cultures and plans, leading to intolerance and bloodshed. Really, man is trying to find the meaning of love if you can read between the lines. Now, how one religion becomes a major faith or not is not hard to figure out.

"We can conclude this talk with the Big Bang Theory. You might think science shouldn't be put together with religion but you'll be wrong. Because scientists too are searching for the origin of life, who or what started it. Though their big bang theory collapsed like a pack of cards, because before the bang there were particles that had to be explained how they got there. Nevertheless, they are searching, too. Now the scientists, at least, some of them, have come up with the String Theory, which I'm afraid is going nowhere, either, because in this theory there is an element of an invisible particle that can't be quantified or weighed by any scientific means. They believe in multiple worlds. Sorry...that didn't come out right. They have this theory of different dimensions of life simultaneously living side by side. Which leads some scientists to call it witchcraft science--pseudoscience. But the important thing with science is that you have to prove it. What appears to me in China should be able to be replicated by another person in Brazil.

25

Unlike all these religions that say, die first and you'll know or as Fela Anikulapo put it, *'suffer, suffer for world, enjoy for heaven'.*"

John looked around the room waiting for any more response, none. They all got up and headed to the exit as if the lecture was over, all of them with their inner questions and answers, wondering...

As they were all about to exit Den asked.

"What I don't understand is that we are on a path to finding love."

"Like I said before, we are here for something much more bigger than ourselves." Richard reminded the group. The group dispersed. Fred wanted to take the back door, but discovered that it led nowhere. He had no choice but to go through the front like everybody else.

"Skeptical scrutiny is the means, in both science and religion by which deep insights can be winnowed from deep nonsense."
Carl Sagan

"Our beliefs are the foundations we build our lives upon. Our beliefs are skewed, foundations are distorted. Period!"
John

Why I Belong

Jack and John sat under the oak tree. The shade was a welcome relief from the sizzling heat of the sun.

"I can rest here forever." Jack said crashing beside John, who shifted slightly.

"Yeah, it's a nice shield from the harsh reality of nature." He agreed.

"Talking about nature, does it mean we are bound or rather doomed to where we are born?" Jack asked inquisitively.

"I don't understand what you mean." John replied, trying to figure out what he meant.

"I mean, you're born in a certain place and you believe in the religion or what have you in that place. And the real question is what if they are wrong? I mean where you're born, believing wrongly, so to speak. I tell you, sometimes these people scare me. Of course, I don't want to go to hell." Jack managed a smile.

John smiled back and touched him on the shoulder and said. "From a little bit of what I know, I don't think that will happen. I don't know how to break this down for you. But always remember the human nature of wanting to be right even without proof of any reasonable knowledge of what he or she is saying. Another thing you have to put at the back of your mind is, more often than not, where a man lives determines his truth or how he sees life, which carries with it an inherent flaw to begin with."

Jack nodded in agreement. "Yeah, some of these beliefs are without sound basis." He found support.

"But they do create fear, and fear which is the basis of these religions is hard to get rid of sometimes." John added cautiously.

"How does one overcome the fear?" Jack wanted to know.

"There's a systematic way to it." John hinted.

"Systematic?" Jack doubted.

"The first place to start looking for clues is with our parents. Though it might sound so obvious, it's not. Most of us think we are damn lucky or chosen at birth by the real maker to be in the right place or family at the right time. Like a special tool for survival that your god has given you; it's a gift you mustn't reject." John started like a detective trying to solve a crime. "We grow up learning most things from them, their habits; good or bad, ways of talking, eating, their likes and dislikes and so on, because at that age we are impressionable. Faith or belief comes with the package. They drown us in whatever religion they practice. Really it's like a hand me down clothes, because his or her parents probably did the same. More often than not you become a reflection of your parents in the area of faith, and so you pass it down like an inheritance to your own family. You're born in a Muslim family – you become one, you're born in a Hindu family – you become one, too, you're born in a Christian family…(Sometimes with slight modifications)." John was about to finish the sentence.

"You become one." Jack filled in the blank.

"Again," John added thoughtfully. "It's not that cut and dried. Nonetheless, they sell it to you as the right thing to do, the right way to live your life and before you know it, you will be thinking as they think (it could be any of their philosophies in life, too; like lack of faith). Pounding it into our heads day and night makes most of us to yield. Then some children even take it a little bit further to the satisfaction of their parents. Thank God for blessed children.

"The other thing you have to consider is your society. To a larger extent the society dictates your religion, too; the origin of your so-called religion and why that religion. There are two aspects here; your native religion and the new popular one. You see, Jack, since man started walking on earth, there has been religion of some sort. So, religion has always been in man's psyche. Put simply, religion is just trying to find out why man is here, what for, and where does he go when he dies or passes on, whichever one you want to use. And sometimes when something that's mindboggling…some mysterious event in your life that can't be explained happens, you unwittingly attribute it to what the religion (pastor/Imam) in your village says or the new one, limiting your own ability to think or see things differently." John enlightened.

"Then, why leave one god for another or did other gods in other religions die?" Jack said curiously.

"No, no Gods died physically. This is what probably happened in such a case; man's idea of what's God changes with time. He's kind of growing in consciousness or awareness." John clarified.

"Hmm." Jack was thoughtful.

"The other aspect of the equation as per one god dying or not is helped greatly by the conquering race. Like the bees helping the flowers to pollinate." John began to shed more light on the subject.

"So the reason these beliefs spread wasn't because their prayers were answered or they were free of all the things that plagued man and his environment. On the contrary, and, especially Christianity and Islam, force was the name of the game. And once force had been used the rest was simple. Parents just passed it on to their children and it trickled down from generation to generation. Sometimes, societies did the same, whether by overt or covert means. And it didn't stop there; even some nations declared that everybody in the country must be of a particular religion.

"Take Christianity for example. The Roman Emperors made it a state religion, thanks in part to Constantine, who had a dream and in the dream he saw the sign of the cross…a symbol of a small sect in the Judaic religion. Remember the Romans worshipped the sun god amongst many other gods.

"In the dream the symbols of the cross and the sun god merged, and according to his interpretation of this heavenly vision without the two religions coming as one he would lose the battle he was about to engage in. So he ordered his army to put the sign of the cross on their shields, helmets and any of the hardware for battle. (You can still see countries in Europe bearing the symbol today on their flags) As it turned out, he won. So did Christianity in the heart of Rome. And this holy marriage of religions gave us the Christmas day to this day. The Roman Sun god which used to be celebrated on that day, 25th of December, now incorporated the birth of Christ on the same day. Jesus wasn't born on that day. Isn't it ironic, a religion of forgiveness spread and gained enormous acceptance because of war. Don't tell that to the born again and the yet to be. God works in mysterious ways.

"Thank goodness he didn't have a dream about the crescent moon or the Ra's symbol and we'd be saying another story now, and nobody... nobody will be any the wiser! Just like not many Christians know the origin of how the old and the New Testaments came about.

"With Constantine accepting the faith, he unknowingly created the hatred of the Jews to this day by the whites and the recipients of the faith. In fact, he wanted to get rid of the Judaic faith altogether when they refused to accept Jesus as their messiah. He burnt their synagogues and persecuted them. They called the Torah the Old Testament and he got the brand new one.

"The Roman empire was so huge it spread to North Africa. You know empires rise and they fall, and the only thing that's constant is change. So when Rome fell, the European colonial powers spread it like disease to the rest of the world. No place was untouched; Africa, North and South America, Asia and Australia.

"The religion systematically became the only way to see things. It became a White man's burden to save mankind after conquering it. It didn't matter whether other cultures and religions deemed it so. Might became right and miracle took the back seat. There's a famous saying by the African elites that goes like this, 'gun in one hand, bible in the other.'

"But of all the events of the spread of Christianity, the Spanish inquisition, which lasted over 400 years, was one of the worst where you couldn't even practice your old traditional religion. If you did you were put to death or tortured by the Christians. Christianity must be the only thing in your life in Spain and all her conquered territories. Only Christians were allowed to breathe oxygen or exhale carbon dioxide, to buy manure or make yours, to eat healthy meal or junk food, to drink holy water or well water, to be politically correct or just open your mouth and let it rip, to milk the cow or scratch your private part, or to grow more than 5ft or be skinny, or to smile or frown like Oscar, the grouch, or to read the bible or watch the Flintstones, or to steal, lie and fornicate, to have sex or to marry or take other peoples' properties or to cover up abuses either in the house God or in the larger society and, any other basic human necessities denied to people that didn't conform.

"It was more like the mark of the beast back then. They didn't need the computer chip with 666 inscription on the forehead to buy Giorgio Armani, Nike, Fubu or McDonald's, or appear in Soap Opera, or run for the presidency—(forget your birth certificate), or be an illegal immigrant, or do any sport, or be a conservative or liberal, or have your groove on, or join an army of one, or hunt for sport, or to be a fan of your team, or pump iron, or wear an afro and break dance, or watch 1000 channels, or be on no flight list, or wear Victoria Secret and maybe do a sex tape or show cleavage or sleep with children or have children or, even to drink your milk shake...or tweet every second." John pointed out.

"So that explains why so many Mexicans are Catholics today." Jack surmised.

"You're catching on fast." John added.

"Indeed, the human nature is complex." Jack was philosophical. "Despite of what they did to their forefathers in the name of Christ."

"Don't think the mayhem was limited to the outsiders, no, no, the Europeans persecuted themselves too to the point that it gave birth to the United States of America. The fleeing Europeans came in their thousands to the New Land because of religious persecution within Christianity and some minor reasons. The US became a land of the persecuted. Then, even within the US they continued to persecute one another, religiously. Australia was seen also as a refuge by the fleeing Christians from fellow Christians, apart from the other reason of sending bums, prostitutes and criminals to the place to cleanse England of riffraff by the monarchy. Just to show you that man as man doesn't know what he's doing.

"Then, the Muslims in the Northern part of Africa engaged in what they called holy war against the infidels. Of course, they hate the words, holy war or Jihad. Jihad means strive. You tell me what I'm striving for when fighting. Take the Berbers for instance, they were different from the Arabs but were killed for their lack of faith in Islam because they held on to their own faith and fun loving social culture." John added.

"This is like a double jeopardy for the black Africans. Did the Arab Muslims conquer them, too?" Jack said pitifully.

"You can say that again." John replied. "But not in the actual sense of the word. The Arabs couldn't extend their imperialism on the so-called sub-Saharan people like they did in Northern Africa and parts of Europe. But they traded in the trafficking of humans too, just like the whites. The triangular slave trade is somewhat more popular than the one carried out by the Muslims. And this trade went on for over 700 years, children included. You should see the chains they used, even on children to carry their cargo back home! The slaves bought and caught by the Muslims were taken to North Africa, Middle East and other places where Muslims were ruling; however, they were meant for servitude and the females were forced into prostitution by my understanding, but they would prefer to call it an unofficial marriage. They still do unofficial marriages to this day amongst their people. But the services of the captured and sold slaves were mild compared to the whites who had plantations that needed cheap and forced labor in order to function." John elaborated.

"It's a shameful thing to sell your own people into slavery...for what?" Jack couldn't understand.

"To buy guns and other materials they didn't have." John answered.

"With that thought, the intensity to wage war for more goods increased tenfold which tore black Africa apart." John added and then continued.

"Some people who came to the defense of the African kingdoms would like to believe that the African rulers probably were of the mind that it would be the same kind of treatment they gave to their captured slaves. I doubt it though. See how they tear themselves apart in tribal or ethnic wars; killing each other without mercy, even cutting off the limbs of children, in some places they will even kill baby girls in order to wipe out the entire tribe and many more atrocities that will shock even Satan, and these are their leaders—the so-called freedom fighters with nice sounding names—Liberating this, Revolutionary that...I am talking about man here and not color or however he wants to identify himself. This is how man continues to be disingenuous and inconsiderate about others.

"But what can be said in the matter in my opinion is that the Arabs and the Whites with their knowledge of a loving, compassionate and merciful and true God or Allah would engage in this barbaric, ungodly endeavor and turning around to call the Africans ungodly, primitive, savages and inferior goes to show the pot calling the kettle black. You have to wonder which one came first, slavery or Christianity." John surmised and went on.

"And the other reason why the religion spread and took root in Africa was when their kings embraced Islam, like in Mali and Songhai empires. And once that was done, the rest of the people followed suit." John elaborated.

"Hmm, I see." Jack murmured.

"Tell the black Africans that and you're looking for trouble. To them, it was as if God or Allah chose the religion for them through their kings." John went on. "Imagine your president choosing a religion for you in this day and age.

"Now the majority of North Africans see themselves as very proud Muslims, but before Islam, Christianity was the dominating religion. And where there are rulers from outside there will be mixed bloods amongst the people." John added.

"John, it's like one religion leaves for the other." Jack made a comment.

"Like in the present day Iran which had Zoroastrianism as the state religion before Islam and each time man will hold on to it and die for it, not knowing it will change." John concurred. "Each time foolishly saying this is it. Man goes back and forth on the pendulum of progress and regression searching for what is in his heart; one step forward, two steps backward until he sees the light, the true light."

"I won't want to be born in Saudi Arabia where Islam is the official and only religion." Jack said happily.

"Yeah, I can sympathize with you on that. Islam is always saying there is no compulsion in religion and a country of about 25 million people all belonging to one religion. You don't need a genius to elaborate on what's going on." John said bluntly and added cautiously. "But hold it there, rebel. You can say you're lucky this time, because historically, Armenia was the first modern country to be a Christian state. So it's not a new idea at all."

"How ridiculous man has become. We don't even like the same food or color or movie or books or shoes, but, somehow, some people find it necessary to impose a religion (a thought) on an entire nation." Jack couldn't believe it.

"People have always been forced to believe one way or the other. And it doesn't really stop with religion; it could be anything, like a system of government. In the land of the free they persecuted the people that favored communism to capitalism. The government prosecuted the communists amongst them. They just don't do it anymore. They repented." John explained.

"The other thing worth mentioning is the complexity of the human nature, like you said a moment ago. I hope I can help you to understand that, too. There is this need or call it a hunger to want to believe in us. So, when someone comes along with a charming personality and enough razzle-dazzle, we succumb to him or her. And this person carries us along in what he or she claims to be coming from a higher power, and since we are naturally vulnerable to fear and anxiety, this person steps in to fill those gaps with hopes and promises and we are hooked. It's stronger than sex, food and cocaine put together.

"We'll do everything to preserve that image that has been planted in our heads, even losing our lives or taking others' should anyone dare to challenge the leaders or the doctrine, he's done away with.

"Even those who claim not to believe in any God should come across someone that wishes them good luck all the time; they would make an effort to see this well-wisher every time. That's how powerful an ordinary wish is. Now compare that to eternal bliss. Man is a creature of comfort. There is a saying that goes like this, 'our constant craving for comfort doesn't make us wise'." John elaborated.

"Man as man is really a sitting duck." Jack observed, after listening to John's analysis of the human mind.

"You're not far from the truth." John replied.

"What truth, master?" Jack questioned jokingly.

"My goddamn truth," John played along. And they both started laughing.

But the laughter faded quickly like a small patch of snow during the transition to summer. Jack was suddenly thoughtful.

"Seriously, John," he said. "This world or life is rather depressing sometimes. So many things we can't explain; natural disasters, broken dreams, broken hearts, loss of loved ones, countless phenomena of life – ghosts, superstitions, so-called luck, ESP and everything that defies physical explanations." He concluded in a sober tone.

"Yes, I do agree with you totally." John replied. "Man does need something beyond here to place his hopes in. But the very tool that man uses in order to find the so-called meaning to this sometimes meaningless world brings chaos and anarchy, leading to more unhappiness and bloodshed. It becomes a double-edged sword." John said.

"There seems no easy solution." Jack added hopelessly.

"Hey, somehow, some people do break out of the herd mentality." John pointed out.

"Wonder where those people get their strength from?" Jack asked. "The pressure to join any religion in your society is very strong. First they look at you as a lost soul and then in a rather twisted way are scared of you. They become afraid of you because they don't want you to put reasonable, factual and obvious doubts in their minds concerning their beliefs." Then Jack paused.

"Trust me, they carry the doubts already. You see, most of them are not strong mentally. They can't face the great unknown on their own. Mentally, man is not created equal. It's like he's created in an unfinished manner and now has to make himself mentally strong." John said frankly.

"In my opinion, I think there's…mmm…I think man is suffering from mass delusion. Just like in the behavior of mobs during whatever protest. And it's very contagious; before you know it you join, especially when things in your life don't go your way." Jack said, trying to make a point of his own about human nature.

"Well observed! But mass delusion is not limited to religion. A good example would be in the 60s in the US when the governor of Mississippi wowed that segregation would be forever. The whole state was enraged that a black man would join their college. You should see it. Man hardly thinks for himself in most cases!" John said.

"So where is the escape?" Jack questioned.

"There are exceptional cases. You are one, too. You might just not be fully conscious of it yet. But, no matter how few these cases are, man still finds a way out of the rut, somehow. It might take a long time, but I think also that the built-in system in man wakes up and then he gets out when the time is right as they say." John assured.

"A friend of mine keeps changing churches. And I have another who jumps from one religion to another. But what puzzles me is that when they first join a religion or another denomination in the religion, they are full of praises of that religion or the way people there are so blessed. And in a twinkle of an eye, they change. I can't account for such a behavior. Isn't God supposed to be in every group or religion?" Jack was scratching his head.

"People like that are searching further. Somehow they might not recognize it yet, too, but something inside isn't satisfied any more with its present state of consciousness." John explained.

"So, what are they searching for?" Jack probed.

"Well, I don't know. But whatever it is, one thing is clear. Their state of God consciousness or what is God is changing slowly.

"You see, sometimes man changes his perspective about what they tell him is God without knowing it. It can either be individual or a collective change.

"Most of the hard core rituals are watered down from one generation to another, and believe it or not, even religious organizations are not immune to it. A classic case is the First Church. They have broken into many denominations of Christianity, that if Jesus should come back tomorrow, he wouldn't know which church to attend. 'For Pete's sake, what happened to the church I told you to build?' Jesus would demand of Peter.

"There are also exceptional cases of people bypassing the rigidity of religion. There's this story of a man who lives in a country that's divided into three major religions. And anywhere his business takes him; he changes his name to that religion, goes to their worship and gets his business done." John gave an insight.

"Now, that's a man that operates at a different level of consciousness." Jack smiled approvingly.

"And sometimes it's the reality of life itself that helps people change the stronghold of their religion on themselves. Economic survival, which is the strongest reason why man tears man apart, takes the proper position in our reasoning. And all the other sentiments that becloud our judgment to the extent of wasting our lives are pushed to the back burner. You can't fight holy wars when you are hungry.

"Take for example where there is a natural disaster, apparently to them coming from their chosen God, and manpower is needed to cultivate the land and prior to this calamity, women or some special males were excluded from manual labor due to their holy privileges. But in order to continue to eat and drink these laws will be changed or rationalized to allow for common sense to prevail.

"Women gained more voice because of the world wars and all kinds of wars, amongst the various struggles between the sexes. This is when reality comes to play. Once there are not enough men to man the so-called manly positions, women will fill them and with that it will open up an avenue to demand more rights from their loving, understanding and protective men. Something similar happened in Iran during the eight-year war with Iraq, women were then put in uniforms, but the journey for them is still a little bit far; slow and painful. Slow and painful isn't what we want if you get where I'm coming from. It's like the blacks in the US always marching for their civil rights. It shouldn't be this way.

"The women in the US - land of freedom, would attest to the 'benefits' of war. They were employed in record numbers to produce hardware for war. It also helped the European women, too, in my opinion more than anything else. But why wait for major disaster is the question? These wars also gave the blacks power to demand more authoritatively their rights from the whites, everywhere the two lived; US, Europe and Africa.

"And it's because of 911 that the danger of religion now takes the center stage in man's mind, at least in the Western world. Something major has to happen before man wakes up or changes." John expounded.

"And now every religion showcases its importance to man, trying to pull people back into their flock. 'My religion is better...my religion is misinterpreted'. It's like trying to quit smoking, if you're not strong enough, you're back." Jack added.

"But in truth what they are saying in plain language is this; we want to mold and shape your destiny so that in all aspects of life we are able to influence you, but ironically also want you to have your own experience. So the moment you see beyond what they see and put it in practice, for instance like in race, tribe, imaginary borders, materialism (while billions suffer in silence), holy books that stress believing to secure a ticket to heaven while engaging in destruction and hatred and so on, because for some reason you see a whole picture rather than separation and differences. They label you nonconformist; hard to deal with. They would rather want you to be going round and round in circles created by their ill-informed fears. It's a tug of war, trying to get to the top of the pyramid of consciousness." John agreed.

"The words of God on TV, radio and on the streets, in the bus and train; they give you tracts and preach to you while condemning the practice of other faiths, too. There seems nowhere to hide. Thank goodness they haven't started it in the plane." Jack said.

"And apart from trying to lure you back in their midst. It gives them power to tell people how to think, and also a profitable venture. That's an added incentive, maybe the only one." John hinted.

"Yeah, someone said on one Talk Show that God or the quest to find God was a business that couldn't be bankrupt." Jack said.

"It's like man is investing in fear and at the same time in hope of a blissful life after this one." John replied and started smiling. "It's an industry that can't go broke, really. Unless the society is broke. There are certain amounts of your income that you must donate every time in some religion and it's backed by their respective holy books. They don't even pay taxes. And technically the entire society contributes to their religious institutions whether we belong to them or not.

"Then their preachers become entrenched in their work to continue to persuade and put fear into people to contribute to the house of God. 'Hey, he created everything; he just wants to test you.' And the aggressiveness at which they plead to you to sow seeds into the house of God is so scary that your money will jump out of your pocket into the coffers without your knowledge. (Then, again, man as man wants to give less to get much more- $1 to get $1000, and that's where man's greed traps him, too.) And that's what they sing to their followers." John wrapped it up.

Seemed they ran out of things to say. The breeze was soft on their bodies. John readjusted his position. Jack got up to stretch his legs.

"Man makes opinion fact, and fact, opinion."
Frank.

"Our true nature is buried under our culture.
Which suppresses our freedom, and we cry to 'God' to free us from
our religion."
Jack

Question That, Never Question This

Jack was beginning to feel a little bit hungry. All this talk was killing unnecessary brain cells. Better this way than what transpired in reality. Little by little they were chipping away at the notion of being chosen by the maker. Yet, it was amazing how something this simple could be missed by the best brains out there, or maybe being so-called smart had little to do with life.

"Well, I don't know about you, but I am starving and would like to refill my tank. You want anything, John?" who was still sitting on the ground with his legs stretched outward.

"That's nice of you." John used to drink a lot of coke like Jack, but now he was trying to reduce it. "Yes, thanks." This time he would put it on hold. "Could you get me a soda and some snacks?" John begged.

Jack headed to the main building as Den was limping towards the Oak tree.

"You guys have got the coolest place to hang out." He said as he stopped to talk to Jack on his way. "That A/C isn't for me. I like the shade under the tree much better. You're coming back, huh?" Den asked.

He had grown to like Jack, maybe because he came to his defense after he had been attacked by the holy soldiers a moment ago.

"Yeah, I'm coming back." Jack patted him on the back as he headed to the main building.

Den took a seat near John who looked as if he was about to take a nap – a long one.

"I'm fascinated by your knowledge of all these religions." He complimented him. "You must have studied a lot and read thousands of holy books."

John smiled. "Not really, you get these things here and there. And if you're interested, you do a little bit of research with an open mind. And sometimes you don't have to do all that but be observant about how man interacts with one another and pay close attention to nature, the animals, including the chief; man, and try understanding it with a mind of an outsider watching a play unfold. Attach no sentiment to the players; the rich or the poor, the beautiful or the ugly, the powerful or the weakling, the host or the visitor, the successful or the struggling, the stranger or the native, the man or the woman, the friend or the enemy, race or tribe, hate or love and so on. That I find fascinating, an eye opener for me.

"You will know who has the power, who is the underdog, who is full of ego, who is spoon-fed with ideas, who is the influencer, who is acting dumb for a while because of lack of power or money, who puts himself or herself in the upper class, who is trying hard to fit in, who is scared of the heavens falling, who favors culture because it favors him, who is hiding his fears with material comfort, who loves and cares for you genuinely, who will share his precious bread with you and who won't, who calls you friend or brother when it's convenient, and many more. My friend, you will learn much more this way than reading all the holy books combined." John said.

"One question I have is why is it that people don't want others to talk about their religion?" Den asked.

But before John could respond to the question, he posed another one.

"Why couldn't I ask my pastors certain things in the bible? Because anytime I did when I was young, they didn't give me satisfying answers. They just said that was the way of the lord to the point that one pastor said I should not come to church anymore. The way he put it was, 'you can contaminate others.' That really made me sad and terrified of the punishment from God for being disobedient. I trembled and shook nervously at times in my room. And what do you think someone like that should do the next time?" Den queried.

John wanted to offer his advice but Den quickly continued. It had promptly turned into a monologue. But John understood why. This guy had been caged like a wild animal and spoon fed the words of God by force. So many questions he could not ask freely in the house of God tumbled out of his mouth like pebbles racing down to the bottom of the mountain. He had found real freedom to express himself and he seized the opportunity with both hands. He was no longer in the house of fear.

"I should stop quizzing them or myself, right, huh?" Den posed the question to himself and answered it. "But no, I continued as if my life depended on it until they kicked me out by turning me into an outcast. You know the feeling when no one wants you around. Then I just left, to the heart break of my parents and friends. You know the name they christened me; Hell-Boy." He sighed with a chuckling smile.

John listened patiently. He had met one or two people like this before. He knew where Den was going with his questions.

"Now my head is spinning with all these questions," John began, laughing, mimicking Den anytime he was confused about anything. "You talk of dogma." He said softly.

"Yeah, yeah," Den said, all wrapped up in emotion and at the same time wanted to hear John's take on the issue.

John cleared his throat and began. "First, it's not that people don't want you to talk about their religion or faith. If you talk to them in agreement, then you have a friendship. You'll now have someone to share your experiences with; your joy and your weak moments. You'll develop a bond, seemingly, stronger than family ties or nationalism. You'll fantasize about the coming of your savior, if you belong to such a religion. You'll learn more from each other, studying your holy book, and more importantly, your new found friend will be willing to help you in times of trouble, either physically or emotionally. And sometimes that is very helpful in this world, somebody to lean on to weather the storm of life if you can't stand on your own.

"But on the other hand you have to take into account that people are very sensitive about their beliefs, they wrap them around their hearts like a precious jewel guarded day and night from the would-be-thief; in this case, a non believer or a non conformist--a questioner, like you. Once they believe something this much that they can't really prove, they defend it blindly and fiercely, even with their lives. Have you ever seen anybody defending 2x2 fiercely? Anybody in opposition is seen as the devil or evil or a harbinger of evil spirit trying to steal their heavenly gem. They will avoid you like a mad man or you are perceived as an infectious disease, someone to be quarantined in their minds. To a thinking man there's no need for this. But that's the nature of man at that level of consciousness.

"The reason is simple," John continued. "They don't want you to... let me use your words...'contaminate their minds'. They have invested their hopes in that faith and don't want it stirred or shaken."

Den appeared to have a little bit of understanding but still wondered why he had to sympathize with their plight, when clearly he was treated harshly by God loving people.

"Let me put it this way." John tried to use another means to let Den see clearly the issue at hand. "There's a man who goes everywhere with a worthless sea shell in his pocket, everywhere, no matter the occasion, because he has put his faith in that shell to give him good luck and protection. Now if you want to turn his world upside down, take the shell and throw it away or give him another one of a better quality, you will paralyze him emotionally. And when there is no key to start the emotional engine, the physical body will be immobilized. He just won't get himself. On a cold, breezy winter day he will be sweating, he can't function well, if at all. You have to be more understanding when you are dealing with someone like this. In time he will outgrow that superstition. The same applies to religious minds...without proof!"

"I see, but if what they want people to believe is true, why can't they welcome all questions, regardless?" Den insisted. "I don't question why 2+2 = 4." He smiled. "I'm not crazy, or am I?"

"This is religion." John said firmly. "If they are sincere about what to call it, really; it should be called Dogma. So you know what you are getting yourself into from the get-go. I-talk-you-obey-without-question, then if you ask questions, you will be the crazy one.

They only walk by faith. This simply phrase which they will gladly tell you from time to time is not registered in their minds. So they get themselves in deep illogical trouble by trying to use logic to explain themselves, forgetting it's their arch enemy, more fearsome than Satan; major contradiction. But they are oblivious to it to this day. This time don't even try to find the reason why. It's a list that's endless." John concluded.

"What you are saying is I should just follow my parents' or my pastor's words...words of God, like sheep?" Den said defiantly.

"Pretty much," John answered. "As the rats follow the flute player out of town; follow the leader. This is dogma and the insidious nature of dogma is that dogma begets dogma. Once you outgrow your present religious group's dogma, you go to another group of your choice and get entrenched in another degree of dogma that seems appealing to you--what God finally ordered or how he loved to be worshipped. 'Good, I'm doing the righteous thing now, halleluiah.' After moving from dogma to dogma with a slight degree of harshness or intensity, you become dogma full. What is hard to realize by these minds is that dogma as fearful and overbearing and unreasonable as it is, cancels out each other.

"For instance, let's say you belong to a religious group that says you can wear a pair of trousers but you can't put on jewelry. You obey that rule faithfully. 'I can't do that in the name of Jesus, I want to be blessed...can't have that in Jesus name.' After a while or through persuasion by your good friends you change to a group that says you can't wear skirt because it's so fitting, it will mess with the minds of the pastors, but you can wear pants and definitely wear earrings. The fear of either wearing jewelry or not is gone, disappeared within the transition.

"Pig, poor thing, is a touchy and churning issue in the belief of God, yet we have those who enjoy the meaty and tastefulness of it to the despicable sight it creates in the hearts of the same believers in the same God! And then, we have the no eating of cow because it's seen as sacred by some, but delicious in other people's mouths. But this strange reason is not limited to the religious people, alone. The secular people also have unreasonable dispositions when it comes to food, especially meat. Some cultures eat horses, cats, dogs and so-called bush meat that will make other people throw up at the mention of dog meat, for example. Really, meat is meat. The only time we should not eat something is when we are allergic to it, barring cannibalism. Because that will negate the formation of human society, you want to be invited to dinner; you don't want to be it." John paused.

Finally, he was eager to hear the questions that earned him his nickname. "Tell me, what was the issue that got you excommunicated from paradise?" John inquired with a cynical smile.

"There was a time I asked how Adam and Eve disobeyed God." Den started.

43

Genesis Chapter 2 verses 16 and 17
And the Lord God commanded thee, saying, of every tree of
the garden thou mayest freely eat.
But of the tree of the knowledge of good and evil, thou shalt
not eat of it: in the day that thou eatest thereof thou shalt
surely die.
Genesis Chapter 3
Now the serpent was more subtle than any beast of the
field which the Lord God had made. And he said unto the
woman Yea, hath God said, ye shall not eat of every tree of
the garden? And the woman said unto the serpent, we may
eat of the fruit of the garden. But of the fruit of the tree
which is in the midst of the
garden, God halt said you shall not eat of it, neither shall
you touch It, lest you die.
And the serpent said unto the woman, ye shall not surely
die. For God doth know that in the day ye
eat thereof, then your eyes shall be opened, and ye shall be as
Gods, knowing good and evil.

"And their reply…?" John asked.

"Their answer to that was God was testing them for loyalty. And just for eating from the tree of good and evil we find ourselves in this mess. It was the same God that allowed Satan – the serpent, to influence them to eat it.

"First, I would like to believe that God knew whether they would disobey him or not in the first place." Den continued without waiting for John's answer. "Couldn't God see the future? I test my friends for loyalty because I don't know the outcome. Can I rely on Eddy or Jeff? Will they always have my back or can I trust my girl friend or my brothers and sisters, for that matter? Can I trust my parents? Can I trust my broker? Can I trust the politicians? Can I trust the weather man?" He added with a smile.

"You can add that to list." John jumped in.

"Add what?" Den asked.

"That God not being able to see the future, go on now." John replied.

"Then Adam and Eve saw themselves naked and were ashamed

of their nakedness. Now to be naked is evil, please. But on the flip side, good thing the animals like dogs didn't eat the fruit. My cat is not ashamed of its naked body." Den said angrily. He was becoming agitated.

"Take it easy; take it easy I'm not your pastor." John cut in laughing, shielding the fighting words with his arms raised to cover his face.

"Gee, you must have given those poor pastors things to think about, to wrestle with during prayer time." John deduced.

"Seriously now," Den continued. "It's like I don't want my 15 year-old-girl to experience boys yet and after I have repeatedly warned her, I knowingly let a handsome boy or an ugly one in the apartment. I think I'm the one to be blamed."

'No, he did not or did he just use the most abominable word in the world.' John thought. 'A word that will freeze the believers to death without the weather dipping well below minus 5 degrees in winter and in this case, even in summer. It's like taking the shell away. They become frozen in time waiting for hails or lightning to strike them dead at any moment by the utterance of the B-word. Translation in modern society; I won't get my prayers answered; my husband will leave me or vice versa; my student loans won't be granted; that handsome man won't look my way; my journey to the western world won't happen; I will be denied my visa; I won't be able to save Africa and the world; I won't be able to save all the poor in the world; I won't pass my exams that I have vigorously studied for; my children won't obey me; I won't have good friends; I will be fat; they will fire me at my job, though, I'm the brain behind it; I won't be a star, doing violent and sexy scenes; I won't grow tall to be a hunk, a 6 footer; I won't be able to buy that new car, even though I have the money ten times over; my dream of buying that mansion just to show off won't materialize; I will not be able to live long on earth, though, you can't compare it to heaven; God will not give me the strength and wisdom to kill all the infidels; God will not allow my congregation to grow so that I can save souls for Him; I won't manifest all the great potentials that God will grant me someday, yeah, someday; God won't bless me with children; God will hate me so much that I will rot in hell for eternity; God won't let me join the right and true religion; my favorite football or soccer team will always lose because God will be getting back at me; I won't be able to score the winning goal; and I won't be able to buy that Rolex watch that will tell me when the end of the world will be upon mankind, so I can prepare and, so many more cool stuff that I can only get from God and not from Santa Claus, just because…just because I said or allowed the B-word in my mind.'

"So you did get to ask many questions?" John was satisfied.

"Listen, even if Adam and Eve committed this grievous or eternal sin, why should I suffer for it or anybody else for that matter, and for how long? Maybe we should follow this God's way of punishment. The head of each household does something wrong and we punish the entire family and relatives, too. Now we suffer and die, and God, Himself, cursed Adam and Eve. After everything is said and done, they tell us that wishing your fellow human beings bad is ungodly. But we do have a great example in the words of our Maker! How can we go wrong or stray from the path of holiness?

> *Genesis Chapter 4 Verse 16*
> *Unto the woman he said, I'll greatly multiply thy sorrow and thy conception. In sorrow thou shalt bring forth children.*
> *And thy desire shall be to thy husband and he shall rule over thee…And unto Adam he said …cursed is the ground for thy sake, In sorrow shalt thou eat of it all the days of thy life.*

"The curse was even extended to the poor animals and the fish and they didn't eat the fruit. Have you heard or seen a shark eating apple for lunch, hee, he, he." Den laughed at his own joke. To him this was a fairness issue or lack of it in what they told him was the Maker's character or rules. It was as if Den was just going to keep the questions coming one after the other, and his own reasons why he couldn't believe or rather needed more explanations than the rest of his peers at that tender age. He let out a flood of questions he had bottled up for so long, questions that would sink Noah's ark in 40 minutes and 40 seconds.

Suddenly he stopped and looked John straight in the eyes as if to say, what a dilemma.

John could now put in his two shekels.

"Den." He called out sharply with a tone filled with understanding. "They are coming up with what constitutes life as we know it. And you have to come up with a premise that can…well, almost, sufficiently explains living and dying and from there you build in whatever you want to add to life or remove. Really it's the struggle of man with his environment, trying to make sense in the world he finds himself. For you to have everyone in line in your community you need an element of unknowingness. In this case, God or whatever name you apply to the Beginner or Maker to scare the living hell out of every man to do what's thought best for the society, and the non conformists will be punished severely to serve as a deterrent to your rule or God's. Then you concretize it with the things everyone can observe in life; like living and dying of all things. Fairy tales, movies of their heroes, celebrities' endorsement, paintings, and symbols are also employed to further their hold on you, to solidify God's reason in your mind and heart and all your endeavors. And then there is the question of fear.

"First, the fear factor is embedded in man, and it affects us in most areas of our lives, and others use the same weapon to cajole us to do their biddings. Sometimes it's so subtle you will think you are carrying out your own wish. Now multiple that a million times in the hands of a forward looking religiously or ambitiously inclined leader and the fear spread, consuming every fiber of your body and the community, and on top of that you start creating your own, too.

"You start living in a bubble; you will be scared of this and that. Is having money harmful or not? Is eating and talking at the same time ungodly? Is making love for pleasure sinful? Is walking backward to your room bad? Is dancing in the house of God sinful? Is having a time for you, a minute forgetting God, evil? Is kissing on the first date, right? Is having premarital sex okay? Is abortion evil even if it happens by itself or am I responsible one way or another? Is using condom or contraceptive pills evil like Satan? Is marrying outside my tribe or race a sin to God that created everybody? Is using electricity a terrible thing? Is working on Monday sinful? Is working night bad? Is having a job done on my face ungodly? Is looking at the moon with my telescope evil? Or is Botox from the devil? Is farting while praying to God a big sin? Is eating what eats what we are not supposed to eat a sin? Is looking at the first ray of the sun a sin? Is eating with your left hand a bad thing? Is passing a non believer on the right hand side a sin? Is sitting in a train with a woman that is menstruating unlawful in the sight of God, whether you are a man or a woman? Is wearing men's clothes a gender sin? Is wearing kilt sinful? Is going to church on Saturday a no, no? Is going to church on Sunday evil? Is going to church on Monday bad? Is moving to the land of the unbelievers evil? Is sleeping facing north ungodly? Is having a long beard sinful? Is having a short beard sinful? Is exposing my beard bad? Is flying a jet plane from point A to B evil? (Because my prophet didn't mention such a thing) Is giving economic freedom to women a sin? (Men are superior to women because they use their wealth to care for them. This is a holy book that's static. The prophet, when he was 25 married a wealthy 40-year-old woman that took care of him. You can see many examples now, even then. Superiority is measured by wealth, ha!) Is it a sin if a blind man approaches God? (In the bible) Is it not a sin to stone stubborn children to death? (In the bible) Is it a sin for a flat nose man to approach God? (In the bible) Is it a sin if the dwarfs come close to God? (In the bible) Is it okay to kill gays and lesbians? Is it a sin for a woman to grab the testicles of a man in a fight? (Yes, in the bible) Is it right to kill my daughter who turns into a prostitute? (But I can have concubines like Solomon) Is it a sin to kill my daughter that prophesies? (In the bible) Is letting women have hair on their heads a sin? Is killing witches okay?

"The long and short of it is that they are trying to explain life; why we have free will, why we are good and bad, why we live and why we die, including the animals and the fish," John smiled. "Why there's so much sorrow and also happiness in our world. Your story of how's and why's has to cover every spectrum of life or else they won't believe you. Every religion has one for its followers and the story is different from one to another. And once you understand that, you won't be afraid of some Gods burning you in hell forever." John explained.

"But that's not what they say. They make it sound like if I don't believe them I'll go to hell, and hell is real." Den defended his reasoning.

"That's why it's faith." John reassured. "All religions of the world try to explain why we suffer here and why things are the way they are. And the followers hope to go to one paradise after the life here. But I understand where you are coming from and I don't agree with them, either, in a story that scares people. It doesn't match what they are calling a loving God in one heaven, period. Really, the problem with them is that they think they know the truth; the origin of life." John tried further to calm Den down. "It's left to you to set yourself free of dogma.

"Consider the Islamic version of why sin entered the world. (*Surah 15.19*)

After Allah created man from the black molded loam, he then commanded all the angels to prostrate before him, but Satan, whom God created from smokeless fire said no to Allah, because man was mere mortal. Then God cursed him till the judgment day. But Satan managed to bargain with Allah to give him chance to tempt mankind, except those ones that'd be faithful to him.

Allah agreed not to give Satan power over his servants, but the sinners will end up in hell with the devil. (Mortal and immortal will burn! But surprisingly, both won't die but suffer for eternity.)

"Now, that takes the cake." Den said despondently. "Simply because Satan didn't bow down to Adam, God would cast him to hell. But before that he would permit Satan to lead us astray first."

"Do you understand now about having what is considered by many a water tight story from the beginning and building on it, thereafter?" John pointed out, trying to demystify it.

"The Hindu religion on the other hand explains it differently. To them everything revolves around Karma and Reincarnation. There are good and bad karma, and it's up to you to learn the good karma, and then after a series of rebirths, for...like hundreds or thousands times of your spirit coming and going, you become enlightened, stop rebirth for good and become one with the Maker.

"You can even make some people in the same society second class citizens for life, no problem. You have the magic wand and you can wield it however you desire or your God wants! In Hindu they practice the Caste System. They have what they call the untouchables or the low caste, where your name determines your status and not your color this time in the society, forever.

"To overcome this obstacle just move your family to another part of the country and have your children change their names. You'd have fooled them by taking a high caste name. Just like some really fair skinned blacks used to fool the whites in America during the segregation era. The whites couldn't tell the difference, and so treated those people like humans; like their own. They 'Passed' as whites!

"Or change your religion and join the one that sees you as equal, at least. No wonder many low caste are joining Islam and Christianity all over India, and that is one of the principal reasons why Hindu worshippers clash with these two religions there. They don't want to free their low caste; 'who am I going to be superior to now that you are gone.' Just like the freedom of religion is partially sanctioned by one religion in Iran. There, Muslims can't be preached to by any other religion; it's death by law. And this is not a new practice by man. It's part and parcel of a dominant religion or sect, or race in a geographical location.

"And we individuals do the same thing, too. Most families don't want their members to be in another religion or to be without one. This is not a great evil by religious people alone. It's a human phenomenon. It's because most of us just don't have the power to enforce it. Just like we won't want our sisters to marry or go out with another race or tribe, and many more ways that I can't count here. It's just that when it's religious it sounds devilish; these people who are supposed to give others freedom to express themselves are now denying others. But it is the same thing.

"Some explanations are scary and some are challenging, making you decide whether you want to lead a life of good, loving human being or not, it's left to you and the consequences." John paused again.

"I see now that my work is cut out for me. But I'm happy I broke the dogma." Den said finally. "If there is any dogma in my life it has to come from me."

"You're lucky indeed as you said. I think you have outgrown your faith, even at that tender age. Millions can't find their way out of the trap, you know." John added. "They are lost in a maze of straight lines.

If you look at it really all known religions have broken away from the original and by so doing, done away with the established dogma. But the interesting thing is that after breaking away from their first dogma, they turn around and set up their own dogma and tell their followers not to question it, just like I've been telling you.

"Usually, if you have charisma and you are blessed with money and political clout or will, you can successfully do away with any dogma, or just being stubborn.

"And the silliest things sometimes make people break the overbearing dogma. King Henry the 8th told the Pope no one could tell him not to marry his wife's cousin, Anne. He went on to found the Church of England because of the disapproval of the Pope, amongst other reasons he favored. The Pope at that time spoke God for all mankind. The church still think they do! But looking at the whole story, you will find that the tyrant-beheading-king was actually right in God's eyes. God allowed Abraham (father of all blessed people, may I say had sex without marrying the slave girl) to marry his sister. Jacob married two sisters. The logical answer why God allowed this to happen will be that God didn't know what he was doing at that time. A God that raised hell over praying to another God suddenly looked the other way when it came to marriage by his favorites!" John indicated.

"I wish I knew you when I was young, I wouldn't even have felt scared in the first place. Tell me, how many dogmas are out there?" Den said.

"Like I said, the Catholic Church…look at how many denominations they broke into. But you have to take into account that even the Catholic Church kind of broke away from Judaism." John explained.

"Now we have Nestorian church, also known as Assyrian, founded because of the dispute over the title given to Virgin Mary. The moment you find anything slightly different from your understanding of the bible you start your own. You will always have followers. The Amish church doing without modern technology. The question for them is when do we say something is modern? You will think in their minds that change is not constant. The Baptist church was founded over what age was right for baptism. You have to give babies the right to grow up first before being baptized; you can't just dip them in water straight from their mothers' wombs. So you start your own church with people of like mind." John said, shaking his finger like a college professor.

"The Calvinists on the other hand believe that hell and heaven are predestined for people. Why bother to pray in this church? Why bother sending the only begotten son and killing him, too?

Then we have the Lutherans founded by Martin Luther, the reformer. Having clashed with the Catholic Church, he ended up marrying one of the Nuns. We have the Methodists that methodologically read the bible. The Presbyterians and the Quakes, and a million more different groups with their different dogmas scattered around the world, all vying for the one true dogma of God. And with the same breath strongly condemning one another's dogma, how tragic. The repercussion is a heavy price, at least in their good hearts, to pay-- eternal damnation in hell. You might as well not even try to be a Christ follower in the first place. You will get the same token a non believer gets; lake of fire.

But if you want to know who broke the greatest dogma in human history, considering the group's number now was Mohammed." John said.

"How," Den said eagerly.

"I will reveal how the business man did that. Remember these famous sayings.

> *John 3:16*
> *For God so loved the world that he gave his only begotten*
> *so, That whosoever believeth in him should not perish, but*
> *have everlasting life*
> *John 3: 36*
> *He that believeth in the son hath everlasting life: and he*
> *that believeth not shall not see life; but the wrath of God*
> *abideth on him*

"That right there is the backbone of Christianity. Millions of people put their hopes in the son of God for deliverance. Mohammed came around, condemned the statement, literally calling those who believed in Jesus as the son of God fools and infidels. And the entire Muslim world whether they appear respectful and humble or not are calling the Christians fools, as well." John said.

"Remember the words I used a moment ago, 'follow the leader?' John asked.

Den nodded his head.

"Likewise, the Christians are saying the Muslims are fools, too. The question is who is fooling who? How will this conflict in dogma and counter-dogma be settled? On earth it's through bloodshed and all the negative consequences that much we know. The one in heaven is up in the air. Your guess is as good as mine.

"Now a Muslim, unbeknownst to him, is not afraid of calling Jesus a prophet of God. A Christian on the other hand would have a fit thinking Jesus other than the son of God, or even not God. Also a Christian wouldn't think twice calling Mohammed a fraud, but a Muslim would shake in his pants even slightly thinking Mohammed was not a prophet of Allah...Now switch the Christian to a Muslim, and vice versa." John said theoretically.

"Why?" Den was lost.

"Because they always change to the opposing religions and by so doing they would have cancelled out their initial dogma or fear. Remember I told you how dogma erases dogma without them knowing? Even the newly converted ones who practiced no religion before, never having any fear in this area, now would carry around their necks the burden of dogma like a slave chain...

You see what I've been trying to tell you clearly now?" John asked seriously.

"Crystal clear, John." Den replied without hesitation.

"Man jumps from branch to branch of the same tree and still claims enlightenment. As always with the things that don't compute in their minds, you can add this to the long list." John continued.

> *Surah 4.171*
> *Jesus, was no more than God's apostle*
> *God forbid that he should have a son.'*

"And that Jesus actually died for the sins of the world; shedding his precious blood for you and I as we have been made to believe.

> *Corinthians 15: 3-4*
> *For I delivered unto you first of all, that which I also*
> *received, how that Christ died for our sins according to the*
> *scriptures; and that he was buried, and that he rose again*
> *the third day according to the scriptures.*

"This is what Mohammed had to say about it. (*Surah 39: 7*) No man is going to take away anyone's sins, period.

"So dogma depends on you accepting it as unquestionable, something direct from The God's mouth because what I can piece together is that one man's dogma is another man's nonsense. Am I right?" Den said.

"I couldn't have said it any better. One man's fear is another man's laughter." John agreed.

"But it gets better, even Islam, the only uniting religion, broke into sects. You see, when Mohammed died, his son-in-law became the first true successor by family ties. And some wanted the leadership to continue in this vein. Mohammed didn't have a male heir, so a group known as shia, meaning partisan wanted a kind of a link to their prophet's life, a kind of hereditary system. Another group known as the sunni, meaning majority wanted to choose the leader democratically.

"And also many more factions surfaced in Islam just like in Christianity. A popular singer, Fela Kuti, sang a song about unity, and one of the lines was *'what is united in united nations?'* So in the secular world we have the same problem and that should give you a clue in understanding man, regardless." He continued after a brief digression.

"So the Sunni gave birth to Maliki, the Shafi, the Hanafi and the Hanibali. The Shia group on the other hand was further divided. We now have the Twelvers, this group boast of the largest Shia group. And get this; they also believe that the twelfth Imam in the line of Ali, the son-in-law to Mohammed will come again as the Almahdi – meaning the chosen one. Tell me whether that doesn't sound like reincarnation.

"Also, we have the Seveners, the Druzre and then the Alawite – this sect incorporates the elements of Christianity, and important for you not to forget in a hurry is the resurrection of Jesus Christ that they believe in. Remember Mohammed said that Jesus was not crucified?

> *Surah 4:157*
> *'We have put to death*
> *Jesus son of Mary, the apostle of God.*
> *They did not kill him, nor did they crucify him,*

"Now, if Mohammed could somehow see that there isn't one type of Islam, so to speak, he wouldn't know who to call an infidel anymore. All the Muslims are in trouble all over again. Another holy war by Mohammed just like in the age of ignorance would be needed to make Islam pure again, because he warned them not to break into sects.

"Then we have the Zaydis. This group got their name from the Shai Imam that was deposed. But there was one last group that split way before the Sunni – Shia breakup, and that was the Ibadiyyah group. They traced their history to one of the numerous wives of Mohammed,

Khadijah, believing in practicing the true Islam. It was Khadijah who restored Mohammed's sanity about the revelations that were coming one at a time from God's angel, Gabriel, and not from a raving mad man, as he sometimes replied his critics." John explained.

"So I'm not crazy," Den said, feeling elated. He had been moving from doubts to uneasy confidence, up and down like a yo-yo in the hands of a manipulator. What if these people were right in the end? What if that was actually the ways of God? There were times he was strong in his condemnation of the whole thing and times when he just wanted to give in, to accept Jesus. Those were the moments when life was hard to bear; things were upside down, nothing was going right, and the conclusion he reached was if he lost things here on earth, at least, Jesus would make everything heavenly, that became his last great hope for some sanity and bliss in the so-called afterlife. He nearly gave himself another nickname, prodigal son. 'Daddy, I've come back home, please take me back, I'm very, very sorry.' But all that silly thoughts went out of the window for good. He took a deep breath and relaxed in the comfort of what was unfolding before his very eyes.

"They are the ones under a dogmatic spell and can't face their fears." Den said authoritatively and victoriously.

John saw that his body language had changed from the agitated, uncertain guy to one of calm and fearlessness. The transformation seemed to be swift but from experience he knew it was a gradual process for him, just like for many people. Fear of this or that was hard to get rid of that easily. He patted him on the shoulder, giving him support. But support was not in the touch on the shoulder like a queen anointing a knight with a sword; rather it was from a deep understanding, coupled with sound knowledge of the craziness that was going on around him.

"My friend it's time for me to tell you a story a good buddy of mine shared with me a long time ago. It's about consciousness." John cocked his head to the right to face Den. He began.

"There were four villages. I'll call them Villages A, B, C and D. Of all these villages, only Village C people dressed beautifully, and they became the envy of other villagers. One day a witch from Village B was so green with envy that she decided to cast a spell in the well that village C drank water from. So everyone in the village started drinking the water except the King who was away on a sacred and secret mission.

When he came back, instead of seeing his people with their elegant attires, they were stark naked, dancing to welcome him. The king for some reason knew what the witch had done, but didn't know how it would affect his people. And the spell couldn't be broken just like that. It would take some time; some very long time."

"What did the King do?" Den was captivated by the story.

"At that time there was nothing he could do." John went on. "The king continued to dance with them as if nothing had happened. Then suddenly one villager noticed something strange with their beloved king. He was wearing gorgeous attire! She shouted, 'the king is mad, the king is mad, oh, the king is mad.' The drums went dead, silence turned into an eerie sound. If a pin dropped the deaf would hear it hitting the ground. The joyous dance froze in time. It was as if time itself stood still, the dust that rose with every welcoming step defied gravity, it wouldn't rejoin mother earth. Everybody and everything knew something was wrong. All eyes were starring at the king. The king looked like a double-headed ghost that must be rid of or made human again. And all of a sudden they all shouted in unionism, 'the king is mad...the king is mad.' The earth shook to the heavens, the angels moved nervously around, waiting to see what would happen next. But the unexplainable thing was that their eyes and hearts were filled with genuine sympathy, love and care. Improbable as it might sound.

"So, they rallied around and discussed what to do, how to make the king sane. They gave the king three days to be normal or they would elect another king like them, naked. The herbalists went to work on the poor king. The king pleaded for seven days because by that time he would be able to reverse the spell. But the crowd shouted only three days. So they took the king to his palace and started treating him of his illness. On the second day, the king thought long and hard about it, couldn't sleep, nothing was coming to him how to solve the problem in the short time given.

"There are unwritten laws to be followed in this world. Certain things you can't rush, you just have to watch them play themselves out. Or it will be like rushing a cup of water down the throat of a man dying of thirst, you will kill him faster than a speeding bullet to his thirsty heart.

"On the third day the king had to come out to speak to the people, and if the villagers found him insane, he wouldn't be fit to lead them anymore or could be killed. The king came out on the appointed day; fully dressed. There was a ghostly silence amongst the people. The herbalists had failed. The gods had abandoned them. The king was beyond redemption. A new king must be elected. Wouldn't have a deranged king on the throne or the land would not be fruitful, women wouldn't give birth, men wouldn't be men anymore, volcanoes would erupt, the earth would swallow people, goats would turn into lions and all hell would break loose on earth. Children's growth would be stunted, prosperity would vanish, and their land wouldn't be blessed.

"As they were coming to dethrone him, he began peeling off one by one his eye-catching attire until he stood there naked, stark naked. In this area he wasn't very gifted. Then all was well in the land of ignorance. Sanity had been restored. Thanks to the gods. Rain would fall in time now. Harvest would be bountiful and joy would spread all over the land. The people would retain their purity of blood; no outsiders would invade their land and corrupt them with new and better ideas. The crowd cheered, the drums sounded and the villagers started dancing, happy that their king was no longer mad.

"That's man as man in a nutshell! Sanity is measured by number in man's world." John finished telling the story.

"So if the people had the same info as the king they would be wiser." Den assumed.

"Man can read all the books on earth, invent the greatest machine to help him do the bulk of his work, calculate the circumference of the globe, governs the largest country well, or it could be opposite everything intellectual and still be ignorant and brainwashed about what constitutes life here, and the dreaded afterlife. A classic case will be Sir Isaac Newton, the apple guy; mister gravity.

"Someone comes along to alter our ways of thinking or consciousness and carries us along with his charms, fears, power and all the other tricks of the trade. He implants his own idea of what is right or wrong, the meaning of life and how it should be lived, like a computer chip. And no one can question it because we are all under a spell. So when man is drunk with something, be it cultural supremacy or nationalism or class, it disguises itself in different ways, we lose ourselves in another person's conflict-ridden goal.

"A man in Muslim-controlled-Afghanistan, not Taliban-controlled, decided to be a Christian and for that reason he was sentenced to death. The lawyers had to claim the man was mad.

"There are so many dogmas out there, you might as well just close your eyes, ears and suspend your thinking, though you think you have it, and choose one or two and you'll defend it with your life, just as the next guy is doing the same with a different dogma." John elaborated.

"Someone said something funny about this issue. He said I should imagine every child in Saudi was moved to the Vatican City. They would grow up praising Jesus - 'thank you our savior.' Then I should imagine moving all the Vatican children..." Den looked confused. "Hey, play along, pretend they have children…to Saudi – they would grow up praising Allah, 'thank you Allah for sending your last prophet to the Arabs.' (You will get the same result with the so-called nationalists)

"If the same thing was done with language, we all would understand, no divine intervention, right? Or we might as well say to the Africans and all conquered people by the British that English is the language God speaks. But something as simple as this to a believer is like trying to swallow two golf balls. Add this too to the list. Remember the list?" John asked.

Den nodded again. "It's growing."

"So even if you choose any religion, then how do you pick the group you will belong to? Be careful, wrong choice and you can lose your life. They have attacked each other's dogmas and even tried to wipe out the ungodly churches and mosques. And they will still engage in the destruction of other groups continuously if not for the sake of secular laws. Even this doesn't stop them at times. Man's law takes the back seat, they always boast. They have to make the ways of worship of God pure.

"Judaism is no exception in the dogma or no dogma problem. You don't see them still stoning people to death, do you? That is one of the many laws they don't obey anymore, but the food thing must still be followed." John continued. "There are orthodox, conservative and reform Judaism. Even the Rastafarians have sects. And their dread-lock look is not unique. The Yoruba people have children that they believe come with that kind of locked hair from their own God, which to them means a special baby, called Dada.

"Now in Buddhism there are so many different sects, even challenging Buddha regarding one of his theories. He too, if he steps away from Nirvana for a minute, he will have to learn from so many different Buddhist sects how to get back home." John said.

Den smiled at the remark.

"I'm not kidding. Imagine having Buddha around now, do you think he will agree with what different sects are doing? Remember he moved away from Hindu religion. They will have one Buddhist temple under him, period. These groups don't respect one another but they mask it so well, just like the Irish and the English…pretty much any tribal or racial interactions, because most of us are still not sincere with one another." John defended his point.

"I'm curious. Is there a religion that hasn't been influenced?" Den asked.

"It's hard to know for certain, but I have it on record that both Judaism and Hindu religions had an outside influence." John replied.

"How do people cope in a dogmatic society?" Den asked.

"It's a living hell for people like you, Den. They can't voice their disagreement out in the open or there will be repercussions, and the consequences are not going to be good, even from their own family. These cultures or overbearing religions suffocate them. They try very hard not to lose their sanity when they see the effects on the less fortunate in the society and there is little they can do about it. Even during the slavery days some whites, few though, tried as best as they could to treat the blacks like humans. Some fell in love with their 'slaves' and had to pretend to go along with the majority in the society that was ignorant so as to avoid being seen as 'mad'.

"Oh, that reminds me about this guy I met by chance. I think you could as well be him. You both have similar stories.

"This concerned boy told me how he suffered wrestling with the faith that his parents handed down to him. He was born in Lagos into an Islamic family, but his extended family comprised of Christians too, and he loved them all. They all celebrated each important religious holiday together. There was no argument about which faith was following the instruction of The God. But their respective pastors and Imams filled that blank. They all got along well until the grandmother died; who was a devout Muslim, she prayed five times daily and went to Mecca, once. Then something pricked this young boy's conscience. Where would his beloved grandma spend eternity? According to Islam that'd be heaven. All he had to do too was to follow the footsteps of his grandma and Mohammad would welcome him to paradise, but what about the others in his extended family?

"One of the daughters of his grandma was a Christian; in fact, another son was also a Jesus follower. The simple reason was the grandma married twice, once to a worshipper of their native ancestral God. And the other was to a Christian. So, where would the Christian children of his grandma end up in the hereafter, and their children, too? Hell, of course, according to the Koran. He wanted to know so badly whether the children of his grandma, especially the Christian side, agreed that their mother would be burning in hell forever. Were they kind of blaming their illiterate mother not to have taken the right path or faith...path that any moron would know without a teacher? Did they agree, at least, that their mother was good, caring, wise, fasting and prayerful? That in hardship, sickness and good times she was there for them, whether consciously or otherwise. They chose the right path and mother headed to hell.

"There was nothing he wouldn't have given to know how the Christian children handled that thought. But suddenly, the beloved of the children of his grandma died unexpectedly and this young boy loved her very much, just like his mother. She was so supportive of everyone in the extended family; she was their backbone, physically and emotionally. Whatever situation anyone faced she was there for them.

"Now, how would Mohammad and Allah judge his aunt? That was the beginning of his dilemma; the beginning of reading the two so-called holy books and really seeing for himself...after all, he too went to a Christian school that was orchestrated by his aunt. That meant the Christians educated him for his betterment in life. How could he deny their help in his life? And so he started to question everything. After a long search without bias, he realized that these two religions had poisoned his family's true humanity.

"One of the interesting things he told me was when he stopped going to the mosque and ceased praying to Jesus, because he was influenced by the school he attended, some members of the family came to him and just wanted him to choose one religion. Because now he believed in nothing, not because he didn't want to believe, but to him it was a wrong belief any human being could have.

"And this made him to question whether man knew or understood what love meant. Whenever he started talking about God, members of his extended families would get up and leave. They really thought they loved one another. He jokingly asked whether they would see each other in the so-called heaven, since they prayed to two separate Gods.

When his own father died when he was still in secondary school he didn't carry out the instruction of the Imams that said he should pray to Allah to send his father to heaven. Not that he was conscious of what he was doing at that time, but looking around in the burial ground, seeing signs of the cross and the crescent moon and some without any, he wondered whether that was all it would take to get to paradise regardless of any atrocities; simple prayer and just being a believer!!

"Then, when he was in college a popular televangelist came to his campus to preach and everybody from far and wide, young and old, the sick and the dejected at heart went to listen to the pastor. This guy saw it as an opportunity to see firsthand the miraculous power of God he had seen on TV. The night was electric according to him. He had no mistrust about the whole thing. He kept an open mind. He would be more than happy to see all the people on the sick beds and wheel chairs healthy again, that the relatives or family members brought for healing that night.

"The preacher came on stage, praised Jesus, boasted about heaven. Praised God, boasted some more about paradise. The crowd cheered happily and sang. In fact, to him that night was enchanting. The preacher with his white counterpart told everyone to raise their hands to the heavens to receive the blessings of God. Everyone did as told willingly, even though some elderly with rheumatism defied their pains and kept up with everybody's hands pointing to the heavens, waiting for the blessings. He prayed and amen was on every lip.

"After the long prayer he asked for donations. He carefully instructed the people not to put their gifts just in any plastic bags that they should put them in green ones that the ushers would be carrying around. This guy guessed some people were cutting into the donations meant for the house of God.

"And after that the pastor left with his entourage back to his five-starred-hotel; heaven on earth. The guy was dejected. The pastor was a well-fed, well-clothed, well-housed, and well-cared for and went back to his well-provided life, leaving the poor and the sick holding on to plenty of advice on patience, endurance and hope ; hope to feed their hungry children; hope to send their sons and daughters to school;

hope to have children and fulfill all human wants; hope for a cure of a sickness; hope for their corrupt government to stop lying to them; hope to enjoy the meager fruit of their labor, not stolen by their God-sent preachers. Nothing but one big false hope!

"Not one miracle was performed that night. He guessed the Holy Spirit was on vacation. And he wondered what man had become, selling hope to the hopeless for a price. Maybe, they didn't have enough faith, maybe, God wanted to know whether they just came for the miracles alone and not loving him, maybe, maybe...but there was no maybe about the donations. And every year the crowd grew larger and larger. He had heard enough. He had seen enough. This was nothing but a sham. If he was a nationalist, he would have seen that as a replay of slavery when the African leaders and the whites sold their kind to the New World. Now the African and the white man had returned with a slightly different kind of scheme to dupe the people; renewal and perpetuating mental slavery.

"And as if everything couldn't be clearer, one of his nieces in the post-911 world, adhered to Islamic tenets. It wasn't forced on her, apart from the parents' religious-hand-me-down choice of faith. Lagos has freedom of religion for now. One group in a society can one day outnumber others and impose their faith on the rest of the groups and call it a Revolution. They shared stories, laughed together, ate together, he helped out in financial situations, even took her to the swimming pool, but she wouldn't swim but secretly told him she liked it but... And they argued about life; what it was, religion or no religion, right or wrong, husband and wife?

"One day he asked her if there was a fight between him, the infidel, and Islam, which side would she be on and whether she would kill him? She clearly said that wouldn't be right for her to do because there was an incident like that when a son wanted to kill his father who was on the other side of Islam, but the Prophet said the son shouldn't do that, but should allow other members of the group to fight his father. And to her, that was right; holy justice. At least, it's clear she will not kill him, but will staunchly, without regrets be on the side of Islam. Needless to say he too re-educated himself and broke the dogma the power that be established for him. No more drinking from the well." John said finally.

"Thank you, John." Den said.

"You are welcome." John replied.

"One more question, John?" Den asked.

"What?" John was curious.

"How did you handle the fear of all these religions? I mean in your personal life." Den wanted to know.

"Mmm," John thought briefly about it and said. "Apart from some unexplainable events in my life that challenge earthly understanding, I drew courage from them. The fearlessness of all these believers in one another's fears, especially the heaven and hell ones, makes me fearless of all their imagined or believed fears. That is the antidote. And my wife has this saying, something about being cocksure of yourself like a mathematician. I don't remember exactly, but I will try...she would say, it's not enough to be right, you have to know why you are right, something like that."

"Thank you, again." Den said gratefully.

"You are welcome, again." John said smiling with Den."

All was understood. Now it was time to set yourself free, if you could.

"Is easier for the camel to pass through the eye of a needle
Than for a brainwashed man to know he is brainwashed."
Den

"Love is not a matter of belief."
Nameless.

Love In Question

Jack came back to the tree and sat down beside the two men. He had in his hands three cans of soda and three donuts. He longed to lift something heavy, bar bells, anything that would challenge his body. He was already missing the gym. He gave one each to the guys.

"What have you guys been up to?" Smiling as if to say, what did I miss? Jack asked.

"Nothing really, we were just wondering about the universe as usual." John answered, sipping his coke.

"What have you been up to yourself? You certainly took your time over there." Den said in a jest.

"Oh, I ran into Bob and we had some talks concerning the project. Then I went to get something to eat, there I saw Ahmed and Fred sharing a burger." Jack answered.

"Why were they sharing a burger?" Den asked.

"I guess that was the last one. And I don't know who bought it. But they were hungry, I guess…," he replied.

"Talk about the ninth wonder of the world." Den was surprised.

"Once in a while I actually believe act of kindness like that gives mankind hope, but…" Before Jack could finish his sentence, John's skeptical face said it all and Den caught on fast.

"Hey, don't you share the same sentiment?" Den queried.

"It's not that." John assured. "It's obviously a commendable gesture to see the true nature of man shinning through the thick layers of misguided concept about one another…" Then he paused to think of what to say next and that gave Jack the chance to finish his thought on the issue.

"But…," Jack said finally. "I've seen act of kindness like that everywhere, and especially in terms of religious differences, it makes me want to jump for joy and happiness, and then in the twinkle of an eye, the opposite, which is terrible, occurs. Then you start to scratch your head about what has just happened. Is the generosity genuine or fake, can it be counted on every time? Or is it like a split personality disorder that makes you kind and generous in the name of God/Allah and also torture, hate, condemn, kill and massacre in the same vein.

Surah 5:47
Believers take neither the Jews nor the Christians for your friends. Whoever of you seeks their friendship shall be one of their number.

"My sentiment, too," John said. "So over the years I try to look beyond the irregular acts of kindness. I now look at man differently, what makes him do what he does, what influences him, the root of his natural tendencies and what have you, who or what is pulling his strings and why, and for what purpose?"

John held his breath for a while then went on.

"Before we jump into this seemingly easy topic, I have to ask you guys if man truly comprehends the concept of love. What's love? How do we love? Why do we love? Do we give partial love? Do we give love just because…? What makes us love? Then, what is the ultimate goal of love?

"Of course, we all rush to give ourselves a pass mark when it comes to love; I defend the right of those people; I give alms to the poor; I have a foundation; I give to worldwide charities; I help my fellow human cross the street; I find job for the homeless; I get up for a pregnant woman in a crowded train or bus and also for the elderly and the injured. All this is praiseworthy and noble, but…?

"A friend of mine is of the view that humans are naturally caring and we love to share, but we get sidetracked from our natural ability to continuously do all those good stuff regardless of the recipient because of a number of reasons that becloud our pure, heartfelt and unconditional love. I can list a million things, but in one word, vanity. Our vanity has robbed us of love; we now love just because we want to make it to heaven; we love just because we want to get into that girl's pants; we love just because we want to get our hands on that rich man's money; we love just because we want peace; we love just because we have been promised everlasting sexual pleasure in paradise. We love just because that guy is so good looking. I am sure there are many more I love just because…we all can fill in the blanks.

"How can we carry this heavy baggage and still think we are genuinely good. I'm a good person - we keep saying, because it makes us feel good inside. I don't wish anybody bad or harm. I love my neighbors. I understand the plight of foreigners, and many more love inspired things we do on a regular basis. I think we only have lower degree of true love but all claim to have ultimate love for our brothers and sisters, fathers and mothers, friends and all people; but what we have is a mere semblance of the real thing.

"Because if we can look deeper inside ourselves, what most of us beat our chest for becomes…what can I liken it to…mmm…yeah, like a KKK giving food to a hungry black baby. Or like a slave seller and buyer taking good care of their slaves' health. We are all climbing the ladder of love which extends to infinity yet man takes the first rung, balances himself, and claims he understands fully what love is." John pondered.

Jack and Den shifted nervously in their positions. This area could reveal their own flaws in the avenue of love--true, genuine love.

"Love never changes; this is not a new-age talk, it's our lack of understanding it that puts man at loggerhead with another. We should love simply because of love, but man as man demands to be loved.

> *II Corinthians Chapter 6 Verses 14-15*
> *Be ye not unequally yoked together with unbelievers: for*
> *what fellowship hath righteousness with unrighteousness?*
> *and what communion hath light with darkness?And what*
> *concord hath Christ with Belial? Or what part hath he that*
> *believeth with an infidel?*

"And once we understand love." John continued. "Do we do it for a while or endlessly? And do we put conditions on it? Who should our mentor concerning love be? Can we love and condemn at the same time? Can we put fear into somebody to love or accept us? There are so many questions about love that mankind hasn't really answered. And lastly, do we love and care for generations before us and after, or the suffering and bloodletting of the past were not that painful back then? It's a long time, forget that!

> *John Chapter 3, Verse 18*
> *He that believeth on him is not condemned; but he that*
> *Believeth not is condemned already, because he hath*
> *Not believed in the name of the only begotten son of*
> *God.*

"Oh, I was going to say something before I got sidetracked by love. Now I remember. I had a discussion with a black American guy about where people who didn't accept Jesus Christ in their lifetime would be in the afterlife? He just said without any concern whatsoever that they would go straight to hell!

> *II Thessalonians, Chapter 2, Verses 7-9*
> *The Lord Jesus shall be revealed from heaven with*
> *his mighty angels, in flaming fire taking vengeance on*
> *them that know not God, and that obey not the gospel*
> *of our lord Jesus Christ: who shall be punished with*
> *everlasting destruction from the presence of the lord,*
> *and from the glory of his power.*

"Then I asked him a question that I knew was close to his heart. Where would Malcolm X go? I asked. At first he was speechless, his jaws dropped. Maybe he had not thought of it that way, and the reality of it dawned on him. It shattered everything he was told to believe.

"To say that Malcolm X did not contribute to the struggle of the blacks in Christian-nation-US for equality would be absurd. And to say that Malcolm X would go to hell because he died a Muslim would be equally absurd. Then the only thing he could do was to fight back blindly, totally disregarding the issue. He felt empty and hypocritical, but rather than taking it out on himself he directed the anger at me for asking that touchy question. To this day we don't talk.

"Other blacks would further delude themselves, the Christians, that Malcolm switched his faith right before he died to...you guessed it--Christianity. Then where would all the black people; men, women and children in the struggle for equality that were beaten, raped and made to disappear into thin air who were neither Muslims nor Christians, be in afterlife? Even Muhammad Ali won't be able to float like a butterfly and sting like a bee pass the loving minds of the Christian hell.

"The hatred and torture by the whites would be like a nuisance to them, lasting for so many years, compared to their brethren sending them in their brotherhood and sisterhood minds and hearts to hell for eternity. Someone should tell them they can't eat their cake and have it too, and they should stop the pathetic excuse about crossing that bridge (judgment day scenario) when they get there.

"But, please don't get me wrong, I believe and know that people naturally mean well, it's just that it's not coming from their religious beliefs, but rather from the core of their true humanity. They have just been robbed of it by the religion of hatred, and it's hard to see!

"And the funny thing is that these acts of kindness and love are erroneously perceived by them as endearing them more to their respective given Gods.

"It gets even weirder when you consider where Malcolm X pitched his tent. Fighting for freedom looks confusing. I fight for you here; you fight for yourself over there. Where should the real fight be, here or there, years or eternity?" John dug into the heart of love.

Surah 5.64
Unbelievers are those that say; God is one of three;

He spread his hands out in a gesture to say those were my reasons. Jack and Den nodded in agreement, and John continued.

"I was in the US and the police, four of them, all white, we were told shot this African guy forty times or so. That's another story in itself. But pertinent to what we are saying, the whole country went berserk. But was the whole country truly serious about caring deep down for this man? And the number one guy in the forefront of the crusade for justice was a reverend, who in his view was fighting injustice in America for the fallen African. But it is the religion of the reverend that is in question here, needless to say - his act was a good deed.

"So the guy died a terrible death at the hands of his fellow men, but he died a Muslim--that changes the complexity of the whole situation when you factor in the true meaning of love as we are trying to understand.

"We know where the reverend's God is going to send this poor African - If you ask me, this guy did pretty well dying for his own sins. But seriously, you weigh the forty or so bullets and eternity in hell roasted by a loving God, and then you tell me which is worse or what justice the reverend should be fighting for? And the whole black and white Christians cried for the poor guy.

"Then we should ask ourselves? Is this love we are showing in cases like this or our own meaning of it. The love we give becomes pretentious and superficial, failing to see clearly the whole spectrum of what we agree to be life; can't see the forest for the trees. Remove the religion of a God like that and you have the reverend in flying colors." John said frankly.

"I couldn't have said it better." Jack said, smiling, trying to sound like John.

"Also, when I see mixed-religious-marriages where I come from… you have to wonder if you can call it love." John added. "Although what most of them try to do in these inter-religious-marriages is one partner tries to change the other, and if that fails…"

"I bet the man is always trying to convert the wife to his religion." Den interrupted.

"Yeah…90% of the time, based on his little dangling thing," John answered. "Like I said, if that fails, they just stay together anyway, especially when the fear of staying single comes to mind. They settle. Just like some women will settle when the alarm clock is ticking or some men after they failed to find that perfect figured woman - and we call it true love. Sometimes it's what makes us accept other tribe or race after our own treated us bad or didn't show interest in us; we suddenly become understanding, sometimes we marry up and delude ourselves its love; generally the successful people from the conquered race or tribe engage in this act because they lack backbone, expect its real love, which is far and in-between. And some just can't marry down, so to speak, not because of lack of love but rather because of class status.

Man engages in this madness to find an appropriate companion as if we have to find a mate to perform that single obligation of marriage in life, and if we don't we are seen as a disappointment.

"This is after we are worried sick that our family and friends might not like the one we say we love. Who says we like the way they look or behave in the first place. And even when we find someone to marry, we make it a do or die affair. We force ourselves to stay together in a loveless relationship not wanting others to see us as failures. And when we do part, we can't part amicably; it has to resort to hatred and violence. We kill or harm the one we boast of loving. But truly, love is not by force, no matter how we look at it and no matter how long we have been together or sacrificed. If someone says I want to go, you let him or her go.

"Marriage is just one of the many ways to learn love and good partnership. Some religions have made love synonymous with marriage, just like to be a Christian is equal to love. It's a holy matrimony sanctioned by God. It must work, like it or not, like salmon returning to their birth place to spawn and then must die.

"Then what about all the other relationships that don't have to do with sex and partnership and still fail woefully, like brothers not on speaking terms forever, family members hardly seeing eye to eye, friends with or without benefits and they still fight and never reconcile, talk about mothers and daughters becoming lifelong enemies. And lesbian and gay marriages (rude awakening to women) failing like 'God sanctioned' ones. Man has had sugar-daddy-marriages, kingdom-alliances-marriages, money-marriages, arranged-marriages, sport-marriages, film- marriages, fine-people-to-fine-people-marriages, ugly-to-beautiful-people-marriages, cousin- marriages, sugar-mummy-marriages, underage-marriages, holy-marriages, choice-marriages (you like him, you marry him), and many more…still we fail to see that we are taking a class in love. We keep forcing all these relationships to work! How long are we going to deceive ourselves? There are numerous areas to learn how to love. We don't have to marry in order to only have the chance at learning love, true love. This is a social lie!

"So when the Catholic Church reluctantly allowed people in Chile to divorce, the courts were overwhelmed by so many women wanting to leave their loving husbands. The bird is out of the cage, if it returns to you, it is love. By the way, did the beloved David love his wives? Maybe, all these holier than thou bible-clutching-women would have loved to be amongst David's wives.

"Also, because we are talked about shamefully when we can't

find somebody to love physically and emotionally, most of us take whomever, with less demand on religion. Some even think you are not responsible if you are not married. But the hardcore drenched in fear, would sacrifice a good man or woman for the sake of heaven. The moderate will conveniently 'love' and marry the unbelievers, 'hey God/ Allah I can't obey you here. He's very caring and loving. Don't worry, I will try and convert him.' " John surmised.

"So, it's not true love, but kind of a contract." Den added his two cents.

"That's what religion has turned man into; it doesn't bring unity and harmony but separation, misunderstanding and deep discord, as if we don't have enough of that around already." John said philosophically.

"Some marriages are broken up based on religious issues. Since we are always changing, a wife or husband can come home someday and say 'I have found God and this is what God says, I cannot stay with you unless you become like me, religiously.' They even think twice before they marry someone in a different denomination, that's how pathetic it is. And when they do, they start fighting over which denomination their poor baby should belong to, even before the child leaves heaven." John continued.

"Hey, what love has put together, let no religion put asunder?" Den was on a roll.

"That's a good one." Jack smiled.

"But seriously, it's apparent that we do not know what we are doing most of the times." John said sadly. "Some of us consciously or otherwise condemn others we call family; fathers, mothers, brothers, sisters, relatives, friends, citizens, fellow human beings because of a difference of beliefs and ours, of course, is the right one. 'How can I not understand the words of God correctly, it's me, after all. Or am I not spiritual enough?'" John was acting out the sarcasm for all to see, beating his chest like a silverback or a player that scored a winning goal in a tight match as if he was the only one in the team.

"And we pretend to truly love, help and care for people. We don't even remotely think of all those that helped us along the journey of life to come to this conclusion of self-righteousness and heavenly bound path." John went on.

"They are all dispensable like pawns in a game of chess; the driver that drove you to school every day; the teacher that taught you how to read and write, and many more; the roadside vendor that sold you food so you didn't go hungry; those that helped you up when you fell on your holy feet; the nurses that cared for you as a baby, and now that you are grown, have you even thought of them? but nevertheless they are going to hell; the midwife that delivered you into this world; the doctor that prescribed medicine when you were sick and your faith did not come through for you; the barber that cut your hair so you were presentable; the employer that gave you job so you could feed your family of God-chosen; the men and women who discovered vaccines for deadly diseases so you could stay here longer before rejoining your God; the inventor of your glasses so that you could clearly see who to hate and who to condemn to hell; the kind hearted atheist that sheltered you when you were homeless, how did he find the kindness in such a heart without your Jesus or prophet's help?; the slaves that built your country with unbearable hard labor, the millions of African slaves tossed into the sea en route the promised land and holy places; the farmers that grew all your holy foods; the babysitter that cared for your holy children while you worked, (still, they are heading straight to hell); the mother that carried you for nine months and fed you her precious milk; the father that cared so much for you; the friends that put a smile on your face when you were down; the entertainers that took your mind away from the chaos of the world - even for a brief moment; the infidels that sold you weapons to continue your holy wars; the donors of money and materials to rebuild your lands when your loving God sent in 'natural disasters'; the inventors of radio and television and computers that kept you informed and entertained, and with which you reached thousands of souls, preaching hatred; the producers of oil to run your economy so that you could keep contributing to your house of God; the builders of your holy cities.

"Where would they all go in the end of their lives serving you, in your loving mind and heart? What about the police and the army that fought on your behalf because another sect from your religion or another religion wanted to send you and your family to an early paradise? What about the fire fighters that helped to stop the fire in your house, saving your holy self and your children before your loving God would send them to hell fire forever. Secretly you have boasted that no fire fighter could put out the fire of hell. So when they leave you safe and sound, don't say your hypocritical thank you; 'God bless you'...say what you really believe. 'See you in hell.' After everything is said and done, you claim it's your God-given-right to have your personal belief.

"And yet, we hold our heads up high and declare, 'I love these people.' Please!"

John paused, took a sip of his coke. He was getting emotional about what he was saying; crying inside for the world of man.

Den and Jack looked at each other and did not know what to say, and just kept silent.

"You know it's hard not to get emotionally involved sometimes, but the thing that takes the cake for me looking at how every race had interacted among themselves is the delusion of the black people." John regained his balance. "The black people make a perfect example of how man claims to see and understand but still very blind and hypocritical. I don't think I can find a better example to illustrate what religion mixed with fear has done to a peoples' thinking. The English starvation of millions of Irish pales against it, the Jews anti-Semitism can't compare, either--though they never let people forget that in a hurry. The Armenia genocide by the Turks takes a far distance, and there are uncountable instances out there. But the thing that separates all this man's inhumanity to man is that within the black people they now knowingly or unknowingly condemn their own to eternal hell by the religion of their former masters or should I omit the word, former? If their former colonial masters condemn themselves in religious arena, should the blacks in diasporas or within black Africa follow suit?

"Can anyone in their right mind say that all those black slaves that worked in such conditions in America and Europe and everywhere else hundreds of years ago would go to hell, (I would like to see a black pastor damn the unbelieving slaves to hell, based on his faith in Christ on national TV) forget those that died on the sea because they were packed like sardines, and when they did, they were tossed into the sea - thousands, wonder what black Christians think...I know what Moby Dick thought...dinner forever. 'Thank you, goddess of the sea.'

"Their cry for unity is instinctual rather than pure love among themselves for survival. Naturally, groups do this. The Indians under the oppressive rule of the British Empire came together to fight the injustice and having won, separated themselves under religion which is worse than the rule under the British. They now deny Indians like themselves entering paradise--depending on the religious beliefs. So also the Irish banded together to fight the British, but they too, divided themselves based on the same religion not only on earth by killing themselves, but also in heavenly matters. Did you hear the Chinese crying for the emancipation of the blacks? No. Did you see the Arab Muslims and Muslims alike marching to condemn the genocide in Darfur? Even the animals engage in this kind of same group mentality, but in their case it's limited to earth and very pragmatic for survival.

"Of course, the ridiculous argument by the so-called holy men and professors of theology is that, those people were not Christians. Christ did not teach that. Does that really matter though? Christianity maintains that as long as you are not a Christian - it does not matter what another man does to you, he can fry you for dinner - you are still going to hell.

"The other defense mechanism they hide behind now in the so-called modern time thinking is, 'I have a personal relationship with God. It's not religion that I am in.' That translates to shut up; I don't want to think of the terrible things a loving God did in the bible. I am not capable of looking in the mirror to truly see without blind eyes or rather blind faith. I am scared of what to find. Just ask them if their personal God is the creator of everything!

"The modern day Christians who would never have enslaved or, be racists or segregationists and all that happened in the past was when man never truly understood Jesus' message of love should ask themselves one question. Why didn't the Holy Spirit teach understanding and compassion to the early Christians? Like 50 years ago...

"Then again, slavery was permitted in Judaism and Christianity, so how can you blame the followers; like father like son. The Church of England just apologized for their involvement in slavery but so many churches are still keeping mute on the topic, like the Baptist. But what is the apology for? If it's man to man, we can say its okay, we can brush that under the carpet as one of learning disabilities. But the issue transcends the physical; it's celestial, which is punishable by eternal condemnation. What would the offender get and what would the offended get? Your guess is as good as mine.(So that it happened a long time ago becomes baseless) The magic portion that will save man from evil now looks like a nice, ripe and juicy apple on the outside but rotten and smelly in the inside. How can anyone reconcile that?

"Sometimes I just would like to be a fly on the wall when the righteous, both blacks and whites and whatever color; the superstars that Jehovah has blessed, the influential Talk Show hosts that the cross of Jesus dangle around their necks when they are giving profound advice to man and the world, the philanthropists that won't go to bed without the bible or Koran under their pillows, the successful actors and actresses, the president of a multi-religious people, the singers and entertainers thanking God for the awards, the social reformers in communities, the agape lovers and the save the children campaigners, get to certain passages that truly reveal man's inequality to man according to the Holy books and God's sound judgments regarding the issues; like genocide. Do they skip it and rush to the passages that promise them heavenly bliss for their work and their strong, unshakeable faith in God, the son and the Holy Spirit?

> *Leviticus Chapter 25,*
> *Both thy bondmen, and thy bondmaids, which thou*
> *shalt have, shall be of the heathen that are round*
> *about you; of them shall you buy bondmen and*
> *bondmaids. Moreover of the children of the strangers*
> *that do sojourn among you, of them you shall buy,*
> *and of their families that are with you, which they begat*
> *in your land and they shall be your possession.*
> *And ye shall take them as an inheritance for your children*
> *after you, to inherit them for a possession; they shall be your*
> *bondmen forever; but over your brethren the children of*
> *Israel, ye shall not rule one over another with rigor.*

"Or do they say in their hearts, yeah, good judgment. Go God!" John said in a hypocritical manner.

"We don't have to verbally voice it before we condemn or judge others. It's self-contradictory and full of hypocrisy." Jack said.

"It's a kind of hidden hypocrisy I would say." Den added.

"It's apparent; crystal clear, my friends. Accepting it by the billions of people that close their eyes to it is the herculean task. Just to let you know that it is clear. Ask a Muslim who claims that it's the same God that they all worship as the Christians to go to church instead or to go to the shrine of a pagan god and bow down. Same God plea that all humans worship is a ridiculous excuse. You will get your answer." John answered and continued.

"A black woman in the land of the free stopped me one day and said, 'can't you see God's touch in my life, my personal life,' proudly. And I thought about it for a minute. I thought about what she would say if I asked her where was God for those black men and women who lived in slavery for hundreds of years, generation after generation without a break, comparing her finding a job to a life of slavery. She might never talk to me again. But I do understand her confusion and fear.

"There is one thing that man fails to put in the right perspective here. We lack comparative analogies as one of my lectures used to say. Spotlighting the struggles of the blacks in the US; this group of people, at least majority of them, thought Jesus led them to the promised land of freedom. Jesus didn't do it! If you know your history, you'll know of Mohandas Gandhi that practiced Hinduism, also led his so-called people to freedom and victory against the mighty British Empire through passive resistance and sustenance of his faith. The feat was achieved not by the blood of Jesus or by the Nation of Islam or Mohammed, but through Vishnu. A logical explanation from this is that all these people's Gods were irrelevant in their plights. I think it's more like the human spirit that was at play. Even Martin Luther King had to go to India to learn the act of passive resistance from Gandhi's legacy.

"Also my wife's friend would like her man to change because of fear of hell. She wanted her husband to convert to Christianity. They never stopped having this argument, until one day he told her that her father-in-law died a Muslim - 'so where would my father be after judgment day?-hell, burning, and me in heaven, dancing, rejoicing, and watching my father on the other side in flames for eternity.' She became speechless, looked embarrassed and walked away. They never had that discussion again." John said.

"Hmm, that's a powerful argument. But then, how do you really love your lover or wife and believe in your heart that your God doesn't approve of her. Isn't love supposed to come from the heart and conquer all?" Den said in a preachy tone.

"Not that his father-in-law's position was encouraging, either. At least, if he truly knew what the Koran said.

Surah 4.56
Those that deny our revelation we will burn in fire.
No sooner will their skin be consumed than we shall
give them other skins

Surah 14.42
The day will surely come when those who disbelieve
will wish that they were Muslims.

"Even when death occurs you can still see this sympathy displayed by these religious people of different faiths. You can't but wonder what's going on in their heads and hearts. But truly I believe people feel real sympathy for the dead apart from their inner fear that it will someday happen to them, too." John said and gave an example.

"So, when one of our co-workers died, we all went to pay our last respect as expected. Everyone was in tears including the Christians amongst us. I had to ask myself, were they crying because the guy just died or because the Christian God would burn this guy in hell forever?"

"How can you love their neighbor and condemn them to hell for eternity just because they don't believe as you? No matter the religion I accept, if I become the only one that makes it to this lofty paradise of God, God will have one very sad guy on his hands." Jack said.

Den and John glanced at him in a questionable way.

"The question is how can I be the only one and the rest of mankind is burning in hell? What did I do to deserve it? Even if this God chose me, shouldn't I decline? Knowing how hard life could be." Jack reasoned.

Then he paused for a while as if searching for the answer from the heavens. "I think love is hard to understand like you have been saying. Consider even Jesus' love. He came to die for the sins of mankind, whether we begged him or not, so we could go to paradise and have a big party demanded we take him as our savior or we are staring hell in the face." Jack said.

"Our pastor said that if all the other religions can take us to paradise, then it means that Jesus died in vain." Den added quickly.

"Shouldn't love be given freely without conditions? Say I saved a girl from drowning, risking my own life, then I turned around and demanded that she must love me. What kind of love would that be? Shouldn't I feel something when I am making love to her, like guilt… embarrassing guilt.

"We all know that some of the so-called sinners, many as they may be are able to be so giving that if God - Jesus' Dad, had requested a volunteer, hundreds of people would be more than willing to die for the sins of the rest of us." Jack assured.

He looked at John with an expression that said yes, I would.

But John decided to inform him that that would not be necessary.

"Actually, my sacrificial lamb, according to the history of the Aztec religion, there had been occasions when the society demanded some people be sacrificed for the general good. And people willing volunteered. So it is not a new idea in the history of man and God or making the world a better place like the Christians are holding on to the blood of Jesus." John pointed out.

"Really," Jack replied.

"Yeah, really," John confirmed.

"But in my case, I would not attach any condition, like…going back to heaven." Jack continued. Obviously happy that what he thought of had already been done. It gave him hope that he was not crazy.

"I never thought about it that way." Den said.

"What do you mean?" John wanted to know, too.

"I mean going back to heaven. If Jesus did not know whether it would be heaven, if he thought it could be eternal hell, would he have done it? That is where the true love should come in." Jack surmised.

"I get it now." Den said laughing his head off.

"Most of us would do the sacrifice at the drop of a hat." Jack said seriously.

"But according to God, only a sinless person can do that." John informed them.

"So we bargain with two sinners for the price of one sinless man." Jack couldn't help laughing this time. "Ha ha ha"

"I keep telling you guys, man is trying to understand why we are here. This is just the story of a sect that broke away from Judaism. There are hundreds of other people's stories that don't add up. The reason why most of us discuss these popular religions is easy to understand. It was imposed on many of us." John regained his outlook on life.

"So it's the fear of the unknown that drives beliefs, not love." Jack said.

"I strongly agree with you, Jack. It's a case of a sighted man groping in the light. We are easy sales. We do not question why we are so important to this creator called God or whatever name you call him. We fail to look beyond ourselves, our family and town or society, to see other people like us that go through the same love and pain as we do, because man is easily flattered; that is his weakness. God has chosen us, somewhat, is the highest of all flatteries and billions fall for it, live by it and die by it.

"Also, they have hammered so much fear into man's head that he would choose heaven. Whatever heaven is over any thing that stands in his way, even a-day-old baby will be crushed en route paradise because he has been conditioned to fight for his own eternal paradise at the expense of anything and anyone. Man is substituting shadow for substance, hatred for love." John concluded.

"I think I'm in good company. I don't know where this big story of if's, why's and how's will end, or even if there is an end. But I'm grateful to have met you guys." Den said thankfully.

"Hey, you want to know the most frightening thing? Most people who are in one religion or another are ignorant of what their respective holy books say on any topic. But the moment you bring it to their attention and they read it themselves, they are shocked, but stubbornly defend it. It's not that they don't know what they just read is evil or bad, but they do not expect it from their beloved book. A Christian even said to me that that wasn't her God when I showed her some quotes in the bible, but still believed in the God of Jesus. They are in big denial and one of the reasons why this is, you make them look as if they don't know what they have been doing and saying all these years; they don't want to appear stupid. Man measures life in terms of years. You hurt their pride.

"Then again, it is also scary for them to leave their comfort zone; truth be told, they have been brainwashed and drenched in dogma. But no one will agree to that openly. They proudly think they have an open mind, but no, they have been blinded by heritage, tradition, culture and religion. They all dance to the rhythm of the past, sacrificing their humanity. Their culture, religion, color can't be compared to others' in their minds, and God even speaks their language! And of course, they reside in God's own country. This pride in one's self is nothing short of hatred in colorful attire. They are scared of living in the present; reliving their fore-father's whim and caprice, and they pay with destructions, wars, ethnic cleansing. And you can't really pity the conquered or blame the conqueror, because they are birds of a feather. We are all victims, unless we open our eyes!

"Stepping outside that 'holy' boundary is frightening, too. You see, reasoning and loving the way they know will cease. What's left will be the reconfiguration of everything in their lives. They will feel empty and lost, so they hold on to their faith for dear life. The harm has been done to their minds, hearts and spirits 'forever'." John concluded.

Just as Den was about to ask another question concerning man, there was a call from the general office to see the model of the complex about to be built. And off they went.

"Humans are searching for the meaning of life and
reaching out to whatever they perceive as 'divine'.
gambling for salvation."
Jack

One Shot, No Second Chances

"I guess that call is important. Let's go see what it's all about." Jack said.

They all got up and headed to the conference room. Everyone was already there, seated. It was a full house and there was a distinctive new face in the midst.

The introduction was done by Bob, flanked by his boss and the stranger. And once in a while Frank would chip in a word or two. The third guy remained silent.

The model was nothing anybody had seen before and it seemed to speak volumes about openness, real love and care - in full detail, and how people who would inhabit the complex would live. There was an aura of peace - not falsehood, and nothing but harmony oozing from the model.

Everyone was in awe of it - like pure paradise was found again, but this time, lasting and all inclusive, with individual freedom entrenched. But how to translate this from a mock-up to an actual reality as man knew it was left to be seen. But this group would have a shot at it.

"And...I sincerely hope that with every hand on deck, this group - this unique group can build it with nothing but love, apart from the materials needed, of course." Bob concluded.

Everyone applauded and broke up into small units discussing what it would take to accomplish the task at hand.

"I think it is beautiful, Jack." Den was blown away.

"I'll give anything to make it come true." Jack was full of praise for the project.

Bob and Frank left the company of the men to attend to more details in private. And the new guy tagged along. Maybe he had a special talent or something. His job remained a mystery for now.

After the excitement faded, everybody settled down, each one with his inner thoughts.

"You know what? If it's true that people do come back, there are so many things that I'd love to do that I did not do in my teenage years, and even now." Den voiced his thoughts.

"You only live once my friend." Fred eagerly answered him. "So I guess your wish will never come true."

Hebrew Chapter 9 - Verse 27
And as it is appointed unto men, once to die
and after this the judgment.

"Really, people who believe in such are foolish. The Koran does not acknowledge such devilish desire." Ahmed also put in his two cents. "I can never believe such; it does not make sense." He continued.

Surah 17:10
fate of each man we have bound about his neck.
On the day of resurrection we shall confront him with a
book spread wide open

Den's personality whether thinking out loud or expressing his feelings always stirred the hornet's nest. Arguments seemed to follow him like a cloud of rain; a magnet for controversy.

"First, because you have been told not to believe it doesn't mean others won't. The belief predates the birth of your religions. Am I right, John?" Den looked in the direction of John who just nodded in agreement.

"And second, it is illogical to disprove a belief with a belief. It's all belief - you catch my drift. Now if you tell us and show us the irrationality of it then we'll know the belief in reincarnation is wrong." Jack finished the argument for Den, who was basking in the support.

This was round two and he was armed to the teeth with much insight into the conflicting human stories of how things started on earth. He could defend himself without the big brother, Jack, but he would take any help to battle the hounding spokespersons of God.

"All I know is that reincarnation talk will land you in hell." Fred charged back, this time looking for his own moral support from Ahmed. Den was quick to pound on that thought.

"Hey, what's going on here? Have you guys forgotten you have an unholy alliance? You condemn each other in your so-called one religion. Now you want to speak with one voice? Please, please, how can water and fire coexist? Continue to drink from the well." Den stressed.

They both looked bewildered, wondering whether Den had gone mad. But he paid them no mind.

"What does drinking from the well have to do with this discussion?" Ahmed was curious.

The atmosphere was heating up and the sympathy that Den was told to have for hell and heaven believers was out of the window.

"Before this gets out of hand," a calm and commanding voice cut in and all turned to John.

"Christianity and Islam are in the minority in terms of not believing in reincarnation. You'll be surprised to know that some people who practice Judaism (the mystical part, Kabbalah) believe in rebirth of some kind.

"I'm sure the Buddhist here believes it." He turned to the side of Richard, who just nodded with an expression of surprise that some people didn't believe in what was so obvious. And likewise Thomas was shocked how some people didn't know any better.

John went on.

"But Christianity and Islam command a larger followership than the rest of all other religions." He pointed out.

"You got that right." Ahmed jumped right in.

"Through force, wars, bullying and the fear of hell," Den countered quickly.

"Like I was saying...that does not mean they are right in not believing in reincarnation." John continued again. "I think most people don't understand what it means."

"It means I don't want to come back as a goat." Ahmed said jokingly.

"Well, like I was saying." John was trying hard to control his own frustration. Sometimes people pushed others to the extreme, but over the years he had stopped to let that be of big concern to him. Man as man would use any tactic to shout down another man's point, thinking that by drowning the voice of another would make the uninformed point reasonable. And also they would keep repeating the same sentence over and over as if that would make it suddenly be right or true. So he ignored him and continued.

"It simply means the spirit or energy of man that cannot die, keeps taking a human form as the case may be and comes back to learn one thing or two. And it's also tied to karma. Which is more like in learning certain things, you make an error and you return to correct the errors and move on, not necessarily with your present mother or father or anybody, but by yourself. Maybe in another family or the present one, but roles could be changed; you make the error, you get your reward or you learn your lesson. But it's not that simple either. This is just scratching the surface of what karma entails. It's deeper than that." John explained.

"Hey, Ahmed," John called out his name. Ahmed started trembling inside because he did not want to look like a fool. He had witnessed the way they had crushed Fred's holy arguments, some, he had agreed with, anyway, those Christians with their incomplete knowledge of the words of God. But now he was afraid to be made a fool of his own knowledge of the Koran, which was shallow. Whatever, he had to show consolidated view point whether it killed him or not. He wasn't going to put his dirty laundry out in the market place for ridicule. Also he was quite aware of the conflicting interpretations of the Koran by the numerous Imams he had passed through in his study of the words of Allah. But more importantly, he was worried about keeping his temper in check. How much should he take from these infidels? What would Mohammed do if anyone attacked the Holy Koran?

"Maybe it's because of the big ego of man that he could not imagine himself having the body of an animal. So, if Allah, that can do anything, and being the one that created you, can you tell Allah not to put you in a goat's body?" John asked.

Ahmed did not answer. After all, to him, it wasn't a direct question but more of a general view. He played dumb and avoided the question. Similar to all the religious people when cornered with a question they couldn't answer. They played dead and sometimes they would throw a red herring. Only a fool would run after the bone.

"Some of us, with our rational minds in a mysterious world, view the concept of reincarnation as nonsense. Man is so full of ego he can't even see himself being in the body of a woman, and vice versa. Yet he can't precisely say how he found himself here. Some of us will tremble with great fear to picture ourselves in another skin other than the one we are wearing. I can't be white, I can never be black, I don't even think I could have come as a Chinese, God forbid! Look at those people. I just can't be anything but this beautiful color. Still, some of us can't even imagine for a moment that we can be born into another religion or in another country. I can never be born a Christian--a Muslim will say, thanking Allah, while a Christian too will say the same. Some will even say they will swim the seven seas, climb the highest mountain, and travel the lowest valley to get to the religion they now practice. Some can't even imagine themselves born in ancient times. Man is mass produced, yet he foolishly thinks he is the most magnificent being. Man as man is forever on an ego trip.

"Needless to say, our ego even touches on the kinds of jobs we do, or not to be seen with an ugly person. 'There are certain places I can go with that guy though he's nice!' It pervades our entire life. And the terrible thing about our sense of self is that it's full of vanity but sugar coated with our humility.

"Even people who say it's the big bang effect, fools. They too in their scientific thinking would have collected all the atoms together to look that fantastic." He paused and seemed to be looking for Fred.

"I've got something in your Bible for you to consider, too, Fred. But before I get into that, I'll say this. I don't want to lose my train of thought." John continued.

"Really I don't know whether we can call reincarnation a religious term. It's just like saying that dreaming when we sleep is religious. Well, whatever anyone thinks, there are many tribes that believe in reincarnation around the world.

"A classic case is the Yoruba people in Nigeria like I hinted before. Some of the names they give their children give validation to their belief in it. Say, a grandfather dies in a family and a new baby is born in that family, the elders of that family will come together and name that baby, Babatunde - meaning the father or the great grandfather has come back, if it's a boy; in the case of a baby girl, she is named Yetunde or Iyabo - meaning the mother has come for another experience.

"The interesting concept here is that the Yoruba people believe that the spirit can come back either as a female or male. Now, how they know, that's another story, because not all the children are named that way." John paused to see whether they understood what he was trying to explain to them.

"Do they still believe that? I mean rebirth." Den wanted to know.

"Yes, they still do, even though the two foreign religions that majority of them tend to follow now don't believe in it. So, they sort of mix beliefs because if you voice out rebirth openly, you are not considered forward looking, just like they would like to speak like the white man or speak Arabic to elevate their status in the society. In reality people still practice their old ways, not openly though, especially in terms of protection from evil and courting good luck." John added extra information.

"Do they still have those names?" Den asked again.

"Oh, they still do. Thank goodness, but with a twist. They now have mixed names that the new generation doesn't know which name is native and which is foreign, anymore. You either reject your native name outright which sounds to them as un-Godly or take the Arabic or the Jewish name, which is Godly. After all, they could not distinguish themselves by their names before. They have to use clearer, better sounding names in the bible or in the Koran. So the Mohammed in Lagos is not related to the one in Saudi, he belongs to an Islamic brotherhood. They, the Muslims, also discard their language and speak Arabic in order to approach Allah in prayer, after all, Allah only hears Arabic! Sometimes they would joke about English language being a slave lingo, but when it's Sunday they rush to the church and on Fridays you know where they go. It's so sad!

"I know of this Yoruba guy who discarded the name his parents gave him. He was named Ishmael. (Yoruba version—Ismaila) They asked him why he would do such a thing, that his name was a prophet's name and he should be happy with it. He replied that he was not against the name, but would like to take some Yoruba names as gifts to the Arab Muslims to give to their children, too. He believed strongly in cultural exchange.

"And man beats his chest proudly shouting that he is a man, 'I'm a man!' And I wonder what that means...does that mean I can no longer

speak to God in my own language? I have to use those people's words...
mmm...to me it's like...let me sleep with your wife because I have holy
sperm!" John said disapprovingly.

"Why don't you change your own name?" Fred charged.

"It doesn't mean anything to me; it's just a name, but to those
people they have attached heavenly importance to them. Satisfied?"
John answered.

"If I may add to what you just said." Richard said running his
hands through his grey hair. "I think there is an upward progression of
soul from the so-called lower animal to the so-called higher one--man;
unless that 'spirit or soul' is really wicked, I mean so wicked, that's when
it re-enters into the so-called lower animal to restart from there."

"I don't care what you guys say about rebirth or reincarnation
and your explanation, it's not true. And on judgment day you'll face
Mohammed." Ahmed said defiantly.

"Okay, let's say reincarnation doesn't exist, that man only lives once,
dies and then, judgment day." John began to counter. "What about
millions of babies dying of one disease or the other. And their parents,
God forbid, are in the wrong religion. Where will those children go
when they die?"

That was a million dollar question that Ahmed was trying to deflect
until Fred opened his mouth. "Everyone born of a woman is a sinner.
No exception, okay" Fred paraphrased a verse of the bible. "And the
only way anyone can be saved is through the blood of Jesus Christ."

Revelation Chapter 20, Verse 15
And whosoever was not found written in the book
of life was cast into the lake of fire.

Ahmed looked at Fred with a muddled mind. The one guy that
knew why Ahmed was confounded was John, and he tried to make it
clearer to Ahmed to see the contradiction.

"You got something to say, Ahmed?" John played the devil's
advocate.

"Jesus didn't die for the sins of mankind. It's your handy work
that Allah will judge, and believing in the last prophet, Mohammed."
Ahmed stated.

"Don't start again, guys; I don't want the holy alliance to crack just yet." Den continued to tease them. "Drink, drink, drink some more, the well is full."

Fred looked at Ahmed pitifully. "That's where you guys, you Muslims are lost.

"All have sinned and fallen short of the glory of God." Fred tried to quote a portion of the bible, again. "It's man's sin that has caused all these diseases. Can't you understand?"

"Hmm, interesting defense." replied John. "But why are they getting their hell before judgment day? That's a double whammy. How come you are physically well, are you sinless? Or I didn't sin. Den, are you adding to the list?"

"Yeah, ooh yeah." Den replied happily.

But before John could go on with his points, Ahmed wanted a clarification from Fred about the Muslims being lost. Maybe it didn't register well in his brain when Fred uttered such nonsense; it deserved a good reply. He just couldn't sit there allowing every Infidel, Jew and Christian to insult his religion, especially, the Christians!

"What do you mean…lost?" Ahmed was trying hard to keep his temper in check.

"Exactly what I said, did I stutter? Someone should set you guys straight." Fred charged.

"Are you saying we don't know what we are doing?" Ahmed replied, equally charged.

"If any group doesn't know what it's doing, it's you people, turning the words of Allah upside down. And that my lost sheep was the singular reason Allah sent Mohammed to straighten things out. Don't you get it? The one Jesus spoke of."

"Ooh…, wait a minute." Fred's skin started to glow, excitement shot to the roof.

"Stop right there. Jesus didn't send Muhammad as I recall in the Bible. You must have been reading the bible upside down. Jesus mentioned a comforter…a comforter."

"And the comforter was Muhammad." Ahmed alluded.

It was like the two had taken the argument personally and the rest of the team seemed invisible. Pretty much the way the two religions thought they owned the world; every other religion was not important. John wanted to intervene in order to continue with his points, but Jack cautioned.

Den disregarded not intervening, but it wasn't clear whether he wanted them to just stop quibbling or got fed up with their constant rambling.

"Hasn't it occurred to you two that since you've been fighting for over a thousand years; the bloodlettings, the hatred, the sporadic violence and the countless lives lost to the holy cause that no Allah or Jesus has come to save millions of you in this world as we know it? You keep destroying the only world we know while deluding yourselves about some heaven no one has shown us. I will say a bird in hand is worth two or 72 virgins in paradise. Please, cease drinking from the well." Den appeased.

But it was as if his plea went in one ear and out the other. The two men continued their verbal attacks. Amazingly, Den started feeling sorry for the plight of man, too.

"Let's do the math. Can you add and subtract, my Muslim brother?" Fred started making his point. "Do you at least agree that Muhammad came after Jesus Christ, our Lord and savior?" He added a little defiance.

Ahmed nodded. Wondered why he would subject himself to such questioning. Maybe he was planning to catch Fred flatfooted.

"And the time between them was at least 500 years; Jesus was like 2000 years ago and Muhammad was like 1500 years ago, too, hmm mm?" Fred stated.

Ahmed didn't answer. He was trying to follow Fred's mathematical argument. Whether that was possible in a religious debate the whole world would like to know.

> *John chapter 14 verse 16*
> *And I will pray the Father, and he shall*
> *Give you another comforter, that he may*
> *Abide with you for ever;*

"The question is why would Jesus say to Peter and the rest of the heart broken disciples that they should not worry when he was departing? It was because he was going to send them a comforter. And why would it take 500 years or so to have that happen? Peter and the rest of them would have died ten times over!

"As far as I know, it did happen during the life of Peter and the disciples. Remember the Pentecost? Did Peter meet Muhammad? No, they received the Holy Spirit as the comforter Jesus sent; a spirit, not an Arab man, period. And who would be comforting the disciples immediately Jesus left the world? Definitely not Muhammad, my friend, he was a little bit late...try 500 years late. Somebody must be lying to you, trying to validate his own laws by affiliating with my Lord.

"And all that Greek translation of *Periklytos* (Holy Spirit) or *Paraclete*...all that nonsense trying to weave a web of lies...really, trying to make Muhammad to be the Holy Spirit in person. It's all Greek to me." He laughed. And he went on with more verbal attacks, defending his religion.

"And the so-called book of Barnabas, which is a book that lacks historical substance, copied by a Muslim...where is the original copy? What did you guys really expect him to have said? That he was in the wrong religion. You guys are even contradicting your own Koran, noble book, that Jesus wasn't the messiah, when your Prophet said he was one. And why would your Muhammad say you should read the Torah and the Gospel when he knew they were fake? And why didn't he talk about the book of Barnabas? You guys just want to impose your fake prophet into every religion...see, see...every prophet predicted our Muhammad. You guys are trying to hold on to anything in order to have legitimacy...but it's like holding on to a straw while sinking in a sea of ignorance. Somebody is misleading you. Why are you guys trying to be grammatically correct, anyway? One of your silly arguments is that the Holy Spirit was referred to as a 'he' and should have been 'it'. Even your prophet referred to Allah as a he. Does that mean Allah is a man? An Arab man, too?

"Why are you always saying may peace of Allah be upon him? When he was always fighting and fighting. Tell me how anyone can have peace like that and live in harmony with his neighbors? And why would a peaceful Jesus send a warrior to come after him when he didn't raise a sword to defend himself? Where is the commonsense here?

"And about the nonsense argument regarding the Holy Spirit, Jesus was still with them so they didn't need the Holy Spirit. It's true that the Holy Spirit has always been around. But when Jesus was with them there was no need for the Holy Spirit, Jesus carried everything on his holy shoulders. And when my Lord departed this sinful world he instructed the Holy Spirit to now guide them until his return. And finally, was your prophet able to impart understanding to all Muslims as one unit, the singular reason why God or should I say Allah sent him, that has now broken into sects, killing themselves? So what is the use of sending him...if Allah knows best because the Christians have corrupted the words of God?" Fred concluded in a jest.

Ahmed had no reply. Eyes that could say thousand words were shut down and the mouth was no good, either. Maybe he would think of one later. He was overwhelmed by the spirit of Jesus in Fred. Fred didn't give Ahmed a breathing space to put a word in like a boxer with a quick left and a right punch followed by a knockout-uppercut.

Jack was amazed at how Fred explained his points.

"What do you think of that, John?" Jack asked.

"I couldn't have said it better." John replied softly.

"But how come Fred could be this articulate on this issue?" Den asked.

"Sometimes man can see others really well and still fails to see himself." John said. "Just like in a community of multiracial or tribes, the majority fails to see the injustice on their part against the minority, but clearly sees the injustice within their group. Man sees things in parts but not as a whole."

John slowly eased them back into the initial argument about the effect of the original sin after the side one ended, making Fred's face glowed with happiness, one for Jesus, at last.

"Now, I would like some of us to imagine being born deformed - mentally or physically in this world if we can. Before you do that, I want to ask you whether you feel pain when you fall down the stairs, whether you feel hurt when you cut yourself when preparing dinner and stuff like that...whether you can cry genuinely because some of us are dead to the feelings of others. But we think we are not; earthly and heavenly, we are. And that's just us; well formed humans. These people can't even comprehend why life has dealt them these cards for half or their entire lives. They go through life with excruciating pains, and all the things that we take for granted become a herculean task every second, every minute and every day.

"What about those with cerebral palsies that occur during traumatic complications - binding them to the wheel chair forever. Now imagine one without the wheel chair. I know you will show your compassion as usual. Talk about down syndrome that causes mental retardation for life; think about the series of heart problems, kidney complications, and who knows what this disease will drag along; what about congenital bone marrow failure, resulting in lack of some white blood cells to fight simple sickness, and lack of proper functioning of the red blood cells; what about cystic fibrosis making some people like you and I to be hooked up to a respiratory machine - just to breathe, and when your nose is blocked, you start praying for a miracle cure.

"What about those that are impotent and can't have children, that gives another meaning to 'go ye and multiply'; what about Aids? Sorry, I forgot again. It started because of man's sexual immorality. But Solomon or David didn't catch it, not even one sexual disease to punish them just like God is punishing us for it now. Or were they excused because Jesus was coming from their lineage? So, God punishes us now and then will still punish us later in hell for eternity, why? I didn't read in the holy books that there would be double punishment.

"What about those with Kline Setter's Syndrome that results in being too tall, affecting them mentally and making them infertile. They are not even trying to rebuild the tower of Babel; what about cancer? Something is not in our food, it's our sin; what about those born with holes in their hearts, while yours is full of love and condemnation; what about malaria fever that kills millions every year; what about sickle cell patients - their blood cells make it difficult for easy flow of blood to all parts of the body. They lie hopelessly in bed anytime the attack comes, paralyzing their day to day joy and activities; also, there are people born with male and female organs - somebody didn't make up his mind on time and you say being gay can be cured with prayers; think of the conjoined twins. Their parents must have eaten the apple itself and not Adam and Eve, this is literally a man and a woman as one flesh; the deaf can't even hear the beautiful sounds of nature and surely not the words of your God - you're right when you say, '...those that have ears, let them hear'; and the dumb, they won't be able to speak in tongues; and the blind, the prophet was right about this, too. Wonder whether to say it's a 'good' thing not to be able to see your racism, discrimination, tribalism, paradise exclusivity, and how blind the sighted people are. The animals have all these diseases that plaque man, yet the animals won't get redemption in some heaven?

"Some of these unlucky ones can't even break any of the ten famous commandments because physical life is so unbearable to them to think of taking another man's wife like David, when they can hardly eat solid food. By the way, why are people who are born again still getting diseases? And yes, what about the organ donor that his kidney or lung or heart is beating in your body, giving it to whoever. At least, his heart or part of him will be taken to heaven. What about the thousands of mothers dying at child birth and their dead babies? And just for a moment, forget all these diseases and think for a minute about people who actually worked too hard in my opinion to put food on the table for their families. The poor farmers that suddenly had drought that killed the crops and livestock and giving the last piece of food to their dying children. Where would such people end up in the minds of city dwelling Christians? I am sorry, they did not have the most important thing in their lives…Jesus. So they would be punished by God, and Jesus would stand there applauding!

"Now you don't want stem cells research because you are afraid that they would be doing your God's work - mere man. That would devastate you. And just like you tried to stop the advancement of man through science, remember Galileo's telescope? Copernicus' rotation of the earth around the sun and not the other way as holy people who spoke to God ought to have known. Did he get the rotation theory from Allah because Muslims are saying Mohammed was authentic because he was informed by Allah about how babies were formed, then…Da Vinci must be a prophet, Copernicus must be a prophet, Sir Isaac Newton must be a prophet, Darwin must be a god, himself (we now know how evolution works and, he wasn't even the only one that had the theory). Einstein must definitely be a prophet—he mapped out the universe. (Sorry he didn't believe in your Allah. Who told him?) Carl Sagan must be a prophet, Galileo must be a prophet, Graham Bell must be a prophet, Bill Gates must be a prophet (though we all know about the window technology and the monopoly) and maybe I am a prophet, too…oh, ha, not forgetting Miller Urey and his experiment. And why didn't any one of these guys, especially, Galileo, force the truth down our ignorant throats by killing us like the Prophets?

"And, about the argument that the Arab Muslims invented algebra and some other stuff is not because they were Muslims, rather because they were humans. They always forget that not all Arabs are Muslims. You're doing the same thing now to all the Galileos out there. I bet in a hundred years from now your Pope or Imam will see an apology in order; another useless and senseless apology.

"Sometimes, some of you even reason that all these diseases and misfortunes are God's ways of showing examples in life for man to appreciate what God can do, and what you and I have to be thankful for. My answer to that is - first, how many people have to be such terrible examples? Second, why don't you volunteer? Since you all claim to talk to God.

"The worst, unimaginable crime against humanity is to program these unfortunate ones to condemn people like themselves who don't belong to their particular religion to hell, that to me is 'unforgivable'.

"Now tell me when people like this die; if they die as Christians, they go to hell forever as per the ruling of a merciful Allah; and if they die as Muslims, they go to hell as per a forgiving Christian God. I can't even imagine where people who die as non believers in any God would go or the punishment. It will probably be worse than hell." John argued.

It seemed Ahmed and Fred had taken a leave of absence. Maybe they were thinking of an appropriate answer for this hell bound guy. John decided to give them a break.

"Let's just bypass all that and say, God or Allah spares these unfortunate souls and let them in paradise. The question is, is it fair to them to have suffered such and you two, Fred and Ahmed, make it to your respective heavens? What did you guys do to deserve such workable bodies? How did you guys get such a smooth ride from heaven to earth, with all the tribulations and suffering, then back to heaven to rest forever with awesome benefits?" John paused. Silence returned like a bad rash that refused to heal.

It was a moment to reflect on life a little bit deeper, a moment to truly care about humans like them, a moment to feel the pains of another, a moment to put our feet in other people's shoes, a moment to remove the mask of insincerity, a moment to reach out and touch others like us in the plights we faced in this mysterious world, a moment to reserve a place in our paradise for all, a moment to damn the fear of hell and, a moment to embrace each other, a moment to face the world with all its calamities with true love, a moment to love and not to condemn, a moment to show and teach Allah or God and Jesus or Muhammad how to love.

"Let me share one open secret with you. For life to be fair we would all have to have the same level of understanding and misunderstanding, intelligence and dumbness, honesty, fairness, opportunities, intuition, compassion, happiness, sadness, stupidity, height, weight, beauty, ugliness, toughness, brilliance, wickedness, patience, weakness, strength, discipline and the list goes on.

"And then you can truly say everyone should have one shot at life, and then judgment. We all know that's impossible in the world we live in.

"Just look at man's society and see that the most trivial thing that one man will kill for, another man will just totally ignore. You explain that to me?

"It is simple; man is growing in consciousness to be loving, good and all that good stuff. So, reincarnation would be more than justified. And true love will break the back of bad karma!

"How does one learn all life's lessons in one lifetime that could be cut short at any age? Ridiculous as it may sound; people do not even die at the same age. What will take a man a year to learn, another man will learn it in two months; even in the same family. Hey, they both drank from the same breast milk." John expounded.

Since the men were still thinking of a heavenly response, John kept his points coming one after the other.

"Ahmed." John called out, again. Ahmed's eyes were wide open, looking as though he was singled out for an interrogation by Homeland Security.

"Tell me what would happen to these people when Allah destroyed the whole nation?

Surah 28: 58
Nor did your lord destroy the nations
until he had sent apostles to the capital cities proclaiming to
them our revelations.

"Let's forget the wrong doers for later. What about the elderly, the children and obviously the pregnant women in the nations that were destroyed. Where did they go, heaven or hell since Allah would judge the handy work of man. What could a baby have done to Allah?

"And one more thing, Allah's so-called world, historically and geographically, was limited to the Middle East. There was no mention of Allah destroying kingdoms in Africa and South America, just to name a couple, after sending his prophets according to you. It's all folk tales from the bible that Muhammad expatiated on. That part in the Middle East doesn't even constitute 1% of the world. Since Muslim scholars claim that the religion is science. Let's be scientific. How old is the world according to Allah? Don't generalize now. Be 'accurate' like how babies in the wombs develop." John queried.

He suddenly switched his attention to Fred.

"And Fred, explain this, if we only live once, when the God of Abraham, Jacob and Isaac killed the first sons of the Egyptians, all of them including their cattle, the first 'sons' of cattle? Why cattle? Really, I don't understand. Were the horses spared? They must have been the chosen beast of burden.

> *Exodus Chapter 10*
> *And the Lord said unto Moses, go in unto Pharaoh ;*
> *For I have hardened his heart, and the heart of his*
> *servants, that I might shew these my signs before him.*

> *Exodus Chapter 12*
> *For I will pass through the land of Egypt this night,*
> *and will smite all the first born in the land of Egypt,*
> *both man and beast, against all the Gods of Egypt*
> *I will execute judgment. I am Lord.*

And please don't forget the Amalek, amongst many tribes destroyed by the God of Israel.

> *Samuel Chapter 15 Verse 3*
> *Now go and smite Amalek and utterly destroy all that*
> *they have, and spare them not but slay both man and*
> *woman, infant and suckling, ox and sheep, camel and ass.*

The question again is not of fairness, mercy or justice, but where they would spend eternity?" John said, and was ready to hear their feeble reasons.

"God creates life. He has the right to take it." Fred said in a pathetic tone. He had stopped thinking for himself and was just parroting what one pastor probably said in response to a question like that.

"So why hasn't he killed you? Are you holier than those suckling and babies?" Jack was furious.

"When you corner them with their heartless defense of their loving God or Allah just killing at random, they resort to that famous saying." John started to explain.

"This is by far their tireless argument about the creator being able to take anybody's life, baby or pregnant woman. After all, he is the maker. They have so many metaphors to buttress their point, but the one I like most is the pottery analogy. Here, God is compared to a potter, having made so many pots decided to break the defectives, in this case you and I. Anyone in his right mind would agree you shouldn't hold the potter guilty. He bought and created as he saw fit.

"As far as our understanding of this world is concerned, that answer is justifiable. This argument sounds real logical; but still imperfect. By factoring Jesus in the equation it sheds light on the problem of their thinking. Say, Jesus came drinking, womanizing, stealing and killing and still preached everything we have now as his words, everyone would call him a hypocrite. So, if God didn't live up to a good standard and arbitrarily killed as he did; taking people's land and giving it to others, killing the wrong guys for being counted and countless more injustices, but still would want us, the pots, to be loving and understanding. Then there is a big fundamental moral issue there. Only a believer will think otherwise.

> *Mathew chapter 21 verse16*
> *Yea, have ye never read, out of the mouth of babies*
> *and suckling thou hast perfect praise?*

"On one hand, God, the father, was putting a hit on babies and infants, and on the other, Jesus, the son, was praising babies and suckling. I guess the babes and suckling of other people didn't matter to Jesus' father or to Jesus. Now when a solider kills infants by mistake, there is a great hue and cry in the Christian and Muslim communities. Wonder why? And if the babies and suckling have perfect praise, how is it that they have sinned? I'm sorry again, literal interpretation." John said.

"So we are like stone to this God." Jack said looking sternly at Fred. "If we didn't mean anything to this God, why did he send Jesus to save us and at the same time killing us for no apparent reason?"

Isaac was conspicuously silent.

John sat back and gazed at the ceiling, all the while in deep thought, and then he continued.

"And believe it or not the infamous inquisition stemmed from the God in the bible. The Popes were following the footsteps of their God.

"'Once you love me, you can't leave me or I will kill you.' In order for us to understand what I am saying right now, you have to be familiar with the boastfulness of the Christians always chanting that humans have free will, Adam and Eve had a choice. Remember? And the ever famous phrase by the Muslims...'no compulsion in religion'. (When Mohammed said in the Hadith that once a Muslim always a Muslim, and if you leave you are dead. Why wonder that cults and mafias have the same motto.)

"All these sayings don't amount to anything because according to the actions on the ground, this God and his prophets have denied us our freedom to change our minds because they've taken deliberate actions to counter them; they give us no chance to change, they kill us.

"There have been spirited efforts to explain this double standard and they range from silly to...yes, to silly defense. They have to rationalize bad or evil tendency to be good and loving. One excuse is that God will take your life if he knows you will sin in the future, and he doesn't want that. This applies to his so-called child of God, not unbeliever. Just like taking your children from school because they might fail one day, or from any other endeavor in life!

"Another bizarre one is that the people already signed on for life to worship God--like God would be lonely if deserted. So killing them would be right.

"But there's one more that needs to be said. It's an outstanding defense of God. A preacher said that the reason why God allowed children that cursed their parents to be stoned to death was because at that time people couldn't change. The good pastor forgot about David. You just have to laugh.

"Now back to reason and by that I mean using reason we can

point to and discarding faith that blinds us. I will illustrate this with what took place centuries ago. There were Mongolian mercenaries rampaging everywhere and their escapade took them to a caliphate. I don't remember the name of the kingdom now; however, they destroyed the Muslim Empire and nearly everything was torched. But when they were about to destroy the Koran and some other books, many of them had a change of heart, started studying it and became Muslims.

"Now the plot thickens as they say in a play. Follow this carefully. This is the assumption of Islam. Mercenaries killed Muslims; dead Muslims went to paradise. Mercenaries turned Muslims died; went to paradise. Now, Muslims killed all the invading mercenaries; mercenaries went to hell, and Muslims that killed the invading mercenaries went to heaven.

"If you follow this simple equation of an argument, you will know man changes his mind, his character, now and then. Like a mind that flips from good to bad or the other way round at any moment. So therefore, Moses or Mohammed had no justification to take the lives of unbelievers, and that goes for all their followers, then and now, even God/Allah, too; man as man will fight and kill to prove his point. God or Allah killing unbelievers is therefore wrong. It's apparent to every one of us that this act of change is known in people and should be automatically known by God--after all, Allah knows all.

"And if they are still so proud of the carnage carried out by Moses that was sanctioned by God, they should stop showing him parting the red sea only, but show him making his own red sea with the blood of his own people. I'm sure most Christians would have loved to switch places with the prophet of God. What would anyone of us not give for talking face to face with God?

"Yet all Christians, whether passive or active think this is justice. There is nothing surprising here. The only thing to consider now is what is justice? And just like beauty or fashion is in the eye of the beholder. Justice, I'm afraid, is in the eye of the believer! And this is how man thinks today in this triangular religion.

"Or why are they silent about this, amongst many more injustices; the great Daniel, that they claim wasn't eaten by the lions because of his righteousness and steadfast love to God, but they don't talk about the children and the wives of those that accused him being killed by the lions. They never sing about the lions eating poor, innocent children.

How could they miss this tiny, irrelevant issue, while showing hungry children around the world hardly having enough to eat with no shoes and no school to attend?

"The story of Daniel doesn't even make sense. He knew the law, he was charged rightly, yet the king put to death his accusers and non accusers. This alone should show that people in their billions are drinking from the well. And yet cry foul when similar things happen now. Stories in the bible shouldn't even be told in Sesame Street, because God doesn't teach children, he kills them.

"Another area where these defenders of God don't see in their solid argument is that other people's Gods, whether they call them pagans or not, had their own priests or prophets take the lives of their followers as well. We know the Aztec Gods and hundreds of other Gods that different people of different cultures worshipped did the same thing. Now if the God in the bible is lost in the mix, don't be alarmed. Only a genius can separate one god from another. And by the way, the Aztec priest could have used the 3,000 killed by Moses for good weather, good harvest and fertility rather than just being wasted on jealousy. Also, 3,000 was almost the number of people first reported to have died at the 911 incident. And the uproar went to the heavens...but curiously, the Moses' one has never been publicly condemned by the Christians and the Jews. And they sleep with the bible day in, day out and yet..." John informed.

"All I believe is that once you have Jesus as your savior you are saved by grace. All your sins are washed away." Fred managed to speak.

Hebrew chapter10:17
And their sins and iniquities will I remember no more.

"That's another shortsightedness of the Christian faith. Repent of your sins and everything is okay." John shed more light on the topic. "Have you guys thought of the consequences of your sins? Say a killer repents, what about the dead guy or guys, first, where would the dead guy end up? Say, he was a heathen. And maybe, he might one day be a believer like you, just like you were once a thief, a rapist, a divider, a fraudster, a fornicator...probably used cocaine and also a former prostitute spreading deadly diseases, but his life was cut short by a repentant born-again now heading to paradise. I tell you that's one man that won't make it into the kingdom of God.

"Also, what about the chain effect of that singular act that just needed the blood of Jesus to wash it away on the guy's family? It's okay, 'I'm in heaven and forgiven my sins?' That reeks of man's selfishness if you ask me.

"And what about the president of a country for another example, stealing the people's money in a country that can hardly get by, suddenly the president gets caught and he is truly sorry and full of repentance. Can anyone imagine the sometimes irreversible bad effects of his actions on his country? It could even lead to civil war, but, never worry, he would be dwelling in paradise with Jesus, just because…How can I forget Idi Amin who ran to Saudi after finding Islam? Allah is most forgiving indeed. Someone should inform Muhammad that millions of people and especially children and elderly died because of that man.

"Well, does it matter to Islam, too? As long as they were not Muslims, they could die a thousand times, it wouldn't matter. Justice of Allah had been denied them in the first place and in the second place, Allah would burn them again and again in hell. 'How dare non Muslims come before me, Allah, looking for justice and begging for forgiveness without believing in you and me, Muhammad'?" He suddenly stopped.

John wanted to give these guys room to digest everything he had said. They had it coming. Then he added his opinion on the issue in a serious tone.

"Since we don't know, I mean, us, where we come from and where we are going when we die; to a thinking man, reincarnation will be preferable to heaven and hell. It's like a baby that's trying to walk, he falls down once and you count him out. And the judge's (God/Allah) character is in question. How can that be fair? But we all demand justice and fairness in our earthly life." John stressed.

Fred's face was hardened like Pharaoh's heart, but in this case not by God. His brows were coming close together. He was losing his glow gradually. It wasn't because he was angry; rather, he couldn't digest the information. More was coming though, more indigestion.

"Relax, relax, Fred." John was trying to calm him down. "We are just talking, nothing serious. It's better for you to hear both sides of the story in life. It might not be easy for you to swallow as you desire, but in the end we are all going to be a little bit wiser in our choices that most of the times influence our action or lack of it.

"That being said, think about this in your holy book, I believe it matches what everybody thinks is reincarnation. I had a discussion with a believer like you on this passage, and she believed Jesus used that name as an example in the Old Testament, that it was the spirit of goodness that Jesus was implying, not a particular person. But, you be the judge. In this case, Jesus used the same name twice, and besides, the same name was used in the Old Testament. If this is not specific, I don't know what is.

> *Malachi chapter 4 verse 5*
> *Behold, I will send you Elijah the prophet before the coming of the great and dreadful day of the Lord.*

> *Mathew Chapter 11 Verse 17*
> *Verily I say unto you, among them that are born of woman there hath not risen a greater than John the Baptist, notwithstanding, he that is least in the kingdom of heaven is greater than he.*
> *And from the days of John the baptist until now the kingdom of heaven suffered violence, and the violent take it by force.*
> *For all the prophets and the law prophesied until John. And if ye will receive it, this is Elias which was for to come. He that hath ears, let him hear.*

> *Mathew Chapter 17 Verse 10*
> *And his disciples asked him saying, why then say the scribes that Elias must first come?*
> *And Jesus answered and said unto them Elias truly shall first come, and restore all things. But I say unto you that Elias is come already, and they knew him not, but have done unto him whatever they listed. Likewise shall also the son of man suffer of them.*
> *Then the disciples understood that the he spake unto of John the Baptist.*

"Most of the holy books are stuck in the past and only time will be the teacher of man. Whether one believes this concept or not is not the issue here, many religions have the concept of God - the creator of all things, which is different from one tribe to another, but the idea of rebirth is similar in all cases.

"The important thing here is that it is not something forced on man. No bloodshed here to persuade man that you have to believe it or die and be condemned. It's kind of a natural thing. Like you just know we are breathing, or dreaming, of course, just like we have been brainwashed by the so-called father of psychoanalysis, Sigmund Freud, telling us our dreams mean nothing or is what we think of before we go to bed or because we eat too much dinner before sleeping, or we put wishes together of what we can't achieve in reality and we make them up in the dreams. Buying this logic too is like listening to the people in the triangular religion about what love is." John digressed. "But here... deja-vu would suffice, yes; deja-vu would be a good example."

John was always conscious of what to divulge to people of a particular consciousness. Sure, everybody knew everything about everything! Half knowledge to him was just as bad as ignorance.

"One tribe or race didn't go around saying we shouldn't think of deja-vu. We all kind of know it, not believe it. But the meaning of deja-vu or why it happens is another story." John concluded.

"Maybe we should do a movie about how the Amalek were destroyed." Jack said. "We should show the movie with the graphic details that it deserves, just like *The Passion of the Christ* movie that got people crying when they were watching a grown man being whipped repeatedly. Now I will like to see those sensitive, caring, giving and loving people's reactions when a suckling is being grabbed from her mum, gets stepped on by Saul, or having his tiny head, still unformed properly, cuts off by a big and mighty warrior of a loving, forgiving, merciful and benevolent God. After all, he had to obey God to the letter; 'to obey is better than sacrifice'. I don't why they proudly say this statement when you consider what he was supposed to do."

"That's heavy, Jack." Den mumbled. "You know I'm not that much of a thinking man." Den laughed at himself. "But sometimes I can't help but see that some animals are better behaved and loving than some of my co-workers or friends."

Everyone started laughing expect the usual suspects.

"Funny but true…funny but true." Jack concurred.

John took another look at the mock-up. Only if man could build it with love, he thought.

> *"Man will fight tooth and nail to remain ignorant; He's like a slave that his master wants to set free but begs to remain a slave.*
> *Puts back his mental shackles and stays put.*
> *After all, ignorance is comforting and blissful."*
> *John*

Holier Than Thou

Den excused himself. He needed to use the restroom fast. He had suddenly begun to feel at home with this bunch. He had always stayed away from topics like this, but now, looking back he felt free and no longer had the fear of the unknown that popped up in his mind now and then or the countless times the television pastors on Sunday kept singing the heaven and hell sermons. Now rational and comparative knowledge restored his confidence in himself, and there were no more demons to confront.

He had been told to save himself from hell; alone, maybe with his family, but what about all those people that would be left behind; what about those African slaves that lived and died in slavery. What if a slave dealer of those times truly repented...what about the slaves that died as non-believers, they would all roast in hell? They might not even be able to fathom a God that allowed such man's inhumanity to man in the first place both by the sellers and the buyers, and all those slaves before Rome made Christianity the state religion? But looking around now, even black Christians never gave them a thought. But they would rather engage in a badly informed scholastic argument about their faith. Really, man was either selfish, saving himself alone or just ignorant, maybe both. His parents unwittingly taught him how to hate. Thank goodness he could see clearly now. Money, power and black gold surely helped to strengthen these outdated beliefs.

He came out of the toilet and bumped right into Ahmed, who had also gone to take care of his own business in the restroom, and didn't even feel it. Ahmed rocked back and forth trying to regain his balance, like a boat in turbulent waters. Maybe it was a reflection of what was going on inside him. Surely there were doubts, plenty. But he couldn't voice it out in his community of different Imams with different interpretations of the Koran. He agreed with certain parts of the Koran but how would you disagree with other parts…that would mean Allah was wrong on some issues, how could that be? He would rather wait and see the Prophet himself to provide the answers, or the Imams would send him to an early trip to see Muhammad, to start enjoying all the promises of endless ecstasy in paradise, but he would like to do just that at his own convenient time. Now he had to continue to put on a show defending his given religious belief no matter what in front of the world.

"Hey, look where you're going." Ahmed said trying to regain his balance.

"Sorry, man." Den apologized.

"It's okay." Ahmed said.

"I'll see you later." Den said. "Hey, you dropped some envelopes."

Den helped him gather the scattered letters and handed them back.

"Here."

"Thanks." Ahmed said. "I was going to mail the letters yesterday but I forgot."

Then Den's eyes caught a sort of a title before Ahmed's name.

"I don't mean to poke into your affairs or anything, but I couldn't help but see that you wrote a word before your name. What does that mean? Is it kind of a mister?" He asked.

Ahmed's eyes lit up as if someone had asked him about something hard to achieve; something that required diligence and deep thought before arriving at the true conclusion, otherwise you could be lost forever in the abyss of ignorance. This was a perfect time to show non believer the beautiful side of Islam. This was the time to get a convert for the ever growing Islam by giving shining examples that no other religion could boast of. This was a way to sell the true worship of the one and, only God, and Mohammed being the last prophet. The show commenced.

"Well," Ahmed said, if you must know and I dare say, maybe you'll have the same thing someday."

Den cut him off fast. "No, no, I'm just curious, don't go that far yet. I'm not ready to jump from frying pan to fire."

"Okay, it's one of the five pillars of Islam to visit the holy land once in your life if you can afford it." Ahmed said as if all the wind inside him was knocked out by a charging 300lb linebacker. "Let me quickly use it and I'll explain…"

Good thing self-righteous and heavenly bound believers still obeyed the simple laws of nature. Ahmed dashed into the restroom. Before he came out, Den had already gone to join the group.

Ahmed came out of the restroom, looked around, Den wasn't there. He knew what to come. He reluctantly went to join them. This job of defending the Prophet and Allah was taking a heavy toll on him. When would the trumpet sound? He was beginning to be weary.

Before Den could take a seat next to John, the question raced out of his mouth.

"Hey, what do you think of the holy land in Mecca and all that stuff?"

"You can't just single out the holy place of the Muslims." John cautioned.

"Oh no, I don't want to, either. It's just that I had a discussion with Ahmed about the title he put in front of his name and it led to this question. You've taught me a big lesson that I should not scratch the surface of any topic and that's why I asked you." Den said submissively. "I don't want to be ignorant anymore if I can help it on this topic. And even if what I know about the individual is senseless, at least, I'd know how he thinks and why he thinks that he thinks." He continued, obviously respecting John's wealth of knowledge in this area.

"But still, you have to do your own research." John added gently, not wanting to scare him away.

Sometimes John found it appalling that an average man out there was always spoon fed on things he could find out himself. But he would rather sit on his couch, arguing every point without anything to back his point of view. He would only react when he had been poked in the face literally and that would be when he would start trying to find out the why's of the matter.

As John was about to start speaking, Ahmed came back. He sat quietly waiting for the expected.

"Practically all religions have what they consider a sacred ground or holy land, where believers go to, say, appointed time to worship, in a more private place. And it carries a lot of spiritual significance for them." John stopped. "That's pretty much it." He thought about what he had just said, whether he left something out, nothing.

"Why so many holy lands," Jack asked. "The Muslims have theirs, the Christians, the Hindu, and so on, all have theirs. And I am sure they all believe their holy land is the only one, am I right?"

He sort of threw the question out there.

"So what happens to the other holy lands, unholy?" Jack was looking for an answer from anybody. When he wanted a reply on any topic he knew how to tug at the targeted persons, like a boy looking for his mother's attention.

"Like I said…" John felt the uneasiness Jack's inquiry was causing the group. "Holy land can be compared to a belief in a particular God or so, and in most cases, it's where God or an angel makes contact with man, and automatically the place becomes a gathering place for the followers of that faith." John pointed out.

"So, is one holy land holier than the other?" Jack protested.

"Really, you don't want to go into that argument simply because every religion or denomination in that religion will defend its holy land and disregard the others. Just like they will do with what is God or no God." John answered.

"I see, I see. But I hear stories from different worshippers claiming one miracle or the other in these holy lands." Jack said informatively.

"Yes, you are right about that, but most of the time we can't verify any of these miracles. And you have to take every story with a grain of salt. Be careful of falsified stories, they are meant to impress the listeners of what they are missing in their unbelievers' lives. And to showcase how God or whatever has blessed them.

"There was a man I used to know who went to a particular holy land just to die there. According to what he believed, that it would cleanse him of his sins, and he would head to paradise." John further explained.

"I'm lost, I don't understand." Den interjected. "Say I go to Jerusalem or Mecca or any holy place in India or wherever it might be, but I go there out of curiosity, does that make the land holy to me, too?"

"I see what you're saying." John said. "But you have to understand one thing; people who say or have agreed with others who claim that a particular place is holy actually believe it to be so. You on the other hand, don't. That's the difference. The Christian faith doesn't acknowledge Islam, so wherever holy place Islam claims is not holy in the eyes of the Christians, you see. And Islam doesn't acknowledge the Baha'i holy place, too."

"Why then do they die in record numbers in these holy lands?" Jack couldn't figure that one out. "Since they all claim intimacy within the boundaries of these sacred places. An observer will think that should be the best place to be protected by whatever God they pray to."

"Jack, I don't know how to explain this to you, but I will try." John started. "Way before the convenience of travel by car and airplane, man thronged to any holy land in their thousands by leg, horses and Camels, and they died in their hundreds on the road, few made it to their accepted holy lands. And in not so recent time the pilgrimage by the Mormons to Utah, in the US. Hundreds died, too; young and old. Man is drawn to places like this in their thousands, like moths to fire or like man is drawn to success in a do or die manner, just to partake in the blessings promised by such observance of the ritual; like having children, having a good job, having peace or just fulfilling their obligation in that religion, having long life and so many more that the person might lack or wish for. And some people just want to relive their prophet's or angel's footsteps, which will be heavenly to them.

"Once there is a gathering of a large number of people in a small area, there is always a tendency for a stampede. It can be in a concert or anyplace. But in terms of religion, you would think it shouldn't. You would be wrong. There's still an element of fear of death in them, and also a great disconnect that God should be able to protect them. All is forgotten in the mad rush for earthly survival. There was one incident in India where a mother took, probably, her only child to this holy place, and then there was a stampede caused by who-knows-what. At the end of the commotion she laid dead and a tiny voice was calling, 'mama… mama', she was only four years old. And there are many such losses of lives in Mecca, too. The organizers always try to prevent such incidents but to no avail, sometimes." John paused.

"Why should God allow such to happen?" Den queried. But the question was left unanswered.

"I guess once you convince the world that God appears to you in your backyard, your backyard becomes a holy place and people flock there at appointed times, and it's also good for your economy and social or cultural or religious superiority amongst nations." Jack said frankly.

"Now I get it." Den said. "Holy lands depend on the believer. So, from now on everywhere I step is holy because I say so." He busted out laughing and Jack joined in. John just smiled, but the rest of the group didn't go along.

"Nothing is funny about what you guys just said." Ahmed countered. Fear of being deceived and wrong sipping into his heart, showing in his voice. He felt really uncomfortable seeing all his so-called 'facts' turning into opinions. "I don't know why you guys just want to condemn other people's religion. What's your gain? What do you benefit from it? Why do you want to scare people that have religion to shield them from this life?"

"Look at one-sided moral judge." Jack charged back. "First of all, fighter, your prophet condemned other religions, too. And again, it's a free world, and if anybody claims to know what we are doing here, that my friend should include my own input in the matter. Because it's acceptable to you to condemn me in your mind and attitude about your supposed God, hmm...or it's okay for you to scare people about hell?"

"Calm down, Jack." John stepped in.

"No, no, no." Jack fired back. "I'm not condemning anybody; I'm only talking about it. And besides, if we don't talk about it, how would we know whether these guys haven't gone gaga with fear. There are so many contradictions and you don't even see them, you are blind like a bat. But in the case of a bat it can still use echolocation bouncing back to find its direction, in your case, you wouldn't even see it if it bit you in the face.

"Okay, you can continue to delude yourselves - I have no problem with that. But it's when you guys get political power and start dictating to the rest of us how to think; what book to read; what to sing; what to dance to; what to wear; how to do my hair; what sport to do; when to make love to my lover or to my wife because I might offend your God; where to sit to eat my breakfast; where not to sit for my dinner; and who knows, you might even tell me when to go to the toilet; and where to face doing it. What to watch; what not to watch. What to think and how to think and when not to think and how much to think and when to think that I think.

"If we make a film of the entire bible and the Koran with all the scenes done exactly, the killings; the violence; the many wives; the marrying of sisters; the taking of in-law's wife by the Prophet; the chasing of the infidels and killing them; and the orgies of king Solomon. I bet you all, soap opera can't hold a candle to it. Hollywood can't dream of writing stories like that in a thousand years. Telling women they can't have abortion when God in the bible destroyed suckling and even pregnant women. (It's a woman's choice).

"Do you know how many people have lost their lives and properties because of religion? Christians and Muslims probably started these brainless fights over which religion is better in the history of man and, of this magnitude. Each time they start killing and raping in the name of one religion, both sides come out looking for sympathy and revenge, pointing accusing finger at the other. 'Oh, my religion is a private matter to me but when they abuse my God I destroy pubic properties and people', as if God is lying in some hospital bed bleeding from a head injury and needs you to go fight for him. You keep saying God is all powerful, yet you keep defending him. I don't get it.

"Let me tell you people, God or whatever anyone, past, present or future says made this world, makes it a public matter and not a private one. Or, unless you agree that your God didn't create this Jack," pointing to himself like a wrestler showing off his big chest as if to make it abundantly clear he was talking about no one else. "You have all blackmailed the whole world for too long, and enough is enough.

"On the other hand, if you keep what you believe in your head…. there…, and don't tell me I have to abide by it, then it's fine. I'm not afraid of your God. Please go to your heaven, don't save me. I'm sure God can create plenty of Jacks for you in paradise to play with. You won't miss me." Jack stopped.

"It's okay, Jack." John was trying to restrain him, patting him on the back. "You just have to find a better way of passing your message across, that it's not love when you force or scare people to go to paradise - even if they are right and that's a big IF."

Jack couldn't take it anymore. He needed fresh air. As he was about to leave he caught Fred's face trying to hold back a giggle about the encounter with Ahmed.

"Hey, what's funny?" Jack became livid. "Tell me, what's Jesus waiting for all these hundreds of years while the Popes were cooking and roasting people who wanted to believe or have a different understanding of what Christianity was, just like now? Couldn't he at least intervene from Heaven? I hear he still hears prayers!

"What would you have done in a situation like that with all your supernatural powers? Turning water into wine...or heaven and earth no longer his domain? Or how can..."

"Who's the ignorant one now?" Fred hammered him before he could continue with his barrage of if's and what's and why's about his beloved Jesus.

"Jesus came to die for the sins of mankind and he did just that, gloriously. Thank God." Fred stamped his authority on the subject.

"And while he was here he healed the sick and fed the hungry and don't let me count all the miracles he performed. Oh yeah, he still answers prayers, halleluiah. Now it's left to you to believe him or not, nobody is forcing you. Judgment day is coming. We did preach the good news to you." Fred replied victoriously.

Fred got Jack by the throat now and he wouldn't let go like a lioness claws around a weak baby antelope. No one could wrestle this point out of his grip.

"Hey, hey, remember when he was alive and they came to arrest him and Peter wanted to fight. He didn't even resist. What do you have to say about that? He said he could have sent for angels, thousands of angels, to defend him, but he didn't." Fred added, taunting Jack, waging his forefinger in his face.

Jack had no reply. He was befuddled. The sharpness of his tongue disappeared like a puddle in the hot, scorching sun. Maybe it would be better to allow John to lead all the time. John knew what he was talking about. He spoke their language. Jack was just going by his guts; his principles. But sometimes knowledge of how the wise and the foolish reasoned was needed in this world in order to take the argument to them.

Meanwhile, John was silent and the silence weighed a ton of bricks on Jack's shoulders, though he was all muscle, his legs were about to buckle. He glanced at John for support; any kind would do in this jam he got himself in.

But before Jack was ever reaching out for help, John had wanted to invite him and Den for a private talk about man. Now it was too late, he had to wait for Jack to expend his energy on a dead horse. Sorry was Jack's quick escape from such incidents, but sorry was not good here. John smiled back with an assurance that he was on the right track. Jack readjusted and sat down eagerly. Papa bear was coming to the rescue.

"Fred." John called. Fred turned slowly to John. He knew it would be hard to face him.

"If Jesus were here and they brought to him seven blind men to heal, one every day for seven days, would he heal them all, day after day?" Fred didn't answer. His brain was trying to figure out where John was going with his question. Should he say faith was needed or not. He couldn't decide what the appropriate response should be. He looked at John and remained mute like a stubborn donkey refusing to move. John decided to go on anyway.

"I'm not here to trick you or anyone. Sometimes in order to bypass human biases you present something to man in a way that he has no sentimental attachment to the situation, and more often than not, he will give you an impartial answer.

"Don't be alarmed. It was used in the bible when David took another man's wife. Let me try another angle, hopefully you will understand me. If you call yourself a human right activist and very proud of it and you get involved in the...say...a Chinese woman's abuse in your country because you are Chinese, but won't do the same for a Korean man. Can you call yourself a human right activist?" John asked.

"I guess not." Fred murmured his answer.

"See how easy that was." John said.

"And your point...?" Fred said angrily.

"The point is Jesus did intervene physically, supposedly from heaven after he was crucified and gone." John provided evidence.

> *Act chapter 9*
> *And Saul, yet breathing out threatening and slaughter*
> *against the disciples of the lord, went unto the high priest..*
> *And as he journeyed, he came near Damascus and suddenly*
> *there shined about him a light from heaven. And he fell to*
> *the earth, and heard a voice saying unto him, Saul, Saul,*
> *why persecutest thou me?*
> *And he said, who art thou, lord?*

And the lord said, I am Jesus whom thou persecutest: It is hard for thee to kick against the pricks.
And he was three days without sight, and neither did eat nor drink.

Fred looked dumbfounded. How was he going to explain this away or sweep it under the carpet? The carpet was too bumpy as of now to walk smoothly on, anyway. This lump would trip anyone, even with a strong walking cane. None of his numerous pastors ever mentioned it in their heavenly sermons, the message they all preached was about a mean, wicked man's conversion to Christianity. Matters closed, no one saw beyond that, maybe even the preachers themselves. You couldn't put anything past the blind leading the blind. He didn't have anybody's view to parrot this time. He was on his own. Scary!

Jack tapped him on his shoulder. "The big question is why did he stop? Wake up, Fred; nobody is coming to save your ass. If there's one thing that I'm sure of, apart from dying and not knowing what life will bring, Jesus, or anybody is not coming to save man. You can take that to the bank."

Jack felt relieved. He got his confidence back. All he needed now was some fresh, unpolluted air by mankind and his hypocrisy. He walked into a cool, refreshing breeze. He would rejoin them after a brief exit.

Den felt exactly how Jack's anger could easily be hard to control and there was nothing he could do to console his friend. 'We live in a world that's turned upside down by fear and sometimes it's hard to explain. Jack didn't know about the witch's story.' Den thought.

> *"The world is a very confusing place.*
> *Everyone going every which way,*
> *searching for the maker. It creates*
> *fear, hatred and delusion, and if you're not*
> *strong enough, you will have a*
> *mental breakdown."*
> *Jack*

> *"Man can't distinguish between evil and good."*
> *John*

My Way or the High Way

As the poignant exchange brought on by Jack subsided, the door swung open and a skinny man stepped in. He surveyed the room and its occupiers. There was a calculating smile on his face. He introduced himself.

"I'm Stan." He said confidently.

His head was shaven. He wasn't bald. He just didn't want to be one of those people with problems combing their hair every morning trying to look one way or another. He wasn't much of a look-at-me-am-fine-kind-of-a-guy. Sure he would never worry about having a bad hair day, one less thing to worry about in an up and down world. Not muscular, too. This man had problems with having unnecessary load on himself as he sometimes joked about life; something functional and he was happy.

"I'm here to work with you guys on the field. I'll be in charge and directing how things go on the ground. I'll be the one to stop anything that might go out of control. I hope we will never come to that. In fact, my job is for us to find a common ground; a balance."

Some chorused their welcome. Others just nodded their heads. It was as if he was interrupting Jack from continuing whatever was left unsaid. He had come back with a renewed energy and more questions, knowing that John was there to get him out of any snag.

The moment Stan stopped. He posed a question to John. "Tell me, John, please help here. Why is it that another man is always trying to help me get to his perceived heaven? I don't get it. And in so doing, wants to impose his so-called God or whatever name he calls his creator on me. And if I don't want it, he forces me one way or another." Jack said furiously.

It appeared he didn't want to hold back anymore. The tension shot high again. Stan was making eye contact with each and everyone. Whether he was beaming calm to everybody was left to be seen.

"I don't know how to address this question, Jack. Historically, man has always wanted to rule his society one way or other. A dominant male establishes his rule by force, thus becoming a king or mobster lord or warlord. And in the case of the old age phenomenon, God or creator, he uses scare tactics, rewards and punishments, in short, the fear of the unknown." John gave his insight.

Fred inched a little bit forward in his seat, wanting to hear everything that John was saying. Maybe irrefutable facts were sinking in after all.

"First, you have to understand that it's very hard to be a leader, even amongst three people. So, most leaders employ ruthless means to achieve this goal. Very few come up with an ingenious way. The most popular God, the one in the bible, couldn't hold his kingdom forever, too. He was rejected by his chosen people.

> *Samuel chapter 8 verse 7*
> *And the Lord said unto Samuel,*
> *Hearken unto the voice of the people*
> *in all that they say unto thee: for they have*
> *not rejected thee, but they have rejected me,*
> *that I should not reign over them.*

"Well, a typical case of a leader was Osei Tutu of old Ghana Empire in West Africa." John elaborated.

"This I got to hear, sounds interesting already." Den leaned forward in his seat, too.

"This was way before the white missionaries came to save Africa - seen as the Dark Continent from their own myopic view, arrogantly calling their mission 'white man's burden'." John said as a matter of fact.

"What happened was the current king at that time died, and normally the son was supposed to be the heir to the throne, but in this particular case the kingdom was divided.

"One fateful morning, the son, Osei-Tutu, called all the Chiefs to his father's palace to tell them about a revelation he had just received.

"They all came and he presented them with a golden stool never seen before in the kingdom. It was a spectacle to behold. You can say the land was paved with nothing but pure gold, nobody would doubt you. It was so unbelievable that it was nicknamed gold coast by outsiders. But this particular stool was beyond comparison. It was simply celestial.

"To say everyone was captivated was an understatement. They never saw anything like that in their entire lives. Osei-Tutu got up and gave the speech of his life.

"He told them he was worried where the kingdom was heading; the state of uneasiness, the fear of its collapse, and all the work everyone had put into building the empire would end up in vain. And what kind of legacy they would hand over to the next generation was uppermost in his mind.

"Then he said as he was praying in the backyard for a solution, all of a sudden, a golden stool appeared and a voice from the heavens said whosoever sat on that golden stool should be accepted and respected as the next king. That was how he became king, regaining his father's throne and ruled. In fact, he was one of the greatest kings in that part of the world." John said.

"That's an interesting piece of information to have." Den was sold.

"This simple idea was what leaders used back then to manipulate people's minds, whether for the good of mankind or not. Your guess is as good as mine. And don't think you can't be manipulated even today. We are living in a manipulated world, either thinking of ourselves as culturally or religiously superior or in a higher class. And don't forget your media and your so-called chosen leaders skewing the obvious, the self-acclaimed gurus (and their secrets) that will bring out the best in you in any situation with a hefty fee so that you live a life of luxury forever or win forever." John warned.

Ahmed's face was begging for the connection between that story and what he believed. His entire body was pleading for an explanation. John suddenly became a mind reader and answered him.

"Hey, Ahmad, your Mohammed went into the cave every time to get what? - Instructions (Surah) or words of Allah dictated by angel

Gabriel. Mohammed hardly ever started a Surah without saying all the good attributes of God and ending it with the punishment that awaited the people who did not believe him. And all the time the Surahs were concerned with the events of his days. Whenever a new situation surfaced that needed a solution or how to handle the matter he would conveniently have a revelation regarding the problem and put the wish of Allah on the subject. End of story. Wouldn't it have been possible to have all matters of human problems answered in one shot, one time, one revelation by the all knowing, all wise, Allah?" John pondered.

Ahmed sat back as if decked by a crushing blow to the brain. His eyes were bloodshot. But more clarity was on the way. Sometimes John used a sledge hammer to kill an ant. According to him, it was called for to drive home a point where partisan humans were involved. You had to spell it out like a-b-c, and sometimes that wouldn't work.

"There was a time the worshippers were told to face Jerusalem, because it was regarded as the only holy city to face when praying to Allah, and this was recorded, of course, but something probably happened between him and the Jews at that time...some sort of a disagreement. It was probably his rejection by the Jews because he claimed to be a prophet to them, too. That made...should I say angel Gabriel or Mohammed to change the position from facing Jerusalem to Mecca to this day when praying. There are many more examples of him shifting to accommodate the situation on the ground.

> *Surah 49:14*
> *true believers are those that have faith in God and*
> *his apostle, and never doubt; and who fight with their*
> *wealth and with their persons in the cause of God.*

"This was when some people decided not to fight anymore after they were defeated. The believers would never tell you their prophet lost some fights. They would only shout about the ones he won.

"And there was a time when he promised one of his wives that he wouldn't see another woman he knew intimately before. But he went back to her anyway. And he was caught by his favorite wife...yes; there was a revelation to put that to rest, too." John buttressed his point.

Surah 66:1
Prophet, Why do you prohibit that which God has made
lawful for you, in seeking to please your wives?
God has given you absolution from such oaths…

Ahmed sat still, thoughtful. His mind was doing all the comparisons over and over.

"There you have it." Jack exclaimed.

"Most of us think we are not that gullible to fall for such a scam. But take a look at yourself - if you really can, and then at the society you live in. You are bound to see what I see or, you might just not be able to see through it.

"Guru Nanak of the Sikh faith, he too claimed to have disappeared for three days from the river bank. Where did he go and who did he consult…God? He came back and started the religion.

"And don't forget in a hurry, Prophet Mirza Husayn Ali of the Baha'i faith, the last prophet. If you can't see a trend here, you must be from another planet." John was laying out the clues.

"Or submerged in the well," Den offered his explanation. "That gives a new meaning to the word, last. Don't you think?"

"It's a way to rally people to your cause." Jack said perceptively.

"And Moses was in the 'cave' too for his famous ten commandments to reinvent himself." John added. "The moment we declare other people to be 'my people', man assumes unrealistic notion that it is his responsibility to steer the ship of his fellows without their inputs or compromise, whichever way he deems fit. And this is only for his selfish glory. But he cries day and night that he does it for the general good of all. How many people did Stalin kill for his vision of a Soviet Empire? And where is the Soviet Union today? Mao also died without remorse like one particular Pope; I don't remember his name now, still urging the maltreatment of infidels on his dying bed. Mao even wanted the whole world to be communist. Man is in trouble; revolutionaries kill him to lay a foundation for a better society, religious people do the same to help him get to heaven!"

"Whoa! I didn't know there was a God of communism, too." Jack laughed.

"It's also helpful if you become a no-nonsense guy. If somebody disobeys you, you make him a scapegoat. But Moses made three thousand of the chosen scapegoats." John informed.

Isaac looked nervous. He had hardly said anything. Once you mentioned a man's hero, he would be ready to defend his flawless character.

"It was Moses who first told the world, 'thou shall not kill' and it was him who first broke it, but not with one but with thousands of lives. Yet, amazingly, his only sin in the face of God was striking the rock for water, twice. And the punishment was not seeing the Promised Land. Talk about punishment fitting the crime.

> *Exodus Chapter 32 Verses 26-28*
> *Then Moses stood in the gate of the camp and said,*
> *who is on the lord's side? Let him come unto me. And*
> *all the sons of Levi gathered themselves together unto*
> *him. And he said unto them. Thus saith the lord God of*
> *Israel. Put everyman his sword by his side, and go in*
> *and out from gate to gate throughout the camp, and*
> *everyman his brother, and everyman his companion,*
> *and everyman his neighbor.*
> *And the children of Levi did according to the word of*
> *Moses; and there fell of the people that day about three*
> *thousand men.*

"Can anyone imagine the pool of blood flowing in those camps at that time? It could rival the red sea. Another miraculous crossing of the real red sea would be needed.

"I want you, a believer, to close your eyes for a minute and imagine yourself at a concert or a sporting event. I'm sure you have had that experience or better still, imagine yourself at a crusade for saving lost souls, see hundreds of people cut down right in front of you, all around you dead bodies falling and shaking with terrible force, and at the same time blood spitting out like a water fountain all over you. Don't you worry; you are the fortunate one, the spared one, the chosen one forgiven by a loving God. And all because of what, let's make up a sin for them, like not paying their 10% or not eating their vegetables.

"Then go home and take a shower, washing all that blood away like Jesus did on the cross for you, and tell me how you feel inside and out. Give us your testimony. Tell us how your God helps you secure a good job and how he takes care of your family, providing sound health care, how you are able to buy that new car and have a loving husband to match, or blessed with children, almost like Jesus; perfect." John provided graphic view.

"That gives a new meaning to 'Thou shall not kill'." Jack said shaking his head, pitying man. But if he wasn't careful his head would roll off his shoulders because the attached muscles would be slackened. He had better find other ways to express his empathy.

Isaac readjusted in his seat. Heavenly laws beginning to have its origin on earth; born in the minds of men. Disapproving the other religions would be totally useless - it would be a bottomless argument.

"Then we have the most talked about man in the world, Jesus. It's always hard for anyone to look at the man, Jesus, critically. He is considered untouchable, even by non believers." John said.

> *Mathew Chapter 13, Verses 41-43*
> *The son of man shall send forth his angels and they*
> *shall gather out of his kingdom all things that offend,*
> *and them which do iniquity*
> *And shall cast them into a furnace of fire: there shall*
> *be wailing and gnashing of teeth.*
> *Then shall the righteous shine forth as the sun in the*
> *Who hath ears to hear, Let him hear.*
>
> *John Chapter 14, Verse 6*
> *Jesus said unto him, I am the way, the truth and the*
> *life: no man cometh to the father but by me.*

"Jesus too did the disappearing act. From age twelve he vanished, only to reappear at age thirty to start his ministry. So many theories have been given as per where he was at that early age in question. I can't go into that now. But some just think it's not important...these are strong believers, just accept him, they yell. Yet they all claim to talk to Jesus on a regular basis, and not just one time will ask where he was from age twelve to thirty or, they only talk about give me, give me, bless me, bless me all the time. If I were Jesus I would ask…hey, where is your curiosity? Don't you care about my childhood and teenage years?

The inspired writers by the Holy Spirit (Remember, holy spirit keeps the book of life, everybody is recorded, every second of every day of our lives just like cameras everywhere now) were so meticulous in tracing the genealogy of Jesus to the day he was born but kept mute on mere gaps in the years of the savior.

"But since Mohammed got direct instruction from angel Gabriel, I would think we would know where Jesus was during those years because he referenced Jesus in the Koran. Well, it's still a mystery to this day. But it was so easy for Muhammad to tell us that Jesus mentioned his name.

"Between Jesus and Mohammed, in order for their followers to follow them, they sang the heaven-reward and hell-punishment song all the time. This puts fear in the minds of men to this day. Or how do you explain the toughest mayor of New York City, the hardest city to run, to stand in line for a piece of bread from his Pope, threatened not to be given him by the Bishop for being a disobedient man. 'No paradise for you'. And the charismatic leader of Great Britain who, on one hand, wants abortion to be legalized, and on the other hand, wants to be a good catholic. We know that fear is contagious and it's hard for this man not to be confused. And in the land of the free they still swear their President in using the bible, promising fairness to all…mmm.

"But the irony of it is that these religions preach against fear. I don't think they know what fear means. Though, most people might beat their chests in the open about not being afraid of dying or the fear of hell, but in their rooms it's another story and that's where the religious ones console them and win them over to their Gods, especially when they are about to face death. The question of the unknown takes center stage in our minds when death approaches or as we grow older. Maybe, that is why the mayor wants to run a city in paradise instead of one in hell.

I have to say I do not know who sang the song of hell more than the other. It's a draw. In a chart topping world now, both leaders (Jesus and Muhammad) would be number one on the billboard magazine forever. Look at the numbers of their fans. Michael Jackson's album, Thriller, would be out-sold billion times over." John said.

Jack glanced at John and smiled. "Man is an incredible animal."

"Did Jesus go away for that long to study the Old Testament and then implanted himself there as the messiah? Because I hear he belonged to a fraternity called Essenes." Den asked.

"We'll never know." John answered.

"But believers say his birth was predicted in the Old Testament." Jack said.

That's just mumbo-jumbo, self-filling prophesy by the Christians. The New Testament was written decades (60 years or more) after Jesus' death. Yet they could quote Jesus correctly. Only in the bible! Even the Old one was written by different writers, like a sequel." John replied and went on as if the point was irrelevant.

"Then we have Buddha who broke away from the Hindu faith. At least, he just sat under the bohi tree for enlightenment. No cave here. And still he got people to follow him in his message to mankind." John continued. "And we have the religion of Jainism. The founder was Mahavira who went wondering naked and led an ascetic life that nearly killed Buddha, before Buddha decided to quit the Hindu faith. After twelve years of suffering, he achieved kevala (omniscience), and at the age of seventy-two, he broke the bonds of karma and achieved enlightenment, just like Buddha.

"He had some profound teachings, including not enslaving your fellow man and being a vegetarian. The vegetarian part is in question because they have this rule about not killing anything. They sweep the ground in order not to step on ants. That will take you years to travel to work on foot. But then again, isn't plant alive?" John questioned.

"Both Buddha and Mahavira used opposite methods, and both got enlightened." Jack was curious.

"Yeah, at least from what both leaders claimed." John replied.

"How come Jainism is not as popular as Buddhism?" Den asked.

"Most religions are not popular and many just fade away. It's all trial and error. Most of the ones that people follow today are just lucky to still be around. It's like all the millions of tiny sperms swimming toward the ovary hoping to be the one to make contact with the egg. It's luck and coupled with favorable historical events. Jainism and Buddhism are similar and both promise achieving enlightenment. I guess the rigorous method of the former is too burdensome for many. I hear Mohammed too had to reduce the number of worship a day from

50 or100 to 5 times daily. They say he bargained with Allah just like Satan did." John said.

"Then within Christianity, there were people who used the same method employed by the founder with a little twist of their own, and guess what, people followed them.

"This is where the founder of the Jehovah Witness comes in. Charles Taze Russell said he alone understood the bible the way it was supposed to be taught. By condemning other churches, salvation now depends on being a Jehovah's Witness. Despite the fact that he predicted the end of the world in 1914, nevertheless, the followers still stayed with him. The followers now would tell anybody that's ready to listen that their leader was not wrong, the world misunderstood him. To that I say we are sorry.

"And apart from the debacle of predicting the end of the world so many times, they also, like Muhammad, have what they call 'new light'. That means they still get revelation from God. For instance, they used to celebrate birthdays, Christmas and pledged allegiance to their country, but new light changed that. God stopped that nonsense. Also in the same vein, William Miller of the 7th Day Adventist broke away from the Baptist Church, predicated the return of Jesus, first in March and when Jesus didn't glide down from the sky, he said, sorry, people, I meant 22nd of October (in 1844), but Jesus disappointed again. Yes, there are still followers to this day, rationalizing their faith and denomination." John stopped.

"So if we think we cannot fall for the same scam then we are kidding ourselves." Jack said thoughtfully.

"You have to conquer the fear of the unknown first and then you can be free." Den offered his thought.

"But Joseph Smith replicated everything from the original method of making people to follow only you just like Muhammad." John continued. "They both had angels visiting them, Moroni to Smith and Gabriel to Mohammed. They were both told to make anew the old religions. Both of them also believed in everlasting revelations from God. Between the two of them we now have the correct words of God or Allah. Smith said that Jesus, after the crucifixion, appeared to him in the United States of America and gave him some gold tablets, instructions or laws - the real one, and he had to translate it into English for the benefit of mankind. This gave birth to the Mormon's Bible. Now they have two.

"Most of these new churches have two bibles, too, so it is not a new thing. And salvation also depends on becoming a member or you're condemned - it does not matter whether you accept Jesus as your savior. Jesus has now become irrelevant, how ironic!

"And just like the ark of the Lord is still not found by the 'true Christians', no gold tablets have been found as well by the Mormons. The search continues...who has the burden of proof? Though, the Christians are always lying about having found the ark, trying to prove their faith with physical evidence. Infighting goes on.

"This is a group (Mormon) that was not all inclusive at the beginning; I guess God did not remember all his creations. They would not allow the black race in. Then, in the late 1970s their leaders got a revelation that it was cool to allow the blacks to join the family of God.

"You see these revelations never end, it's two for a penny and everybody's got one at the appropriate time. You won't believe it, blacks are now joining." John said.

"How the hell did they convince blacks to join? Den asked in disbelieve.

"Maybe they bribed them with goods and...they even have churches in Africa, now." John added.

"Talk of complexity and irrationality of the human nature. This is beyond me, man." Jack couldn't figure it out.

"Even Joseph Smith could not save himself from the mob. He died at their hands. There are over five million followers today and growing, the fourth largest church in America, the only land of the smart, the wise and the knowledgeable." John went on.

"And many uncountable churches around the world have their own twist on the age old bible and their leaders breathing in fresh understanding not known to Moses and Jesus. There is one in Lagos, Nigeria, not to be confused with Lagos in Portugal, where their leader instructs them not to wear shoes. Maybe, because everywhere to them is holy...remember the burning bush, except where there are broken bottles or nails that can puncture the foot. There is another one in South Korea (Unification church) where the white and black people have to belong to now for salvation. I guess power is really shifting. McDonald's and Coca-cola are not the only franchises, anymore.

"If God is rational, he won't be able to choose the right religion not to talk of the right denomination.

"Now the second part of the heavenly scheme is simple, too. You're supposed to spread the word once you're hooked.

> *Ezekiel Chapter 33 Verse 8*
> *Thou dost not speak to warn the wicked. His blood will*
> *I require at thine hand.*

"It has nothing to do with liking you. It's an obligation. They have the biggest task in the world, to spread the word to 6,000,000,000 people, and growing." John answered.

"Gee, what if they can't get to an infant that dies suddenly before they could preach the word to him in a remote jungle...they get punished?" Den joked.

"I have often wondered about people going out as missionaries, old and young, to preach to others in the cold, rain, snow or heat, like the US postal service slogan, promising to deliver your mails in any kind of weather condition. Now I know in their minds they see me going to hell or will be destroyed by God if I don't join their group. So it's not as if they would do it in the first place. They are saving their asses." Jack was surprised.

"Even if you join any of these religions, your battle has just started. You would now have to pray to God to get you into the right group." Den said in wonder.

Before John or anybody could respond to the last comment, Bob got up to leave.

"I have to call my wife." Bob said, getting up. "But hey, please keep me posted, will you, Jack."

"Definitely," Jack promised.

"See you later." Bob said.

He dialed his home number from his office. The phone rang a few times but no one answered. He called her office and no one picked up, either.

'Where can she be?' He thought. He was still wondering about his wife's whereabouts when Frank stepped into his office.

"How are you getting along with your heavenly team?" He teased.

"Quite nice, I must say…interesting discussions so far." Bob replied.

"I'm glad you feel that way. Next time you see them the party is over. Work starts tomorrow. Everything is in place. Let's see how they work together." Frank said.

"Okay, Frank. It's about time." He felt relieved that physical work would start and before he could continue, Frank disappeared.

"Frank." He called out, no response. Seemed everyone was in a disappearing mode.

He decided to take a nap. He would call his wife later after a good siesta. At that moment his mind became restless and it started churning over everything that was said and to his utmost amazement, he felt he was not missing anything from the group.

"Where we have strong emotions,
We're liable to fool ourselves."
Carl Sagan

"Man's main quest is to free himself from being a man."
Bob

Pandemic Spread

"You know something? I'm really tired of all these religions. Somebody please stop this spinning ball. I want out. When will this madness end?" Jack exclaimed.

"Very soon, very soon," Fred said optimistically.

It wasn't clear whether he was saying 'very soon' in order to be vindicated or whether he was himself showing signs of waiting for too long to know whether it would be true or not.

"You must be kidding, Fred. You guys have been singing that song forever," replied Jack.

"John, is anyone coming to save us all?" Jack continued sarcastically. This time he was not shaking his head.

"Many people have predicted the end of time and nothing has happened so far as you can see. But it's making people restless. You see, something else is built in man's psyche that makes him want to rest; take a break from all the hustling and bustling, toiling day and night and night and day…ooh God, when will it all end? And the triangular religions are crying the most. It's like dangling a carrot in front of a donkey; some wishes just fade away, some people take it with a grain of salt, some pray for it every day and night. A popular evangelist, the presidents' pastor, they nicknamed him, in the US wakes up every morning looking up in the sky asking Jesus whether he is coming today.

"They say it's this generation and not that generation. This is the special generation and it goes on and on like a parrot that has just discovered talking for the first time.

"Some claim their savior comes in every age to defeat the evil that plagues man. This is actually attributed to Krishna." John said.

"How long does it take to do that?" Den was eager to know.

"You have to ask Krishna." John answered. "On the other hand, Islam is sort of waiting for the return of Jesus Christ, too."

"Really," Den did not believe his ears. "Is it that entangled?"

"Yes, really, they just don't shout it like the Christians do every day." John said.

"Jesus is supposed to come back to this world, get married and have children and then die at 40 years of age or so. This is because he didn't get to do all this the first time, and in Islam there is no celibacy. You have to do it. But we all know that not all men can do it. Maybe all Prophets have to do it. They belong to an exclusive club. Prophets can't be impotent. This is an interpretation by some Imams.

"Another interpretation by a different Muslim group concerning the end time will be that Jesus comes back to fight the anti-Christ and defeats him, of course, like the good guy, bad guy Hollywood movie. Then the world will be no more."

"Interesting," Jack was shaking his head in disbelieve.

"And then." John continued. "The trumpet will sound to signal the end of your worries according to Islam."

"Indeed, like everything with man there is confusion on this issue about the coming of the messiah." Jack said.

"I bet every one of them is claiming to have the final word on the matter as well." Den added an obvious thought.

"You guys are right, but you have to put this at the back of your mind that this issue of the messiah coming only applies to what I call the three-pointed-religion; Judaism, Christianity, and Islam. So, according to the Christians their messiah had already come, but will come again to draw the final curtain." John said.

> *Matthew Chapter 1 Verses 23 & 25*
> *Behold, a virgin shall be with child,*
> *and shall bring forth a son, and they*
> *shall call his name Emmanuel, which*
> *being interpreted is, 'God with us'*
> *And knew her not till she had*
> *brought forth her first born son, and*
> *he called his name Jesus.*

"But the Jews are still expecting their messiah. Wasn't Jesus a Jew? How come they did not believe him to be the messiah?" Jack asked the question looking directly at Isaac. He wanted him to answer this one.

Isaac, who had been a spectator apart from saying few words here and there all along decided to break his silence.

"We are not a foolish and rebellious people as most people would like you to believe." Isaac responded.

He tilted his black hat forward. He was built like Stan but the difference was in the hair. He had to wear his beard long and bushy as God ordered with a strand or lock of hair at both sides of the head, dangling like earrings. The Mormons copied that appearance before they got a revelation to change that way of dressing, to cut it off and look more like mainstream Americans; a GQ look. Seemed the Jews didn't get that memo or revelation. Needless to say Isaac was wearing the long black coat with matching pants and a spotless, white shirt underneath. But if you shaved every strand of hair on his head he would look very much like Stan. God would find it hard to spot his chosen.

"The fact of the matter is not that simple." Isaac continued. "It's rooted in history and you can't just pick one topic in peoples' history and think you will have a good understanding of their story. You'll be doing a great injustice to those people. In this case, to my people: the chosen people.

"With any human group you'll agree with me that there are good and bad people, and with our history, there had been claims by some individuals to be the messiah sent by the God of Abraham, Jacob and Isaac, and had been found not to be true." Isaac stated plainly.

"Did you hear yourself just now?" Den said in a lighthearted manner.

"Hey, I'm serious here. I know what you mean," replied Isaac. "I was just named after him. Back to what I was saying, according to the old testament, Prophet Isaiah prophesied that a messiah would be sent to the people of Israel and there would be everlasting peace amongst other things." Isaac said, stressing every word.

"Hey, look around you. Is there peace?" He asked. That was another million dollar question that needed no answer.

> *Isaiah Chapter 9 Verses 6-7*
> *For unto us a child is born unto us a son is given and*

*the government shall be upon his shoulder and his
name shall be called wonderful, counselor. The mighty
God, The everlasting father, The Prince of peace, of
the increase of his government and peace there shall
be no end, upon the throne of David, and upon his
kingdom, to order it, and to establish it with judgment
and with justice from henceforth even for ever. The zeal
of the lord of hosts will perform this*

"So my friends, we are still waiting, unfortunately." Isaac said soberly.

"But some Jews during the trying periods, especially during the holocaust claimed to be the messiah." Jack played the devil's advocate.

"To all of them, including the celebrated Jesus of the Christian faith, they should read the book of Isaiah properly and pray for the spirit of discernment or understanding. They are all liars, at least, going by what the prophet saw." Isaac said.

"If I'm a believing man," Jack cut in. "I will agree with you totally on this passage even without the spirit's aid. Please tell me, Isaac, why is it that non-Jewish people like the whites...don't look at me. I don't do the herd mentality in any case...blacks and Arabs hate you guys for killing your prophets, especially Jesus and John the Baptist? I find it hard to comprehend. Even Bob Marley sang about it in a non supporting way. *How long will they kill our prophets and we stand aside and look."*

But before Isaac could respond to Jack's inquiry, John stepped in, very unusual of him. Maybe he was trying to protect the chosen one. Doubtful though, judging by his nature. That would be the area of the Christians now, but before it was a different story. The Jews had to live a double life in good ole Europe; they either changed their names to Christian names or were expelled from the 'promised land'. Pretty much what the world wide Christian missionaries did. 'Change your god forbidden names before you can go to our schools and hospitals.' Whoever said preaching the good word was enough to convert must be a liar.

"You can't quantify human behavior, Jack. The complexity of man is far beyond what you can analyze in a lab. There are so many facets to consider, the environment, good upbringing or lack of it, level of education - formal and informal, the person in question, social standing, understanding, really, it's endless, and considering the unknown reasons…jealousy, rivalry, it goes on…'

Isaac cut John off. "I'll tell you, Jack."

Isaac had been trying to get certain things off his chest, things that you wouldn't say in the open. Who said it was a one way street. Everybody hid their true feelings in a multiracial society, even in a family.

"Honestly, it beats me. Most of us can't answer that question, either. But, I strongly believe you could trace it to jealousy and misguided views about us way before Hitler capitalized on it in Europe. The much praised Martin Luther by the Westerners of the Protestant fame was a Jew hater. Once an icon in a society says something people are more likely to believe him or her. I personally blame him for his careless utterances. We were the go-to-guys to get different kinds of businesses done. We were enterprising and from our business acumen we became wealthy, and they were envious of that amongst other things. The silliest one was that we kept to ourselves." Isaac declared.

"So you're not blaming Adolf?" Jack asked.

"No, my point is that individuals in Europe had the hatred already and Hitler just gave them a powerful and deadly force with which to commit the atrocities against innocent Jews. We moved from the Western part of Europe to the East for refuge and the same thing happened. How can you not see the pattern here?" Isaac replied.

"I see." Jack agreed.

"No leader can do such a thing without the passive support of the majority in the country. Look at the blacks in America." Isaac was trying to explain himself as clear as possible so that no one would have any misconception on where he stood. Whether that was possible in the context of human nature had to be seen.

"When the US passed the segregation and all those inhumane laws, the whites in the society went along with it passively; because most whites had been conditioned to believe they were superior to the blacks, and the blacks were only fitted for domestic services. To the extent that the government scientists and the US Army (Now army of one) conducted their so-called scientific research into black people's brains just to prove their theory filled with bias. But on the other hand, if the society did not support the bad law, it would be dead in its tracks. Some governors even ran their campaigns on segregation as an agenda and won."

"Someone said that Jesus would have been put at the back of the bus because of his skin color." Jack mumbled.

Isaac managed a smile and then went on. "Remember the Jews were affected by these awful laws in the US too, but it was more pronounced on the blacks. Really all the minorities in the US were affected. Can that be done today?"

The question answered itself.

"So, even if we did kill Jesus, we honestly killed one of our own. Why should they care? We have not told any group not to do away with anyone in their midst that's against their social laws. And we know most societies had killed or driven out their so-called prophets. Wasn't Mohammed driven out of Mecca to Medina and had to fight back? You don't see us hating them for that." Isaac said emphatically.

Jack pressed on. "But what they are saying is that you killed God or the son of God. I don't know how they arrived at that, but that's the word on the street. You are accused of deicide."

"Tell me, really, you look like an intelligent fellow. How can man kill G-d?" Isaac asked.

"Thanks for seeing me as an intelligent guy, but I'm not taking that as a compliment because some of the people that are saying this are accepted as such - men and women in the society that are praised and their intelligent advice sought after, day and night." Jack rejected the praise.

"Okay, okay. But tell me, how could we kill G-d?"

"It's beyond me." Jack threw his hands in the air.

"This is our story." Isaac went on.

"Certainly, it's your history and story." Jack reassured.

"The Arab Muslims through their so-called prophet changed the stories of our G-d, turned the names of our people around and still have the audacity to condemn us. Mohammed even had the effrontery to say Abraham wasn't a Jew. That's laughable.

"We gave them their G-d for crying out loud. We even gave the whites their G-d, whether it was diluted through their chosen messiah or not.

"We didn't spread our faith by force or have you read anywhere in the history books that the Jewish people imposed their faith on conquered people around the world? No." He said categorically. "Even Jesus said he was only sent to the house of Israel." He added with an ironic smile.

> *Matthew Chapter 15 Verses 22 - 26*
> *And, behold a woman of Canaan came out of the same*
> *coasts and cried unto him, saying, have mercy on me*
> *O Lord, thou son of David, my daughter is grievously*
> *vexed with a devil. But he answered her not a word. And*
> *his disciples came and besought him saying, send her away,*
> *for she crieth after us. But he answered and said. I am not*
> *sent but unto the lost sheep of the house of Israel. Then came*
> *she and worshipped him, saying,*
> *Lord help me. But he answered and said, It is not meet to*
> *take the children's bread, and to cast it to dogs*

"I thought he was sent to the whole world. And Jesus comparing me to a dog, if I were that woman I wouldn't take the healing." Jack interjected and added, "show some dignity as a human being."

But Isaac just pretended as if he didn't hear the comment.

"Without the Jews some of these people will still be worshipping the sun, moon, sand dunes, rivers and Allat." He said angrily.

"But the Christians are saying…" Jack was about to make another point.

"The Christians are saying what?" Isaac fired back. "My friend, the same Christians are trying to convert all the Jews to Christianity. Can you imagine that? They are saying we do not practice our own religion right. Some Christians are of the mind that the kingdom of G-d has been taken away from us and given to them. Even the Muslims want us converted to Islam.

> *Surah 2 : 136*
> *We believe in God and that which has been*
> *revealed to us; in what was revealed to Abraham,*
> *Ishmael, Isaac, Jacob and the tribes: Moses and*
> *Jesus and the other prophets by their Lord.*
> *If they accept your faith, they shall be rightly guided*

"What these people don't put into account is that G-d of Abraham, Isaac and Jacob promised us that he would bless any people that bless us and would curse any people that curse us.

"I know every Christian that believes in G-d would find it easy to point to Jesus as the messiah, but even the disciples of Jesus were in the dark regarding this question.

"Remember the disciples asked him; 'why then say the scribes that Elijah must first come,' because that was another sign of the messiah coming to the Jewish people. This is the twist. Jesus said Elijah came already but the people didn't know him and they did to him whatever they pleased.

"So tell me that was crystal clear, that it was Jesus who was to come. And where is the peace?" Isaac reminded them emphatically, again.

"So, is Jesus coming for the first time, second or the last time? I'm lost." Den was confused as usual, but it was a confusion that he was beginning to enjoy at the expense of the entangled minds of man.

"Even according to the Christian faith, that isn't clear." John spoke after listening to Isaac.

"What did I get myself into?" Den wondered.

"You mean coming into this world, ha? My man, you've no choice, at least, you would not be here." Jack answered.

"When Christ comes back everything will be clear." Fred's flame of Christianity still burnt on like a candle in the wind. "And what do you mean, ' confusion about his coming'? Christianity might have broken into different denominations, but everyone believes the same on this issue, even the Jehovah's Witnesses." Fred challenged.

"If you must know, Christ was telling his disciples about the predicament that would befall the world before coming back." John replied. "Hear it from the horse's mouth:

> *'And then shall they see the son of man coming in a*
> *cloud with power and great glory'*

"These are the signs of the end, Fred.

> *Luke Chapter 21 Verse 21*
> *Then let them which are in Judea flee to the mountains,*
> *and let them which are in the midst of it depart out; and*

let not them that are in the countries enter therinto
but woe unto them that are with, and to them that
give suck, in those days for there shall be great distress
In the land, and wrath upon this people

"And after counting all the terrible things before he would appear, Christ dropped this bombshell.

Luke Chapter 21 Verses 31 -32
So likewise ye, when ye see these things come to pass,
know ye that the kingdom of God is nigh at hand.
Verily I say unto you, this generation shall not pass
away, till all be fulfilled.

Now, you do the math, Fred. Many generations have passed and still he hasn't returned." John asked. "In fact, some say he came already. Remember the Rastafarians."

Fred looked down, trying to put together a sound reply, finding it hard to mentally elevate himself this time.

"I discussed this passage with a Christian sister and she said I should disregard the words 'this generation'." John said.

"How else are we to look at the word, generation?" Den asked. "It's simple, 50 years or so should be a generational gap."

"Some religious scientists are now trying to figure it out. Their theory is that we now start counting generation from the birth of the nation of Israel, founded in 1948." John went on.

"That's bullshit." Jack added, not believing how far man would go to prove something in order to fit his theory. Man, always wise after event. Man would connect the dots perfectly well after any major occurrence, even 911 was prophesied in the bible amongst other events of the end of the world.

"Hey." John said. "Don't worry your head over that. This quote will provide answer to that. You can use the bible against the believers here.

Luke chapter 1 verse 48
For he hath regarded the low estate of his handmaiden:
for, behold, from henceforth all generations shall call
me blessed.

"Never doubt the power of denial. We do it when it comes to our family, children, friends, husband, wife, sisters and brothers, race, tribe and country, why not in what we believe." John assured Jack and went on.

"There are other indications too, but I keep telling you guys that you are dealing with a religious mindset. They are blind but they think they can see objectively. They can be learned professors, scientists, lawyers and thinkers but when it comes to understanding what love really is or finding real answers to life or why we are here, they are ignorant. But the ego of man pushes him on to claim what he accepts as the truth. Forgetting that close to him in another town, other fellows like him with so-called analytical minds choose the opposite religion or ways of understanding why we are here and where we are going. Education can only provide a better living, everything being equal. A head full of knowledge doesn't amount to love or wisdom."

"How long have they been waiting?" Jack asked.

"Over 2,000 years." John answered like a student who had memorized it because the teacher never stopped telling the story.

"Hmm," Jack was thoughtful. "So, before Jesus showed up, Moses probably freed the Israelites around 3,000 years ago and…from the time of Moses to Adam and Eve, say, around 3,000 years also. So, all together man has spent, say, less than 10,000 years or so on earth."

"You'll be close." John said.

"Then the world isn't that old according to them. But the scientists, real ones, are telling us that the sharks have been in existence for over three million years." Jack said.

"You don't want to make comparisons like that, Jack. You can't compare religious numbers with scientific ones. They are in two separate worlds." John quickly replied and provided more thought provoking insights.

"Even the fact that the Aborigines in the present day Australia dates back to 40,000 years before any white man stepped on the continent's soil doesn't add up in a religious mind. And the so-called third world country, Nigeria, there they found artifacts that date back as far as 39,000 years in the Nok culture. And also we have Lucy, the complete female bone that was found in Eastern part of Africa to be over a million years. And In the present day Israel they have found a Shaman's grave that dates back to 12,000 years ago. Several thousand years before Jehovah created the world. Whoa! Carbon dating is the devil's invention according to the believers. It's a conspiracy, another telescopic denial!" John clarified.

"So, that's like 7,000 years of shoving and forcing and recycling this despicable lie down the throat of man." Jack dropped his own bombshell.

"But like I was saying, there are more statements to consider in their own story, Jack." John informed.

> *Matthew Chapter 16 Verses 27- 28*
> *For the son of man shall come in the glory of his father*
> *with his angels, and then he shall reward everyman*
> *according to his works.*
> *Verily I say unto you, there be some standing here,*
> *which shall not taste of death, till they see the son of*
> *man coming in his kingdom*

"And all this, they are still expecting." Jack was beside himself.
"There's more." John added.

> *Matthew Chapter 10 Verses 21 - 23*
> *And the brother shall deliver up the brother to death,*
> *and the father the child, and the children shall rise up*
> *against the parents, and cause them to be put to death.*
> *And ye shall be hated of all men for my name's sake:*
> *but he that endureth to the end shall be saved.*
> *But when they persecute you in this city, flee ye into*
> *another, for verily I say unto you, ye shall not have*
> *gone over the cities of Israel, till the son of man be*
> *Come*

"Apart from the fact that this is clear, Jesus was to have come back before every city in Israel was preached to. If he didn't mention Israel, and just cities, they can sink their teeth on that and make it sound like it's a worldwide issue, but it was limited to Israel. I'm sure a holy-spirit-filled Christian will claim that Israel now means the world. I can't wait to hear that." Jack concluded.

"But whether we like it or not the coming of a messiah is a very powerful message. Throughout history we hear of people selling their properties when their leaders tell them that Jesus is coming tomorrow. Some will take poison to facilitate their quick reunion with Christ. Remember the Heaven's gate incident in the US. This was a group of elites; the educated, the movie stars, the lawyers, the nurses and so on. They had their beds laid out for them and were dressed as if going to school. They voluntarily drank poison. I don't think we have seen the end of that kind of group. A similar one happened in Ugandan. This one you can say was carried out by the uninformed; illiterates. Does it matter with man, knowledgeable or not. And don't forget Jim Jones of the Guyana tragedy when believers took poison to assist in their quick reunion with Jesus.

"This is because when you start singing about heaven and hell and especially how hell will be, people become afraid and turn converts. Fear is a powerful weapon to make man do what you want.

> *Revelation Chapter 1 Verse 18*
> *I am he that liveth, and was dead; and behold, I am*
> *alive for evermore, amen, and have the keys of hell*
> *and of death.*

> *Revelation Chapter 19 Verse 20*
> *And the beast was taken, and with him the false*
> *prophet that wrought miracles before him, with which*
> *he deceived them that had received the mark of the*
> *beast, and them that worshipped his image. These*
> *both were cast alive into a lake of fire burning with*
> *brimstone.*

So, we succumb in our billions because of fear; not of love." John explained, always trying to show why man was in this predicament.

"Isaac, do you have anything to say about Jesus coming again? I mean the Christian Jesus." Jack said, he could not get enough of his explanations.

"This is their battle; remember we are still expecting the real savior." Isaac looked at Fred, who seemed drained at this time. Blind faith was easy to come by but hard to get rid of.

"What about Judas? Wasn't he paid 30 Shekels for Jesus' head by the Jewish leaders?" Jack asked again, disregarding Isaac's objection to the issue.

But John decided to come to his rescue. "Jack, according to the story of God, the father of Jesus was looking for a way to redeem the world of sins, and so Jesus was offered as a sacrificial lamb for mankind. The problem was Jesus had to die somehow for you and I to be redeemed, and that was where Judas came in. So you can say these two figures were predestined to carry out their missions."

"How come the Christians are saying that Judas will burn forever in hell?" Jack was curious and John gave him a knowing look.

"John, I know what you have been saying about religion and mindset, but that does not mean I should not hear what they have to say. Even though I might get thousands of answers to one question and all claiming their answers come from one Holy Spirit. Let me get a good laugh from their mouths because when I'm down I can recall their reasons and laugh myself back to good spirit. Who says Jesus isn't helpful." Jack said smiling.

> *Matthew Chapter 26 Verses 20 - 25*
> *Now when the even was come, he sat down with the*
> *twelve. And as they did eat, he said, verily I say unto*
> *you, that one of you shall betray me*
> *And they were exceedingly sorrowful and began every*
> *one of them to say unto him, Lord, is it I?*
> *And he answered and said, he that dippeth his hand*
> *with me in the dish, the same shall betray me.*
> *The son of man goeth as it is written of him; but woe*
> *unto that man by whom the son of man is betrayed!*
> *It had been good for that man if he had not been born.*
> *Then Judas, which betrayed him, answered and said,*
> *master, is it I? He said unto him. Thou hast said.*

"Gee, I'm lost again." Den said looking seriously at John, trying to understand what the passage meant. Seemed the confusion this time was justified.

"First, Jesus said it was written to go that way, and then said woe to Judas, and that it would be better for Judas not to be born. How was he going to be sacrificed?"

"You're not lost, Den." Jack shifted forward in his seat. "It's simple. Any rational mind will come up with your question. On one hand they want to be saved, on the other, they don't want their beloved lamb to die. It's either one or the other. Just like they want the world to end, but don't want all the calamities their Jesus said would take place.

"So what could Judas do against such a powerful God? Christians are saying he had a choice. Something was planned by their almighty God…he had a choice, what choice? Some say he wasn't remorseful, a guy that took his own life after the bribe.

"This guy was put here to take our sins, to wash them away. Was he supposed to jump from a tree to offer his life, or to swim until he drowned or better still, to take an overdose of sleeping pills? Yes, that would be good. A suggestion like that could have spared the life of poor puppet, Judas. How the hell did the white leaders persecute the Jews in the first place for this?" Jack was infuriated.

"Hey, before you run out of steam, according to the gospel of Judas…, John informed.

"There is a gospel according to Judas?" Den asked eagerly before John could go on with the information.

"Yes, they just discovered it in some remote area and it contradicts what a true Christian wants to hear." John said.

"What?" Jack was astonished.

"Jesus appeared to have instructed Judas to betray him so that he (Jesus) could go back to where he came from. More like committing suicide.

> *Gospel according to Judas*
> *Knowing that Judas was reflecting upon something*
> *that was exulted, Jesus said to him, step away from*
> *the others, and I shall tell you the mysteries of the*
> *kingdom. It is possible for you to reach it, but you will*
> *grieve a great deal. For someone else will replace*
> *you, in order that the twelve (disciples) may again*
> *come to completion with their God.*

"What I can gather from this story is that Jesus was actually closer to the dreaded, unrepentant Judas both physically and spiritually and not to Peter. And remember Judas was their treasurer. Also, Judas had a transfiguration, too, which was similar to the one Jesus had and, a voice in the cloud applauded the good work he was doing." John interpreted.

"Hmm," Den sighed. "Where do we go from here, so many contradictions?"

"Nowhere, remember it's just one religion claiming to know what man is doing here," replied John, without concern.

Fred desperately wanted to say something but nothing came out of his mouth, he looked shocked. He was slowly rocking back and forth in his chair like those poor children nodding their heads when learning the holy books by force, which would render them mentally useless in a secular society.

"You see, back and forth argument does not make what you believe to be true." John added frankly.

"You guys can rationalize all you want." Fred finally came out of his slumber and was ready to defend his belief. "Judas had a choice. When God made us he gave us free will to know good and bad. You guys are using your free will the way you want and nothing is stopping you. You agree? It's because God allows that."

"What is free will if you are restricted from the get-go from eating from the tree of life? I don't think you guys understand the concept of free will. Also, remember when God hardened the heart of Pharaoh in Egypt when he already threw in the towel; surrendered. But God just wouldn't have that. He had to use excessive force." John answered Fred.

> *Exodus Chapter 11*
> *And the Lord gave the people favor in the sight of the*
> *Egyptians. And all the first born in the land of Egypt*
> *shall die, from the first born of Pharaoh that sitteth upon*
> *his throne, even unto the first born of the maidservant that*
> *is behind the mill; and all the first born of beasts…And the*
> *Lord said unto Moses. Pharaoh shall not harken unto you;*
> *that my wonders be multiplied in the land of Egypt. And*
> *Moses and Aaron did all these wonders before Pharaoh; and*
> *the Lord hardened Pharaoh's heart, so that he would not let*
> *the children of Israel go out of the land.*

"I would say Pharaoh was denied his free will just like Onan and the three thousand people that Moses killed for exercising their free will to worship the golden calf." John stressed.

"John, please say no more. I think it's a hopeless situation trying to talk some sense into people like this. You and I are wasting our breath." Jack said. "I just wish this world would stop spinning."

"The kingdom of God is at hand." Fred echoed. "It was people like you that made God destroy the world in the first place. But this time he would just send you and your kind to hell because of your blasphemy."

"Was the world really destroyed, John?" Jack asked.

"Remember the faithful Noah." John started.

> *Genesis Chapter 6 Verse 7*
> *And the Lord said, I will destroy man whom I have*
> *created from the face of the earth; both man, and beast,*
> *and the creeping thing, and the fowls of the air; for it*
> *repenteth me that I have made them.*
> *But Noah found grace in the eyes of the lord.*

"He was instructed to build the famous ark. To gather every pair of animals in the world and God flooded the earth for 40 days and 40 nights. Everything died excluding Noah's family."

"I know the story, John. They sang it to us when I was young." Jack pointed out.

"But why did he take the rats, the roaches, flies and mosquitoes." Den added, laughing.

"Yeah, like the world would be a better place without them." Jack said.

Ahmed just kept silent. He knew his own prophet talked about the same story. After all, Mohammed claimed to serve the same God.

"Seriously, Fred, why destroy the world in the first place? What was God trying to accomplish after regretting that he created man. Would the next phase be sinless? How come God didn't know we would be back to square one? Tell me, Fred." Den insisted.

"Leave the poor guy alone, he's just holding on to the gospel truth. Never question, just take my word." John intervened. "But they fail due to the fear of punishment from what they believe to be God to realize that they are denying him of knowing the future, biggest sin in my view. It's a wasted effort to destroy those so-called sinners and everything is back to the same-old-sinful-world.

"You see in these triangular religions you can't just but wonder about the character of God. Take the popular man in the bible, Job. He was a man of God. He was perfect before God. All the preachers in the world use his story in their sermon to convey how to endure and love God.

> *Job Chapter 1*
> *There was a man in the land of Uz, whose name was Job and that man was perfect and upright, and one that feared God and eschewed evil.*
> *And there were born unto him seven sons and three daughters. His substance also was seven thousand sheep, three thousand camels, and five hundred yoke of oxen … So that this man was the greatest of all the men of the east.*

"Then one fateful day God turned his life upside down.

> *Job Chapter 1 Verse 8*
> *And the lord said unto Satan hast thou considered my servant Job, that there's none like him in the earth, a perfect and upright man, one that feareth God, and eschewed evil?*
> *Then Satan answered the lord and said, doth Job fear God for nought. Hast thou not made a hedge about him, and about his house on every side? Thou hast blessed the work of his hands and his substance is increased in the land… And the lord said unto Satan Behold, all that he hath is in thy power, only upon himself put not forth thine hand.*

"The long and short of the story is that the poor guy lost everything he ever worked for, including his sons and daughters. Everything perished." John said.

"You guys are misleading people. That's just a classic case of how all knowing God tests humans of their loyalty to him." Fred jumped on the matter. He was just echoing what his pastor had told him, foolproof. He stood up looking down at everyone. Each time trying desperately to win an argument for Jesus, but everybody was not Ahmed. How could all knowing still be testing us?

"That's a perfect example of suffering and still believing in God, even under such a test." Fred said devotedly.

Jack looked at Den and then at John. There was no response from John. He was going to buttress his argument with Job's story, now where was the point to look out for.

John studied the excitement on Fred's face. He hesitated as if not knowing what to say. Man, he thought was growing in consciousness to understand what love really meant without his sentimental attachments.

Even Jack was blind to what to come out of John's mouth like millions of these diehard believers. They kept coming back with dead points over and over as if their points would suddenly be resurrected from the dead.

"First of all, why would God take a challenge from Satan whom he created?" John went on the offensive. "For what reason, shouldn't that God be a pagan god, trying to prove something? Do you guys smell ego? A bet and you tell us not to gamble. Las Vegas is for the evil doers.

The expression of victory on Fred's face started to fade.

"Second, God won. But God won at the cost of the innocent children of Job and all his hard working servants. (There is a trend here; the animals were killed, too.) They all died, used as pawns between God and Satan. And the blind world applauded Job, for what, loyalty! It should be an example about the fact that this God kills whether you are good or not. It shouldn't be about loyalty sermon. They got it wrong for hundreds of years, even Jesus got it wrong." John said.

Before Fred could parrot the God-had-the-right speech in defense of a loving God, Jack gestured to Fred to zip it.

John decided to pound Fred's head with more of what he called his weapon; making people who prided themselves of sound moral behavior and backing it with a book that revealed inconsistencies with what any normal human being would regard as such.

Chronicles; chapter 21verses 1,10,12,13,14,1
And Satan stood up against Israel, and
provoked David to number Israel
Go and tell David, saying…I offer thee three
things: choose thee one of them, that I may do it unto
thee. Either three years famine; or three months to be
destroyed Before thy foes…or else three days the sword of the
lord, even the pestilence
let me fall now into the hand of the lord
So the lord sent pestilence upon Israel: and there fell of
Seventy thousand men. and David said unto God, is it not
I that commanded the people to be numbered? Even I it
is that have sinned and done evil indeed; but as for these
sheep, what have they done?

"The catch phrase you guys keep using is that God is always testing us and you back it with what you think is water tight argument that goes like this, 'you punish your children, don't you if they don't obey you,' same thing? No, because when we mere humans do punish our kids, we don't kill them, because we are training them. China won't be the most populous country if we are like your God. And we don't destroy a whole nation like Muhammad said of his Allah. Stop calling evil love or compassion.

"Even in this passage Prophet David became wiser than God after dodging the bullet, though. Shouldn't it be the other way round? Mere mortal was telling God, all merciful, all just, to punish the right offender. But in this case, there was no offence, really. Nevertheless, to compound this singular issue of census, there are two different verses that will make anyone that can put two and two together say, hey, wait a minute. Is God Satan now or is Satan, God? Is the word, he, not the pronoun of the word, Lord, in the sentence, again? But, as always, we are told to suspend our thinking and see the word, he, as referring to Satan. (Who was always angry at Israel, anyway, God or Satan?) This is a special privilege in English language. God and Satan now interchangeable! Forget this minor contradiction and go with the flow as they say. Blame it on language to language interpretation."

Samuel ll; chapter 24 verse 1
And again the anger of the Lord was kindled against
Israel, And he moved David against them to say, Go,
number Israel and Judah.

"What is the population of the world? Sorry, counting it might result in the end of the planet. Maybe we should stop counting the number of children we have, God might kill us; the parents oh, no. God will kill the counted; the children.

"That huge number my soccer fan is almost a packed Maracana stadium in Brazil. Imagine them not cheering for a fantastic goal, but falling all over one another dead for just watching the game; mere spectators, between David and God this time, forget Goliath for now." John asserted.

The tough talk returned. John was trying to provide irrevocable evidence in what they kept calling fair, merciful and wise God for over 2000 years. But he also knew that evidence like that might not be sufficient for people to see reason, largely because of fear.

Then he went for the jugular. He compared God to a pagan god that both the Muslims and the Christians had labeled unholy, uncaring and unforgiving, god that couldn't talk. And everybody knew how God and God's people carried out that accusation against paganism and their worshippers; through bloodshed. In search of the Maker we crushed everything on our path with the forces of evil.

"Why are you calling people who worship different Gods other than the one in the bible pagans, anyway?" John asked mockingly.

"They're serving their own creation of what they wrongfully think is God. It's not. They sacrifice humans for getting one favor or another from such gods and only God knows what else they do." Fred gave a befitting answer in his view. Wondered where he got his strength from. He was like a boxer that didn't know when to quit after he had been bloodied round after round.

"But Abraham sacrificed too to your God." Den countered.

"He sacrificed a ram. You see, Abraham was the only one that worshipped the one true God. He didn't follow the rest of the people praying to stones or carved images or sea." Fred replied.

"Didn't he want to sacrifice his only son?"

"Den, God won't allow such an evil thing to happen. He was just tested to see if he loved God more than anything else in the world." Fred corrected.

"So, he passed." Jack concluded.

"You haven't answered my question, Fred." John said slowly.

"What else is there to say? Maybe, you missed that part in the bible. Mr. I read holy books with an open mind." Fred said in a jest.

"You don't attack the person, you address the question. Only a small-minded person will say what you just said. Trying to kill the messenger…why don't you listen to the message." Den came to John's defense.

"I take no offense, Den. What's written is written, no one can change it. It's just our lack of willingness to open our eyes, minds and meticulously research whatever we've been told to believe, right or wrong, good or bad, by our society.

"First, it's ignorance. Second, it's our superficial care for fellow human beings in the past, present or future. And third, it's our lack of ability to put ourselves in the shoes of those people who got the short end of the stick from our loving God, Job's wife and children for instance, and the people that Abraham bought with his money. But God wouldn't be concerned with minor things like that," John said.

Then he gently turned to Fred.

"Your answer can't be farther from the truth. We hear how Abraham wanted to sacrifice Isaac due to the holy test.

> *Genesis Chapter 22 Verse 13*
> *And Abraham lifted up his eyes, and looked , and behold behind him was a ram caught in a thicket by his horns; and Abraham went and took the ram, and offered him up for a burnt offering in the stead of his son.*

"This singular event has made the Christians to rejoice in a God of Abraham, and now you have songs like *Abraham's blessings are mine*. Easy to claim the blessings and not the part where humans were bought with money.

"But, and that's a big but. If you read farther in the holy book you will see that God actually accepted the sacrifice of Abraham in a way, by presenting Isaac as a burnt offering! This is where you roast a human being like yourself alive, pretty much what the Popes did. And people say the Popes don't emulate God's actions." John said.

Fred's eyes nearly popped out of the sockets. Like Galileo's telescope reaching into the moon. "What's this guy smoking?"

> *Judges Chapter 11 Verse 29*
> *Then the spirit of the lord came upon Jephthah, and he*
> *passed over Gilead and Manasseh, and passed over*
> *Mizpeh of Gilead*
> *And Jephthah vowed a vow unto the Lord and said, if thou*
> *shalt without fail deliver the children of Ammon into mine*
> *hands.*
> *Then it shall be, that whatsoever cometh forth of the doors*
> *of my house to meet me, when I return in peace from the*
> *children of Ammon, shall surely be the Lord's, and I will*
> *offer it up for a burnt offering*
> *And Jephthah came to Mizpeh unto his house, and, behold,*
> *his daughter came out to meet him with timbrels and with*
> *dances, and she was his only child*
> *And it came to pass at the end of two months, that she*
> *returned unto her father, who did with her according to his*
> *vow which he had vowed.*

"Jephthah promised that if God allowed him victory over the enemy of Israel he would sacrifice a human being to God. Unfortunately for him, or can I really say that, well, it was his daughter that saw him first.

"Wasn't God the one empowering him, like Samson, when God's spirit came upon him? Wasn't God saying I'm with you, I heard you and I'd not let you down?

"You'll never hear a preacher use this good example to approach God. Hey, the story of Joseph the dreamer is overused, or don't they believe every word in the bible anymore?

"You see the Jews and the Christians are always saying the bible is a good book when it comes to sound morality; everything that man needs to function well in any society can be found in there. What am I going to learn from this? They argue every law in the bible and in the end justifies it, only in their heads. But it's not only the laws that are in question; it's also the character of that God. And even with the laws, should we mere mortals now come up with more humane laws than God, who should be wise beyond any man's puny brain in any age.

"Christians say Jesus was with the father (God) at the beginning of time. There you have it, Jesus actually knew of those laws and sacrifice. How can anyone exonerate him now? I'll leave this to the pastors and their congregations to answer." John concluded.

Fred was silent.

"You shut him up. How come he's not defending God as usual?" Jack was surprised.

"He's thinking…" John replied and continued.

"But I took this human sacrifice up with a devout Christian, and his position was that Jephthah shouldn't have made such a promise. This was the same guy I asked the day before whether the Aztecs sacrifice of humans was right and he dismissed it without a thought. He said they were wrong and ignorant."

"That was the same response we got from Fred?" Den was amazed.

"Yes, it's due to their ignorance of their holy book." John answered and continued.

"And according to him once that was done Jephthah had to follow through, to him a promise was a promise. He failed to understand the magnitude of the question. In their blind faith to defend God, they actually turn God into a thoughtless being, degrading their maker."

"I see your point, John. Sometimes I think you have to present to man many sides of an event before, hopefully, he gets it; over and over again." Den said.

"But the discussion got better." John was excited to go on.

"How," Den asked.

"The guy saw me again and he was kind of feeling inadequate, somewhat. He said, 'John, I know I gave you that answer but I was still thinking about it and it didn't make sense to me.' I kept quiet, letting him talk. Then I asked. 'Do you now know the answer; I mean good reason for the burnt offering?' He said, yes. According to him he prayed to God for the answer. In my mind I said this was going to be good.

'And boy oh boy, did he answer or what?' He said pompously. God explained everything to him clearly. There was no burnt offering, and Jephthah just dedicated her only daughter to God. That was the practice in the Old Testament. Samuel was dedicated amongst many others, and the lamenting in the passage was because she would never be kissed, touched and loved by a man.

"I said I would give God an 'F'. Any lecturer would fail God. I said and left.

"If you want to look into how a religious mindset works, this is it. In his mind this is how he sees the passage, 'whatsoever cometh to meet me after my victory is my only daughter that I won't sacrifice to the lord because the lord doesn't take human sacrifice.' Total irrationality at its best, you don't need a CAT scan of his brain.

"Actually to show you, if you can see clearly, if you are not drinking from the well, Jesus provided the answer to this question.

> *Matthew chapter 8 verse 9*
> *Or what man is there of you*
> *Whom if his son ask bread, will he give him a stone?*
> *Or if he ask a fish, will he give him a serpent?*

"Which unfortunately leads to another question to ask ourselves? Was Jesus wiser than his father by saying this? I'll leave the born again to answer this, too. Then as luck would have it we bumped into each other another day and I wanted to ask him about David and the census that resulted in so many deaths. But he refused to answer that. He said he knew the reason why that happened but wouldn't tell me because I wouldn't buy it. Then I said that would be my number one question for Jesus before heading to hell. Actually, a pastor said it was because David decided to do God's work. Only God could count the people. And he preached it so well that it made wrong sounding right." John said.

Fred made an attempt to say something but Jack cut him off.

"So, tell me. Why is it that man sacrifices animals or humans?" He gave Fred a dirty look before he continued…"In the first place?"

"The thinking is that once that is done, all will be well in the community. It's a primitive way of wishing for the goodness of all in the society. There's absolutely no reward in a practice like this. It's nothing short of ignorance. Even Jesus as the sacrificial lamb falls into this category. Christianity is based on this foundation. And we are told to accept it as the gospel truth. But why would anybody want to sacrifice his son or daughter?

"We, the recipients of such blessings don't really care as long as we get what we pray for. This kind of belief still makes sense to us to this day. And the reason why this is a good sales pitch is simple. Man buys into it because he doesn't want to be responsible for his actions. He believes someone should take his sins away, and a similar notion is Allah will forgive me all my misdeeds once I pray for forgiveness and believing in the last prophet. Really, if they tell man to face the ocean to confess his sins and all will be forgiven, he will do it. Anything works.

"Believe is the most useless word we use proudly, everyone uses it as if they know what they are saying. To believe is without proof. Our logical arguments or Godly ones, back and forth don't make what we believe a reality. Yet we are ready to die for our beliefs. Only man as man will engage in something this foolish.

"You see, if man as man is told to get rid of his entire family for the sake of heaven, he would do so gladly and in his controlled and twisted mind, justifies it regardless of his status in society; educated or not, old or young, male or female, wise or foolish." John explained.

"Hey, I just realized something...you know how they tell us so many times that God in the bible loves us so much that he gave up his only begotten son." Jack said.

"Yeah," Den nodded to Jack's wake up call.

"How come Jesus was not sent before the first destruction of the world? Or are we special and our sins are not like theirs'? Killing each other is different now; our stealing is surely not the same now; our enslavement has changed; our raping can't be compared to theirs; our lying is far better than theirs; our hatred is modern; our wars don't result in bloodshed, we bleed red wine now; our back stabbing is way different now; our greed is now understandable; our infidelity is way civilized, too; our gays and lesbians are more sophisticated now and our worship of all kinds of gods is more forgivable also." Jack elaborated.

"You're never going to get a rational answer from them. God works in a haphazard way. Keep in mind it took Allah 500 years after the death of Christ to send Mohammed to save mankind from the corrupted words of God. That means ten generations were in limbo; between hell and heaven. All missed out on the new instructions from Mohammed.

"You know, I think Jesus is arguably the most important religious figure in the world. Go to India, though he came way after Krishna, there's a saying comparing both men, making Krishna the junior of Jesus, 'Jesus of India,' they call Krishna. You'll never believe that Krishna's birth was similar to Jesus'; the three wise men, the gifts and the virgin birth. Somebody is stealing somebody's story. Maybe the real three wise men can provide the answer?

"We have the blue eyed, white Jesus; the black Jesus; the Japanese Jesus; everything but a Jewish Jesus. I bet you when he comes back he'll have an identity crisis. I'm sure the parapsychologists will be able to straighten him out. Show him where he really belongs with a fee, of course. Everybody just wants a piece of him, like most humans wanting to associate with winners." John joked and added.

"And Jesus as the prince of peace - my friends, it's a mixed bag of good and extreme laws. On one hand the laws he made were considerate and, on the other hand, they were worse than the Old Testament laws.

> *Matthew Chapter 5 verse 3*
> *Blessed are they that mourn For they shall be comforted*
> *Blessed are the merciful For they shall obtain mercy Think*
> *not that I am come to destroy the law or the prophets I am*
> *not come to destroy but to fulfill*
>
> *But I say unto you, That whosoever shall put away*
> *his wife, saving for the cause of fornication, causeth*
> *her to commit adultery; and whosoever shall marry her*
> *that is divorced commit adultery*
>
> *Thou shalt not kill; and whosoever shall kill shall be*
> *in danger of judgment. But I say unto you, that*
> *whosoever is angry with his brother without a cause*
> *shall be in danger of the judgment. Whosoever shall*
> *say to his brother, Raca you shall be in danger of the*
> *counal. But whosoever shall say; thou fool, shall be in*
> *danger of hell fire*

"Get it? From the horse's mouth you can't marry a divorced woman because there is no way for her to change. This was from someone preaching about repentance. There are some sins that his blood can't wash away, but killing can be forgiven and, slavery, too! So, therefore,

Mary Madeline could never marry again regardless of being forgiven by Jesus, himself. It doesn't add up. Who should be our mentor, again? Jesus?

"And Jesus as God, because the so-called modern Christians have usurped love, goodness and caring from the entire human race and made them Jesus' and his followers. And in a rather twisted way condemn their counterparts - the Muslims, of worshipping a different God, looking down on them and wondering how the hell can people worship such a God. There is only one conclusion to derive from this and it's simple. It was Jesus that orchestrated all those evil laws in the Old Testament and actually carried them out.

"Well, here is another test for the faithful. This is an experience that money can't buy and the bible can't give you. Go to a maternity ward and carry a baby…a suckling and a prophet of your God rushes towards you and takes the baby from your careful hands and slices the baby's head off. That is just one; now imagine the same fate happening to all the new borns in the ward. But please never be horrified, God is doing them a big favor. He will take them to heaven. That is the divine explanation. One theologian argued that the reason why Jesus or should I say God killed those Amalek's babies was because their parents were 'wicked - wicked - wicked people' and the babies would just grow up to be like their parents, too. So, God was doing them a favor by killing them and taking them straight to heaven. How merciful!

"And it makes me wonder, did those people eat their fathers for breakfast and their granddads for dinner, and when they were hanging out, had two pregnant women fight to death with swords and when the women gave birth to, say twins, the elders came together and ate one baby with some exotic spices.

"Maybe all Christian nations should be punished for slavery, everybody. Because that's the only thing I can consider wicked with a capital 'W'. After all, not all Egyptians had slaves but were punished together with their government by the Christian God. Maybe we should start the reparation talk based on the Egyptians' experience.

"Yet God in his infinite mercy did not send Black Moses to lead African slaves to freedom. What am I saying, when Jesus knew slavery was going on in his time and didn't object to it. He was very silent on this human issue!

1ˢᵗ Timothy Chapter 6 Verses 1-2
Let as many servants (slaves) as are under the yoke
count their own masters worthy of all honour, that the
name of God and his doctrine be not blasphemed.
And they that have believing masters, let them not
despise them, because they are brethren; but rather
do them service, because they are faithful and beloved
partakers of the benefit. These things teach and exhort.

"And before you lay the blame of blindness to all these theologians, even the blacks themselves that were enslaved approve the destruction of the Amalek. For some bizarre reason you can't rationalize the African enslavement to the black people by the whites, but they can rationalize the bible permitting slavery. They say the whites should have known better. You just have to throw in the towel when it comes to understanding human nature regarding reasoning or what is just.

Because if they all don't, why worship the God in the bible? How can one injustice be better than another?

"The crux of the matter is simple: if we are to see Jesus as God, then he destroyed kingdoms, killing everyone including infants, suckling, pregnant women and then turned around to heal, say thirty...Let us all do the math now." John paused after an extended clarification as always.

"I guess once they get you to agree that a particular God is God you are hooked and that kind of puts you in a box. You can't think outside the box. It puts you in an insincere position and it's hard to find your way out." Jack observed.

"Is that why Taco Bell is making us think outside the box?" Stan broke his rule of not saying anything in the matter.

"I agree with you that religion has blackmailed the world and before you say one thing about God or no God, they rush to attack you as if God/Allah lives in their apartment." Den added his two shekels. He always carried some change.

"The other phenomenon like Jesus is Israel. I think Israel is the most important country in the world today. It's not that the Israelites calculated this to be so, just like the original 13 colonies in the US making it into the great country it is today was uncertain from the get-go. (But don't tell that to the diehard nationalists, you will hear a religious argument.) After all, being born a Jew is an exclusive right.

> *'Blessed are you, O Lord our God, King of the universe who has chosen us from all the nations and given us the Torah.'*

"It was the strange turn of events that brought the real superpowers of the western world like Great Britain and Spain to spread the faith of a tribe amongst millions by force, and we have been brainwashed to think the Israelites have the real God and every other God is no God. They, the Christians, sell Israel to the rest of the world like a PC, 'Hey, God is using Israel as the light of the world to all mankind; to teach love and help us grow in spirit so we can be among the counted in paradise. Look, I am a gentile and I believe this with all my heart and soul. I'm not from the tribes of Israel. I'm not promoting myself. This is what it is, period!' Actually, what they are saying is, please be blind like me and together we will fall into the same pit. After all, misery loves company.

"And whether anybody agrees or not, they gave the Arab Muslims their Allah, forget the unseen aspect everyone claims once in a while if they want to make people follow them one way or another. Historically, Mohammed studied with a Syrian Monk who was a Christian, before he started his mission.

"And, that Jesus mentioned Mohammed is questionable, but Mohammed's account is what we have. You know what that means, one man's account of a story that involves two people. You be the judge. I will leave this to the Imams to answer.

> *Matthew Chapter 8 Verse 11*
> *And I say unto you, that many shall come from the east and west, and shall sit down with Abraham, and Isaac and Jacob, in the kingdom of heaven*

"That's the only suggestive avenue where anybody can jump in and claim a foothold in the chosen people's legacy.

And it's not that Jesus himself denied practicing Judaism, nevertheless, he was rejected by his own people; he and his disciples sort of went their own way. Then came a big leap when Saul turned Paul reinvented what he considered Christianity.

"Look around you now you'll see stamp of Israel, a tribe of one family - Jacob and his many wives and twelve children, everywhere.

"We name our children by the biblical names; Europe is littered with heavenly names, Africa, Asia and Australia, not to mention South and North America, and their number one enemy, the Arabs. And it beats me why the Arabs are complaining about their lands being taken by God's chosen people. It was God - Allah that gave Israel the lands flowing with milk and honey.

> *Joshua Chapter 1 Verse 4*
> *From the wilderness and this Lebanon, even unto the*
> *great river, the river Euphrates, all the land of the*
> *Hittites, and unto the great sea towards the going down*
> *of the sun, shall be your coast.*

"And amongst the lands that fell to the Israelites were Jericho, Canaan and many more. Why the quarrel? Didn't Mohammed tell them 'Allah does as he pleases'." John said.

"How does one start to unravel the mystery of man's thinking?" Jack queried.

"To add to the complexity, some orthodox Jews are waiting for their real messiah to come before they claim the land. (So, what are they standing on now?) There's so much confusion that you don't know where to start trying to understand the Israeli saga and its strong influence in the world. Yes, every one of us has a piece of Israel because we are gullible." John argued.

> *"Fear is overwhelming, but when placed side by side with true love*
> *it pales, and seen as it should be seen, shallow."*
> *John.*

Road To Heaven Paved With Sex.

"Knowing what we now know or understand about all these religions, it's funny to me when they poke fun at each other in private as if their hypocrisy could be hidden in public. Look at marriage. The Christians laugh at the Muslims for marrying more than one wife. They should all be laughed at." Jack vented his disapproval.

"You sure you want to delve into holy marriages?" John warned.

"Hey, John, talk about it, you're damned, don't talk about it, you're damned. Why not talk, maybe some people will see the light." Jack smiled at himself.

"Sociologically, the male has always dominated sex in the animal kingdom, suppressing the female, with a few exceptions. So when it comes to marriage men have always wanted two or more wives. If you look at it from the ancient times, many wives translate into many children and that means a large family will be employed in farming, hunting or fishing, and the bond will be strong to provide food for the entire family. And when the head of the family is old and feeble, the sons and daughters continue to fend for everyone, and gradually the family acquires wealth and good social standing. Their survival becomes high on the scale of life. Many sociologists would argue that it was something thought of by the male, like a smart thing, but the answer is no in my view. Behavior like this, in the past or now, has more to do with I can have more females because I am a man than the thoughtfulness of raising a family of workers. How do we explain the pride of lions' sexual behavior, or our nearest cousin, ape?" John lectured.

"I don't think we have left the primitive stage." Jack quickly butted in.

"And on the other hand, it's the selfishness of the male to pick and choose which wife to have intercourse with. And as men grow old, they marry young girls. The wise saying is that it makes them feel and look young again. But only in their heads are they trying to regain their youth. (Women want the same thing but the society rejects it. But as long as there is no force, any adult, male or female can choose who to be with.)"John said.

"That's bullshit." Jack interrupted. It's another manipulation.

"Now when it comes to God in the bible, polygamy was the order of the day.

> *Genesis Chapter 29 Verses 10 - 11*
> *And it came to pass, when Jacob saw Rachel, the*
> *daughter of Laban, his mother's brother, and the sheep*
> *of Laban his mother's brother, that Jacob went near,*
> *and rolled the stone from the well's mouth, and watered*
> *the flock of Laban, his mother's brother.*
> *And Jacob kissed Rachel and lifted up his voice, and wept*

"And amongst his many wives and sexual partners were Zilpah, Leah and Bilhah and from him we have the twelve children that became the tribes of Israel." John explained.

"Something is fishy here." Jack said.

"What?"John asked.

"How can a family turn into a tribe? Didn't he have brothers and uncles before he married? I have to ask my sociology lecturer." Jack said.

"With this story a tree can make a forest. Better let this go for now. But more importantly is this.

> *Samuel Chapter 5 Verses 12 - 13*
> *And David perceived that the Lord had established him*
> *king over Israel and that he had exalted his kingdom*
> *for his people Israel's sake*
> *And David took him more concubines and wives out of*
> *Jerusalem, after he was come from Hebron: and there*
> *were yet sons and daughters born to David*

"See, no prophet was sent to warn David of his many wives, the delight of God to be king. But his son, Solomon, broke the record in terms of wives and concubines. You didn't hear of premarital sex here, did you, under the very nose of God. Even Moses, the man that saw God face to face had more than one wife. And for the record, most cultures frown on premarital sex because it brings shame to the parents and the trouble it will cause the daughter to raise children at that age without a means of livelihood. Some cultures just don't kill their daughters because of it. They deal with the situation in an understanding way. The Christians making it an issue now is nonsense. They are not teaching man a new thing, like every other thing. Even in their bible God didn't rein in the offenders..." John said.

> *1ˢᵗ King Chapter 11 Verse 3*
> *And he had seven hundred wives, princesses and three*
> *hundred concubines, and his wives turned away his heart*

"Wait a minute." Jack interjected again. "What do you mean polygamy? What you are saying doesn't fit that word. How do you account for the concubines and the housemaids that were offered Jacob to sleep with? Were they like desserts after the main course?"

John smiled. Jack was always blunt.

"So why are Christians claiming God only sanctions monogamy? A book that is fraught with polygamy is used by millions to honor monogamous marriages." Den questioned.

"Really, it lacks basis in Christianity. There is no one passage that says a man should only marry just one wife. I think it's more of a modern understanding in man that champions this kind of marriage rather than the religion or, it could be a quiet cultural revolution by the women." John explained.

"This must be the only issue that all the Gods of man and man everywhere concur with." Jack added jokingly.

"But looking at one side of the story is what I don't agree with." John went on.

"What do you mean?" Den asked.

"The Koran allows Muslim men to have as many wives as they want, provided they can maintain them equally." John informed.

Surah 4: 34
Men have authority over women because God has made
the one superior to the other,

"At least there is no hypocrisy here." Den said.

"This idea of marrying more than one is changing amongst the modern ones now. Also, their wives are not allowing that anymore, either. It's a dying idea in countries outside strong Islamic influence whether the husband can afford ten wives or not. It's not that an average woman, whether Muslim or not, wants competition with her man. Humans generally don't like any form of rivalry when it comes to their lovers, even animals. That's why many civilized men still kill their women when they are found with another man or design their faces with their punches. Sadly, women also are guilty of the same crime of passion. Anyway, the Muslims that now practice one man, one woman, find a loophole in the very Koran that says you should not marry more than one if you can't love them equally. But many would rather follow the footsteps of their prophet; what better example can you get?

"Mohammed set the rule firmly when it comes to marriage, not to be broken by anyone, after all, its Allah's law." John said. "The laws say your mothers and sisters are forbidden for anyone to marry; so also your aunts, your sons' wives, your foster sisters and so on. And also this;" John explained.

Surah 4: 25
If anyone of you cannot afford to marry a free believing
woman, let him marry a slave girl who is a believer.

"Better to marry a slave-girl, gee." Den said.

"Hey, the Muslims always give the impression that under Allah's laws everyone is equal." Jack said surprisingly.

"Oh, Mohammed never abolished that kind of slavery. In fact, Muslims could keep other Muslims as slaves." John pointed out.

"Sure?" Jack asked in disbelieve.

"Yeah, sure, he kept slaves too, the slave girls as booty from Allah.

Surah 4: 92
It is unlawful for a believer to kill another believer,
accidents excepted…

"According to Muslims, Muhammad freed one black slave and they made him a champion of humanity. A Black Muslim said it wasn't that kind of slavery that he didn't stop. He was trying to blame all forms of slavery only on the white. Then I asked him, 'why free the slave of his babysitting job?'" John concluded with such sarcasm that it could cause a tremor in the holy land; Mecca.

"I thought everyone was equal in the Islamic world under Mohammed and Allah. Because some blacks in America tended to embrace Islam during those times of segregation and what have you, remember the famous Cassius Clay changing his name to Mohammed Ali? Jack wanted clarification.

"Jumping from one master to the other," John summed it up.

"I'd think people who went through such harsh, degrading laws wouldn't tolerate any organization or religion that would allow that kind of inequality in any form." Jack wondered.

"Jack, you have to understand that the blacks did not know where to turn to when they were segregated and treated as subhuman beings. And they couldn't understand why Christians who claimed to 'love thy neighbor' continued to treat them like animals. So, 'in God we trust' had all the stamp of hypocrisy. So the blacks unknowingly turned to Islam, at least in my view, mainly to send a message that they were no longer their slaves; mentally. To show the whites that they were people and could very much steer their own destiny by themselves; that they needed their own separate social structures; that they needed to educate their kind and not be fed the white man's history; that they needed to tell their own history that would give confidence to their children; to tell the history of their inventors and contributions of their people in the world and definitely in America; and to develop their own cultures; they wanted their dignity that was stripped away from them for hundreds of years back. It was not because Allah or Islam would save them.

"The other point is that people hardly know what their religion talks about, they just listen to what their religious leaders tell them. And these leaders pick and choose the passages that favor them in a particular sermon.

"I was watching television early Sunday morning; you know how every station is showing one preacher or the other. The sermon was about not lusting after another woman once a man is married. And in this case the pastor chose good old David as an example. The pastor did his best to say David suffered greatly for what he did, taking Bathsheba, the wife of one of his generals in the army. So he told the congregation not to do it, but clearly avoided telling them how God decided to punish David. And people think the politicians are not telling them everything.

> *2nd Samuel Chapter 12 Verses 11 - 12*
> *Thus saith the Lord, behold, I will raise up evil against*
> *thee out of thine own house, and I will take thy wives*
> *before thine eyes, and give them unto thy neighbor, and*
> *he shall lie with thy wives in the sight of this sun. For*
> *thou didst it secretly: but I will do this thing before all*
> *Israel, and before the sun.*

"Even after the baby that resulted in David sleeping with Bathsheba died, David went back to her and a son was born, the son's name was Solomon. Like a repeat offender, he slept with her again and again but this time it was right in the sight of God. (By the way, I would have loved to be the one God would use to rebuke David this time. Ha ha ha.)

"So, you see. They tell people what they want them to know and most people go home and never bother to open their holy books. Tell an ugly girl she's the most beautiful, and she will think you are the greatest guy on the planet; she will fall head over heels in love with you." John said.

"Interesting, but the Muslims shouldn't only be shouting about one God, but should also be shouting about having slaves, especially slave girls." Jack was furious.

"I may not know that much about my faith, but in Islam my Imam tells me that women have same rights as men." Ahmed ignored Jack's comment, picking what he felt comfortable talking about, and a way out taken by all the religious people, religiously.

"I don't know which book you're reading from or which Koran your Imam consults for his wise sayings, but what I know is clear. You might as well say when the blacks in America had separate but equal status, it translated into equality." John jolted him back to reality and provided proof.

"Maybe you are deceived by this sentence, but if you read farther, it will become clear.

Surah 2 : 226
Women shall with justice have rights similar to those
exercised against them, although men have a status
above women.

"And I am sure you have heard of Islamic men not taking no for an answer when they want to have sex with their women. A woman having rights equal to man should be able to say no and be respected for it.

Surah 2: 222
Women are your fields: go, then, into your fields whence you
please

Surah 4: 34
Good women are obedient. They guard their unseen
parts because god has guarded them. As for those
whom you fear disobedience, admonish them, forsake
them in bed apart, and beat them

"My friend the good treatments are so many I think every woman should be a wife of a Muslim man even at an early age.

Surah 65: 4
If you are in doubt concerning those of your wives who
have ceased menstruating, know that their waiting
period shall be three months. The same shall apply to
those who have not yet menstruated

"Children are not even spared in this Godly respect for women. The moment they say da-da we parcel them to grown men who already have numerous wives. Remember the Koran was direct from God, Allah.

"A Muslim President defends the definition of a child; I guess he is right that from culture to culture and religion to religion the agreement varies in what constitutes a child. But we know there could be major complications when the body is not fully developed after puberty to start mounting your property. Why the hurry, anyway? Is the population of the world getting depleted?

"There was this case in Ethiopia where the wise parents of this teenager that just started puberty was parceled out to marry this man. She got pregnant and there started for this young girl the backlash of early pregnancy. The husband abandoned her, of course, to wallow in her misery. After she received treatment they asked her whether she would do the same to her children, she gave a resounding no, with tears in her eyes; if every drop could talk...

"Does it have to take a case like this that could be prevented, ruining the lives of who we call our children before we learn? Our ego prevents us from taking help from anyone outside our archaic culture or religion, and this is mostly due to our selfishness because we benefit from it. Men in most cultures and religions don't respect young girls; they see them as their pleasure, their sweet pleasure for one minute or less. He wants to be the first to deflower the girl. He wants so badly to be the only one the girl will never forget; hoping for immortality in the life of another human being, just like dictators putting their faces on bags of rice, money and building figurines of themselves everywhere in 'their' countries. 'You must remember me after I leave this world; put me in your history books, put me in your hearts,' yeah." John said in a condemning manner.

"John, I think that if women can really be equal to men in the Islamic sense, they should be able to marry as many men as their male counterparts." Den said.

"Yeah, like that ever happened in any society," Ahmed replied sternly.

"You may be surprised by that statement, Ahmed. There have been cases of polyandry practiced in India, Tibet, and some Eastern parts of Africa where women actually married more than one husband. Now, whether the woman ruled in this kind of relationship is another story. But it has happened before, believe it or not." John informed him.

"And for your personal information, Ahmed, Mohammed was the one that stopped the Arab women from marrying more than one husband. It was a society that men and women married as many as they wanted. And there has always been this view by the elites in Islam that Mohammed wanted to have an egalitarian society when he met one already, but changed it to favor the men.

"Also there is this excuse that after the war decimated the community of men it was suggested to men to marry as many as they could care for. I don't know how to reconcile the statement but I see a major contradiction which all believers say isn't in the Koran. Mark this as one. There are many more for the world to see. And besides, men have always fought in all societies, reducing their numbers greatly. Is this why men love polygamy, everywhere?

"And the one treatment of women that I find sickening is this punishment in a particular offence that tells anyone with a sense of justice that something is just not right, period. Just like a white-collar thief would be sent to a boys' club and a blue-collar one would be sent to the real 'shit house' (jail) for the same offence or less.

> *Surah 4: 13*
> *If any of your women commit a lewd act, call in four*
> *witnesses…; if they testify to their guilt confine them to*
> *their houses till death overtakes them*

> *Surah 4: 16*
> *If two men among you commit a lewd act, punish them*
> *both. If they repent and mend their ways, let them be*

"And unfortunately they also pass women to their kinsmen after their husbands die. But this law from Allah only half-addressed the issue, it didn't stop it completely. How many women would have the guts to say otherwise, when they have been made too dependent, anyway." John argued.

> *Surah 4: 19*
> *Believers, it is unlawful for you to inherit the women of*
> *your deceased kinsmen against their will.*

"The Jewish people did that too in the bible, right?" Jack asked.
"Yeah, some people came to test Jesus about what heaven would be

like in terms of marriage. But Jesus didn't rebuke the practice; he just called them ignorant about what heaven would be like." John answered and continued.

> *Mark Chapter 12 Verse 19*
> *Master, Moses wrote unto us, if a man's brother die,*
> *and leave his wife behind him, and leave no children,*
> *that his brother should take his wife, and raise up*
> *seed unto his brother.*
> *Now there were seven brethren: and the first took a*
> *wife, and dying left no seed*
> *And the seven had her, and left no seed. Last of all,*
> *the woman died too For when they shall rise from the dead,*
> *they neither marry, nor are given in marriage, but are as*
> *the angels which are in heaven*

"The treatment of women in this fashion was not limited to a particular religion or culture back then. Many tribes practiced this system around the world. The Yoruba people did the same thing.

So, Ahmed, Islam isn't the only religion that treats women this way. The difference is that when man claims it's from an all-knowing God, then the understanding changes. Why would Allah allow such a practice?

"It's like a disease with men wanting to suppress women; their counterparts. The Yoruba men for example still have a way of putting women in their place. When a man is married to his wife for a considerable time, maybe, with children, the man will gradually tell the wife to start respecting and addressing him more or less like a king. 'You can't call me by my name anymore, address me as a chief. And when I call you, you say, sir. Okay.' But customarily call their own Gods by name and don't use a respectable way to address them! This is how ignorant men treat their lovers. Really, this is man's way of showing his petty ego and dominance. It pervades everything he does; might is right. Like a little boy in a toy store, and if he doesn't have his way throws a tantrum.

"And if I may say this. I have never understood how a man would transfer his lack of self-discipline to a woman, a mere weaker sex, accusing her of making him sexually weak. And for this singular reason you burden women with covering their bodies from head to toe, making them suffer in the heat because of you, wearing dark colors. Yet, men still find ways to rape them. This wasn't even the fashion Allah intended for the Islamic women. (Mohammed didn't veil the first wife and it was later when people flooded his compound that he started veiling his numerous wives) But then, once we cover from top to bottom, have we covered our minds of all sexual thoughts? Some women are so brainwashed that they welcome such treatment as coming from God.

"But on the other hand, a Muslim man can be in a suit and tie, after denying the women their natural feeling of attraction. It's a good thing that our thinking can't be seen or the women will be punished severely everyday for thinking those sweet thoughts that Eve had when gazing upon strong and sexy Adam. Who can vouch for what any man or woman does when all alone, anyway?

"Unless all those self-righteous men look at themselves in the mirror when they dress and say, hey, I'm so unattractive today. Thank you, Allah.

"Again, to understand the situation a bit better, you have to look at why men do the things they do, either in the name of one God or culture. The answer is simple, it's Jealousy.

"A classic case was during the monarchy era. The men that guarded the king's numerous wives were always castrated. And some time ago in Europe it was the chastity belt that was used on women. And in some parts of Africa, before the Europeans divided them into countries in a haphazard manner, they used juju on their wives, and anybody that slept with their wives would just die doing it; talk about dying in the arms of a sexy woman. But you have to know one thing here. Nothing was put on the men that had all these wives, no restriction whatsoever either by God or cultural law." John argued.

"With all this sex talk and jealousy, why should we be celibate?" Den was enjoying the moment.

"There's no celibacy in Islam." Ahmed managed to reply after he was hammered by John about the abuse Islam was inflicting on women. Though, he was still blind to it somehow.

Den gave him a look of surprise. "How can you still be defending Islam?"

"It's simple, fear of hell." Jack answered.

"Den, when it comes to sex man is kind of weird. He is torn

apart between what he calls spirituality and his own sexuality; he is confused." John began to explain.

"Some see sex as holding them back from Nirvana or enlightenment or moving closer to whatever they consider spiritually viable. We know Buddha had to leave his wife and child in search of enlightenment. Talk about bad karma, leaving your family, becoming a monk. No more sex for you 'wifey'. Go get it somewhere else. Maybe that was why women also got the short end of the stick in Buddhism way back then. Or maybe it still continues on the down low.

"Then we have the Ashramas of the Hindu faith, becoming homeless, leaving their family too to be closer to God. And in the western world we have the catholic monks denying themselves sex, also in order to be nearer to God. But in this case we have heard catholic monks raping boys and girls alike. Talk of underage and premarital sex in church. They are paying billions of dollars to the victims to wash away their sins before Jesus' blood will do the same in heaven for them.

"But before you rush to judge them, though, you have to consider the fact that it was Lord Jesus that put that fear in them. Many Christians are ignorant of this passage." John pointed out.

"What are you saying?" Fred challenged.

Before John could reply Fred. Jack stepped in to defend him.

"Has this guy ever said something a reasonable person can't read in your story book...sorry, your holy book?"

"I can handle this, Jack."

> *Matthew Chapter 19 Verses 11-12*
> *But he said unto them, all men cannot receive this*
> *saying, save they to whom it is given*
> *For they are some eunuchs, which were so born to their*
> *mothers womb: and there are some eunuchs, which*
> *were made eunuchs of men: and there be eunuchs*
> *which have made themselves eunuchs for the kingdom*
> *of heaven's sake.*

Fred was speechless. There were so many passages that the shepherd never revealed to the sheep like him.

"Couldn't this triangular religion just say, hey, wait a minute. Why all this confusion about marriage, anyway? Why did God create Eve for Adam or, why not many Eves for him?" Jack wondered.

"That's a good point, Jack. But even God wasn't consistent in the bible. There were so many occasions that God employed evil to do his work and yet his son, Jesus, declared he didn't come from the devil. Remember the popular saying, 'a house divided against itself cannot stand'." John pointed out the error and added.

> *Matthew Chapter 12 Verses 25 - 26*
> *'And Jesus knew their thoughts, and said unto them.*
> *Every kingdom divided against itself is brought to*
> *desolation: every city or house divided against itself*
> *shall not stand. And if Satan cast out satan, he is*
> *divided against himself; how shall then his kingdom*
> *stand?*
>
> *Judges chapter 9 verse 23*
> *Then God sent an evil spirit between Abimelech*
> *and the men of Shechem;*
>
> *Matthew chapter 15 verse 19*
> *For out of the heart proceed evil thoughts.*

"When God used evil to carry out his objections, then it's logical to say that God's house shouldn't stand because out of God's heart came evil. So, what's in Satan's heart? I will leave that for the devil to answer. He deserves to defend himself; fair trial.

"Do you remember our lord's prayer, 'Lead us not into temptation, but deliver us from evil...'? You be the interpreter...Who delivered evil to Abimelech? 'Satan, can I borrow one of your staunchest evil spirits. I got this project and I can't use Gabriel, he's too soft. Thanks'." John stopped.

"Just like some gays and lesbians believe that Jesus will forgive them for their unnatural sexual practices, at least, according to nature. When Jesus wouldn't forgive anyone marrying a divorced wife based on fornication. How can he forgive homosexuality when it's seen as an abomination to him and his father?" Jack said. "How would he find it in his loving heart to welcome the gays to paradise? This I've got to see. Front row ticket, please. "

"This gay issue, regarding their conviction in making it to Jesus' paradise is another case of delusion. This group claims to be more understanding and open than the rest of the society, yet, trapped by the fear of hell." John explained and quickly gave an insight into another double-standard in the Koran.

"But the one thing that really takes the cake was Mohammed's reversal of his rule regarding marriage and sex. Or should I say Allah changed his mind." John continued.

"Remember Allah said your paternal and maternal aunts and all other forbidden relationships shouldn't be entered into again. But there was a change of heart somewhere, another convenient revelation by the prophet." John clarified.

> *Surah 33: 38…*
> *Prophet, we have made lawful for you, the wives to*
> *whom you have granted dowries and the slave girls*
> *whom God has given to you as booty; the daughters of*
> *your paternal and maternal uncles and of your paternal*
> *and maternal aunts who fled with you; and any*
> *believing woman who gives herself to the prophet and*
> *whom the prophet wishes to take in marriage.*
> *This privilege is yours alone,*

"If there's ever a double standard, this is it." Jack said as a matter of fact.

"I think women should create their own Goddess and divorce all these men when they misbehave." Den joked.

"Oh, I don't know about that Goddess thing, but they do allow women to have divorce, to some extent. But divorce according to the prince of peace was scary to his followers. Jesus kind of discouraged his disciples from wanting to marry. Because once you marry you can't divorce except for fornication. Where is 'for better or worse'? So many of us have forgiven our lovers, wives, husbands for fornication…I guess we are more forgiving than Jesus." John went on.

> *Matthew Chapter 19 Verses 7 - 10*
> *They say unto him, why did Moses then command to*
> *give a writing of divorcement, and to put her away.*

*He saith unto them, Moses because of your hearts
suffered you to put away your wives; but from the
beginning it was not so.
And I say unto you, whosoever shall put away his wife
except it be for fornication, and shall marry another,
committeth adultery, and whoso marrieth her which is
put away doth commit adultery.
His disciples say unto him, if the case of the man be so
with his wife, it is not good to marry.*

"In Islam it only takes less than a minute to divorce your wife, but the woman is not given the same easy way out. Wonder why? You repeat the words, I divorce you, three times and it's done." John explained.

*Surah 2: 230
If a man divorces his wife, he cannot remarry her until
she has wedded another man and been divorced by
him.*

"That does not make any sense. What if they change their minds and want to get right back together?" Den observed.

"There are so many what if's in this surah to examine till kingdom come." Jack remarked.

"But you will see clearly the resounding jealousy in this one." John couldn't wait to go on.

*Surah 33: 53
nor shall you ever wed his(Mohammed) wives after him;
this would surely be a
grave offence in the sight of God.*

"So you see, Jack, these so-called prophets or sons of God, and many more like them are nothing but social reformers in my own view. Don't tell that to the believers.

"The Muslims give the impression that their prophet was loved by all back then. He wasn't even respected by his entire family. One of his uncles vehemently was against him and this made Mohammed furious." John said.

"The uncle didn't take a sip from the well." Den provided the hindsight.

Surah 111: 1
May the hands of Abu-lahab perish! May he himself
perish! He shall be burnt in a flaming fire, and his wife,

"And to think that a man of a merciful God would start this awful saying with 'In the name God, the compassionate, the merciful', which most of the look-at-me-I'm-a-pious-Muslim will say before starting any conversation. Be careful who you choose as your counselor." John said and added, "even Moses was full of curses, holy curses, like God."

"So, I guess there's a glimmer of hope for man after all, if some members of his family could oppose him." Jack said.

"Hmmm, hmmm, hmmm, there is a lot of information in a book that costs a penny." Den wrapped it.

One at a time they all got up to leave. Everyone went to their respective quarters. These people needed one another. Maybe by opening up this way man would grow a little bit more in understanding and rid himself of a lot of insincerities. It could be cancerous if not treated; it would soon infect the whole body, rendering it useless.

"Truth doesn't demand violence.
The question is, how deep is your hate, and how shallow is your
love."
Nameless

Miscellaneous

Den and John sat in the open field. They didn't need the shelter of the oak tree anymore. The weather was cool and it was getting dark. The rest of the group had moved on to something they had to attend to. And the stars were already visible, decorating the sky with whatever pattern the viewer wanted to see. One star in particular shone really bright.

Den gazed at the sky for a long time, his back turned to John. He was more relaxed now; there was no need for the brows coming together in a frown.

"What is prayer?" He asked almost absentmindedly, probably reflecting what his mind was wondering about amongst many things in the universe.

John looked at him. "Den, stay with me. Where are you?"

"I'm here, John."

"Good, because if you're not careful you'll be overwhelmed with God-thoughts and you might start thinking how to save mankind, thinking you have been chosen. And believe it or not, man will follow you. And you might even convince yourself that God has chosen you, too, and the chaos starts all over again."

"I understand, John. Please answer my prayer." He managed to joke.

"Prayer is nothing but a wish. Something you make to your supposed God to bring good things into your life and your surroundings. Man will pray to anything as long as they think their prayers are answered. They would pray to the sea, mountains, rivers…you name it. But, whether they like it or not, seems everybody's prayer to his or her God is a hit or miss. There is no way to validate the authenticity of their prayers being answered by a God, yet everyone claims their prayers are answered. If that is the case, the world would be a better place." John answered.

"Do we have to pray to God before we get what we need to survive in this world?" Den asked.

"Depends on who you ask, some think your prayer has to be exact; to the point, if you want it answered, as if you're praying to your drunken father. So there are countless books on prayers. You have to approach God my way. Many people speak God.

"And with the Christian faith that heavily believes in miracles, it's another story. Some call themselves prayer warriors, even when Jesus said, 'keep it simple, and don't be like the Gentiles. Your father knows before you ask him anything'.

"But prayer might just be a good way to keep at bay the stress of life; an emotional placebo. It's a comforting feeling that something favorable will happen to us soon. It's hope, nothing more. It keeps you going in terms of hardship.

"Deep down inside us we all want to be loved and cared for especially in terms of danger, having exhausted every action or knowledge humanly possible. A helping hand from above will be more than desired.

"But the reality on the ground is different if you look at it clearly. If a man survives an accident, he praises God for saving his life. But what we forget quickly is that other people mightn't be so lucky. How do we account for that? What have we done to deserve that miracle? It's another shortsightedness of man." John said.

"Hmm…" Den was thoughtful.

"I witnessed an accident where almost everyone died." John continued. "In this terrible car crash you would think nobody could have survived, but this man did; almost unscathed. It was nothing short of a miracle as people would like to say. He walked away thanking Jesus. We rushed to the scene to see whether other people would be as fortunate, but none made it. As one of us was moving the bodies around, a young girl, about 14 years old was lying on her stomach. He turned her body over and the first thing I saw was a shinning silver cross. What was the rationale for God or Jesus to choose who lived?

"There are hundreds of cases like this but we conveniently attribute it in our favor that one God has saved us, but for what? To make the world a better place, to appreciate life better, to love more, to be kind? Of course, most people say it will make us more humane, probably, but not guaranteed.

"Something must be at work here that defies our sentimental understanding in such cases. And there are so many obviously bad people that get away in such nasty accidents. The consoling answer you get is that their time is not up, yet. Crap.

"A short time ago, two women came forward to share their testimonies about one televangelist healing them of cancer. Two months later they died. Here and there you will see the dramatized shows of laying hand on the would-be-healed, and the falling on the floor. The power of the Holy Spirit in one man is too much when he touches the faithful. Even Jesus didn't have this 'superman power' while he walked the earth. He couldn't even just say open your eyes sometimes. He had to use sand with spit and then rubbed it in the poor guy's eyes before the miracle could occur.

"But passing out like that is no mystery. Michael Jackson did it with his moonwalk, affecting his fans; they cried and sometimes fainted without the laying of hand. And some superstars make us breathless when we see them, as if they have two heads and walk on air. We are the ones giving ourselves over willingly to them; we are moved when a song is sung well; we are inspired when we hear a good orator speak. This is just part of the package of being human. And besides, these healing-powers are staged.

"When I was young I told my friend who was deaf and dumb to go see all these pastors that we watched on TV, performing all these miracles in the name of God. He looked at me and saw the care in my eyes and said. 'John, they are lying. I have been taken to nearly all of them.' He managed to force a few words out of his mouth. They probably accused him of not having faith, or not enough faith. Wasn't it faith to want to go in the first place? Or where do we put the Deaf Society of America that was founded because they were rejected by the mainstream churches. Tell me, what more faith do you need to get healed? There are still deaf societies around the world to this day who are Christians." John explained and went on.

"Then there was a time some miners were trapped for days and everybody thought hope for survival was lost, still people kept praying for a miracle; vigils were held at the site every day. Then suddenly someone broke the news that the miners were alive. The church was full of praise. Press conference was held by the families, surrounded by the pastors and well-wishers that prayed for the miracle. 'How could they have survived? Only Jesus has this power.' Someone remarked. Unfortunately, the news was false. They ended up blaming the irresponsibility of the reporter. But no mention of God or Jesus, why? They surely rationalized their faith. We might as well just flip a coin in a case like this.

"Den, if this life is all about saving lives, then the three surgeons that were trying to transplant a vital organ to this patient shouldn't have lost their lives as they rushed to another state by air to get the organ. The plane crashed and no one survived. Maybe God was jealous and didn't want them to play him." John stopped.

"But, is there a way to test God, to test our faith...to know whether God wants us to take this job or something like that?" Den said, still half listening to John.

"Yes, and the answer will surprise you, at least, according to the bible. It lies in the holy book." John answered.

"You're sure?" Den's eyes lighted up.

"His name was Gideon." John said as if he had found a silver bullet.

"Gideon, according to the bible tested God, not once, but twice. And the test was nothing abstract, it was physical. Something similar to this - God, if you want me to fight this kingdom, let there be water in this bottle when I wake up tomorrow. And there was water in the empty bottle. Then, he reversed it on the second day just to be sure, and God answered again.

"So when people say you can't test God, if they are Christians, then they are ignorant. Refer them to Gideon and the Golden Fleece (Judges 6 verses 37-40). It wasn't about faith as they now cry, have faith...have faith. No, it was more like show me the money." John informed.

"So, faith isn't all it seems to be as they make it sound?" Den wondered.

"Let's just sweep Gideon under the carpet and say when a believer gets his prayers answered, they rejoice, saying he has faith. And if not, they say his faith is not strong enough. Even Jesus claimed he couldn't heal some people because of lack of faith. There goes the license to use against you, making you feel inadequate. You now depend more and more on your pastor to shore up your faith. The question of faith didn't come up even by Jesus when he raised the dead. You ever thought about that?

"Regardless of what we know that is clear like the blue sky, they still hide behind the word faith like a shield of armor against reality. The five-letter-word is so colorfully praised it's almost an untouchable, sacred word. It's like you have killed the first sons or so, or destroyed a whole village if you say something against their faith. 'Don't even dare go against my faith, it's mine, you have yours,' as if it's a golden word. But when we strip the word naked, we see the insidiousness of the most used word by believers, a faith that condemns others to burning in hell for eternity is what man holds dear in his heart.

"Faith, we are told is to believe in the unseen, something that's beyond the thinking or thought of man. And to most people the word means something else. Remember, language is made for man and not the other way around. To them, faith actually means that they know. How can they not, after all, they are nice, loving, understanding, full of wisdom, reasonable, helpful and giving. So tell me why they won't have the right faith.

"It's because if they openly say they know, it will open a stream of questions that will drown them and make them look foolish. So they hide behind the word, faith.

"But there is one big lie about the word, faith. Some say you can't think about it, you just accept it. There's no room to analyze it, otherwise, it's not faith. You just suspend your thinking faculty when it comes to faith and be led. This argument holds no water. Because before we accept something, we would have already thought about it, either to accept it or not to. So thinking faith descends on us from above without our input is just the beginning of sliding down the path of hallucination. And since delusion is ubiquitous as the air we breathe, we are ready to see it as sanity. It's not. Here, number is no strength. They are under hypnosis.

"The fact that they can't doubt their given faith but ready to trash others' is a testimony to their lie of just accepting faith as it is.

Now, this is my main concern about the whole thing. If the faith stays in their hearts, all well and good, but it's always played out in the human experience. It colors the way we see others. People who say it's just faith are either confused or not honest with themselves.

"There is a saying that goes like this. If your neighbor eats stomach-churning food at night and you know, but gives no word of caution. You and your neighbor will stay up all night. When a book defines the way we see others, it becomes our self-authorized task to correct the people around us, a book based on disjointed collections of interpretations that is downright ignorant and evil. And when people start asking tough questions about all these faiths, they band together and present a common front, trying to use the UN to ban freedom of speech. It's called an Association of Hypocrites.

"A court in Wisconsin in the US had to sanction a pharmacist that refused to give birth-control pills to this college student. He based his reasoning on the 'fact' that by doing so he would be 'impairing the fertility of a human being'. I'm sure there are numerous ways these holier than thou stick it to unbelievers. We just have to be saved one way or another. Even when you die they will pray to their God/Allah to welcome you to paradise…to forgive you, and bury you the proper way sanctioned by their God/Allah. 'Satan led him astray'. Talk about taking the horse to the river and forcing it to drink.

"Funny how they always fight tooth and nail against abortion. They think these crusades make them look like caring and loving humans, whereas, the God they pray to killed pregnant women and massacred children. This is the worst of all hypocrisies. Or maybe they might want to stop abortion that naturally occurs more than 70% worldwide.

"These holier than thou still have the audacity to lecture us about morality. They are saving all the children for God whether they belong to their faith or not. Then God will roast all the children for not having Jesus as their savoir forever in hell, it looks like they are pouring water into a basket. Their cry is just for show. Look at me; I care about another human being. Give me a medal."

Den smiled at John's answer.

"And don't think faith is a harmless word, either. It's not. It's comes with fear and force. I call it the three Fs. I will give you an example of faith in motion and how it goes with fear." John began. "A pregnant woman was making her way down the street and another woman walked up to her with her 3 year-old tagging along. The pregnant woman stopped and said.

'How are you?'

'We are fine.' The stranger replied. 'I see you are expecting...1st...2nd...'

'My first'.

'Well, congrats.'

'Thanks.' She beamed a healthy smile.

The stranger hesitated a while then managed to say what was on her mind.

'You know you always have to put a safety pin in your purse.'

'Why?'

'You don't know your baby will be born with all kinds of deformities?'

'Who told you that?'

'That's a general belief. Everybody knows that.'

'But we don't believe that.'

'It doesn't matter what you believe. Do you want a healthy baby?' Then she walked away a bit angry that she doubted her divine advice.

The pregnant woman thought about the encounter and became concerned for her unborn baby. When she got home she put a safety pin in her purse and had one for reserve, just in case.

"On the day of delivery she started to panic because for some reason the two pins were gone. She became restless. The doctor and the midwife tried to calm her down but to no avail. She grabbed hold of her mother.

'Where is my pin?'

'What pin?'

'The one I'm supposed to have in order for the baby to be born healthy.'

'Who told you that?'

'A woman I met some time ago. Where is the pin?'

'I didn't put any pin on me when I had you and you turned out all right.'

'No, no mum...'

She was so much terrified that she passed out. Luckily for her the doctor performed a C-section. The baby was healthy.

"Now, take the Sabbath day for another example. God instructed people to be stoned to death if anyone worked on that day. This has created full and partial fear to this day, 21st century.

In spite of the fact that their Jesus said that Sabbath was made for man and not the other way round.

"The people that are fearful of working on that day now transfer the punishment for disobeying their lord to any anomaly that happens in their lives; like losing money or any precious thing, and many imagined penalties from their God. And the society enables it by allowing them to use it as a holy excuse not to perform any duty that day. Sometimes they can even close public schools. You are bound to wonder whether the Christians that do work on Saturday (there is still a big debate on which day Sabbath should be) get punished. Nevertheless, they faithfully keep to the Sabbath rule, maybe by doing so they will get a special heaven or are scared to death that once you break one simple rule, though you die as a Christian, you will still go to hell or made a servant in heaven." John said.

> *Exodus 35:2. Six days shall work be done,*
> *but on the seventh day, there shall be to you*
> *an holy day , a Sabbath of rest to the Lord:*
> *whosoever doeth work therein shall be put to*
> *death.*
> *Numbers 15:32-6. A man was found gathering wood*
> *on the Sabbath so the Lord told Moses that*
> *he must die and be stoned to death outside the*
> *camp. So the assembly took him outside the*
> *camp and stoned him to death as the Lord*
> *commanded Moses.*

"But why would Jesus go against God, or did he really go against God?" Den wanted clarification.

"The answer is twofold. First, Jesus, who always quoted the Old Testament to back himself up, like when he was quick to say that Moses allowed divorce because of the hardness of their hearts, but now no more divorce...expect for fornication, appeared to be ignorant that his father actually had someone stoned to death for gathering woods, just like he plucked something to eat from a tree. Second, he gave an example that it was permissible to do good on that day. But was what he was doing when accused good? He was merely eating just like that poor man would like to by gathering woods for food.

"But the believer's shortsightedness kicks in here also. No one thought whether that man stoned to death had a family to feed. That didn't concern them, as long as the draconian law was carried out. Even Jesus, the do-gooder, was clearly a hypocrite here. He should have addressed it because the fear was real in their minds. They could point to a passage that God, his father, killed someone on a Sabbath day!

"If all this doesn't make a so-called loving and caring person think twice about a faith based solely on fear, then imagine a good Christian walking up to an elderly man who can barely make his way to get food, and says to him that if he dies tomorrow he will be burning in hell forever because...

"But what's fear? Why do we have this phobia? What will happen if we discard our fear? Can we really discard it? And what can help us get rid of it?" Den was known for asking not one question but as many as anyone could take. Luckily, John was ready.

"It is hard to explain...it's like you feel you will lose something precious, like losing your life, or a kind of rejection, or failure to accomplish something in time.

"First, there are numerous fears out there and even though they appear different from one another the result is pretty much the same.

"There are social, physical, emotional, real and unreal, man-made, self- made fears and the list goes on and on. Take the fear of the religion of good versus evil; hell and heaven for instance; it makes me want to run the other way, considering the so-called revelations and the character of the creator; God, Yahweh and Allah and his armies of prophets. That should create enough fear. This is the only time that I embrace fear wholeheartedly." John smiled. Then he continued.

"Though it's common knowledge that no one or prophets can deny this, even if they try, that humans of all walks of life go through the same suffering and happiness; we get jobs, we lose jobs; we get lovers, we lose lovers; we build houses, we lose houses; we cry and laugh; we are fit and we have aches and pains; we pass and we fail; we are winners and we are losers; we are good and we are bad and we live and die and so forth, regardless whether we pray or not, be a Muslim or a Christian, a Jew or an atheist or a pagan. We all experience love and pain in life.

"So, it's amazing knowing all these things how we still allow fear to paralyze us to the point that we will listen to anyone, no matter who and turn ourselves into machines manipulated by someone else's fear; how ironic. The manipulators use heaven and hell since they can't alleviate the human suffering. And the catch phrase is 'wait till you die, you will see.' It works like magic. And we say commercial businesses are full of hidden catches.

"This is what someone told me about getting rid of fear even at the face of death. 'Love in its purest form; unpolluted.

"That I have to start practicing?" Den approved.

"What?"

"True love, regardless." Den replied.

"Well, trailing on the heels of fear is force. In the area of religion, we use clever force to pass it down to our children and there is nothing wrong with that as long as when they reach the age of maturity they can reject the belief, should they choose to. But the subtle persuasions by the family won't let up. You will hear when was the last time you went to church or mosque, or prayed? And sometimes in order to keep your parents or friends happy or to just shut them up, you go to the house of worship.

"Another gentle nudge is when they deliberately make you an outcast and you are the type that wants to hang out with them. You slowly do what they want of you. After all, they are trying to save your damn soul, how can you not be appreciative. Den, you experienced this.

"The one that will make you feel lonely is when you want to get married, if you are rooted in tradition. Hardly will you find a pastor that will join you two in a holy matrimony, why? You don't come to church. It also affects you when you need funeral service or to christen your child if you are the type that thinks without your holy men you can't do these things.

"Before you know it you will succumb to the heavy scrutiny of religion. Social pressure mounts and mounts, who says peer pressure is limited to kids. So if you are not strong enough you will be dining and wining with the chosen.

"It's even carried to the work place. The constant phrase is we are praying for you to change your evil ways, your only sin is not believing in their God. And lastly, as far as I can remember in court they use their holy books to coerce you to tell the truth. Please don't tell the brilliant lawyers and the incorruptible judges. They just want nothing but the truth with a book that's full of unfairness. Other than that, the book scares the truth out of their mouths sometimes." John argued.

"From some of the things we've been discussing, I find one thing standing out and that is…why do we put ourselves down? Why do we do this?" Den asked honestly.

"It's hard to answer that question because there's a thin line between constructive advice and downright jealousy. But with man being man, it's overwhelmingly the latter that's at play." John was trying to explain why man demonized another, even up to the heavens.

"Man as man is selfish and does not want any competition and when forced to have one, wants to win at all costs. It makes him feel good inside and out. It's foolish pride that's at work here. And most people just like in religion are blind to it.

"And once we demonize others, we exonerate ourselves from any pain and suffering we inflict on them. Force is used to subdue the vulnerable. This is really due to man's ignorance. He believes might is right. The weak are bought and sold.

"So, even when the first Africans arrived in Europe, the Europeans did not see them as inferior and certainly the Africans didn't see the Europeans as superior, too. They all mingled together in their society and attended their schools of higher learning. Recorded history even tells us blacks served in the mighty Roman Empire as equals.

"Then came the demonization whisper which soon permeated the entire society, probably because the white indentured servants were running away from their white masters or their terms expired, just like such system around the world. And in order to replace them and not to follow through with the terms, black laborers were brought in and this most likely started the greatest, harshest and most inhumane treatment in terms of slavery.

"And what followed was a tremendous disconnect as living, breathing human beings within the whites and the onslaught of slavery ensued with a passion. And even after that, the principle of might was right lingered on to the extent that the white powers, after slavery ended physically, decided to colonize them all. The major players were Great Britain, Spain and France, and not forgetting the Dutch." John said.

Den looked sad and John quickly cautioned.

"Remember we are talking about man here. It doesn't matter what color, he's the same. The so-called Africans could have done the same to the whites, or to the blue people.

"Another example of demonization would be that of the Incas people of South America, demonized by the Spaniards on the basis of being soulless people, so they became fit to be destroyed. And the Jews were hated in Europe for killing Christ amongst other things, and the slaughter started, too.

"In 2007, a co-founder of the DNA, a white man, re-echoed the blacks-are-not-intelligent-cry. And the cry of any dominant race or tribe that says there's nothing like that anymore is nonsense. It's because it reflects on them.

"Development is no mystery in this world and no one man can claim it. Man is known to borrow ideas from man just like in religion. If they are in a particular area, whatever new information one man has will soon spread to other places and that's how man progresses. Even in science and technology.

"This is where we can't forget Thomas Edison and Tesla, the Hungarian genius and Howard Lewis Latimer, the Black American. Man continues to build on others' ideas to make them better. So the technologically backward people are left behind in most cases by design. And unfortunately this ideology was what some people used to suppress others, calling them inferior as if everyone in their race or tribe from the moment they were born understood calculus or knew how a radio worked, or how to swing a golf club.

"How many whites could think of improving on what Edison invented at that time, but wouldn't hesitate to hang Lewis on a tree if he walked down the street or looked at him with a condescending gaze. Really, that is laughable. See how being brainwashed is shallow and man can't see.

"Sometimes they don't teach the achievements of people considered low in what they call intelligence to their children. Cultural supremacy is as bad as religious fight, maybe, worse than religion. The Turks don't teach the language and culture of the Kurds in Turkey. This is causing a big problem. Now EU is forcing them to change their ways because... The Japanese tried to rewrite the history of their oppression in that continent. This made Koreans and Chinese to demonstrate against changing history.

"This demonizing even happens within a group. Mao, the Chinese now praise for his achievement at the expense of 35 million people he demonized and killed to build his communist state. That's patriotism!

"These rewriters of history books want the past to favor them because they believe it reflect on their good, fair and understanding nature and don't want it tainted. They try to wash away the atrocities of their forefathers, too, just like Jesus' mission. They explain it away also with their rational thinking, making act of violence squeaky clean. They will never acknowledge that they benefit from their hero's oppressions, just like the children of rich parents will make light of their father's help in their lives. They also will deny the exploitation of conquered peoples' natural resources to build their beloved countries that now give charitable donations to the countries stolen from. Whoa! What kindness.

"Well, no matter how Stalin is praised by the history books in Russia, the Ukrainians know what he did to them in their millions. These people are worse than religious groups. At least, the faithful stick to their guns and argue it out no matter how simple-minded they sound. Of course, if the holy books can be rewritten by the apologists, they will do it, too. Remove all the blemishes from their Gods. This will leave us with no story. What am I saying, they have…Bible is getting a makeover like one of the Before and After Reality Shows.

"Maybe the people who demonize one group or another for their selfish reason, either for emotional triumph or economical, fail to realize in their scientific and logical thinking that the highest quality a human being can have is real love and compassion for all, in any case.

"My friend, sad as this may sound, know this for a fact. Many people in this day and age would want to live with their so-called kind. It's only because of commerce that man tolerates another man. And that's two-faced. It's not a sincere way of loving thy neighbor.

"Just imagine during the segregation period in the US, when man thought he made the best laws in order to have peace in the civil society and the end of the world came - remember it was rooted in Christianity at that time. In paradise, whites would say to God or Jesus, 'hey, can we have our own heaven? We practiced this system on earth and it worked like a charm-we didn't even bury the dead together.' They even separated their dung, amazing superior shit!

"You'll be surprised, just to let you know, man is a machine and would act accordingly. Nationalism is treated the same way as religion in the minds of nationalists. They are proud of their forefathers; proud of their heritage and culture; sing their forefathers' praises at any given time, why? Because it makes man feel important and full of pride. His existence is not wasted, as if he would have gotten along understandably well with his forefathers. It doesn't matter what the topic is, man as man will go along blindly for his petty glory.

"I was reading a history book about the founding fathers of America, and the historian almost painted Jefferson (slave owner) amongst others as a saint. First of all, an alien from Mars would think slavery only lasted for nine months, like a human pregnancy with all the pains for a while and then delivery. It lasted over 240 years, and then segregation just ended about 50 years ago or so. And that's according to the law! So, here is where the nationalists should see themselves as the religionists, if they are sincere; they pompously praise their leaders for having sound values they are proud of; they too celebrate their idols (gods) like Jefferson and countless founding fathers around the world; and when the nationalists are forced to mention their founding fathers' atrocities (taking other peoples' land, amongst many bad things), they say it with as few words as possible just like the religionists regarding their Gods. I will leave the patriots to figure this out. Like Moses, the founding fathers would be in heaven, too. After all, they were inspired by God to build the US as a shining example for the rest of mankind. Funny thing, though, some of these nationalists don't agree with the religionists. How do they see the difference?

"Anyway, the historian said Jefferson put ending slavery in the original constitution, but was removed by others. This was someone that didn't free his own slaves and only instructed to free them after his death. This should be listed as one of my favorites top ten hypocrisies.

"Their 2007 president just awarded medals to the men that fought evil Hitler when they were under evil tyranny themselves. This president, though not an historian, but the speech he delivered was the same as not calling it as he should. I guess they call that diplomacy. The speech acknowledged the denial but said that 'in the hearts of Americans' they were not given their rightful respect. Then I told myself…definitely not in the hearts of the blacks." John said.

He was still in the middle of explaining faith, prayer and why we put fellow beings like ourselves down when Fred joined them. Actually, he wanted a private session with John. But John declined and told him to say whatever he had in mind in front of Den.

"I'll like to see you alone if you don't mind." Fred begged.

"For what?"

"I can understand some of the things you said, but some, I don't."

"So why don't we stay here together with Den, maybe, he did not understand certain things, too." John insisted.

"Okay. You want me to put man above God?" Fred asked.

"No, I don't." John replied.

"What?" Why all that talk about Christian God not being of love?" Fred wanted to know.

"I want you to question everything you've been told and put yourself in those people's shoes that the God in the bible took their land for instance, or one of the servants of Job." John argued.

"But I can't question God." Fred replied.

"What they have made you to believe is God. There is a big difference. You sure can question Allah. Can't you?" John pointed out.

Then all was quiet. Fred thought it would be easy to persuade John to see things his way.

"So, if you always want to obey God then answer these questions. Just go along. These are no trick questions. Trust me."

Question: So you're a believer in God?
Answer: Yes, with all my heart.
Question: In which God?
Answer: There's only one God.
Question: Then where can I read about this God?
Answer: The Holy Bible.
Question: So you obey all God's commands?
Answer: I try within my power, I'm not perfect.
Question: Could God have made you in the period of the Old
           Testament?
Answer: Yes, God has authority over everything, and time.
Question: Did God choose Saul as the first King of Israel?
Answer: Yes.
Question: Would you disobey God like Saul?
Answer: To obey is better than sacrifice.

But as the session continued, Fred got wiser. "I know where you're taking this question to."

And he left. The luster faded finally.

"Wait a minute. The last question is, would you kill babies and suckling for your God?"

The question seemed to follow Fred as he disappeared into the night, pounding hard in his Christian heart.

They both knew the answer to that.

"Is he going to be okay?" Den was concerned.

"He will be fine." John replied. "He will outgrow the fear someday. We all do, few of us sooner than later.

"Back to what we were saying, prayer is not limited to a particular religion. The Buddhists too pray to Buddha to free them from the cycle of rebirth. Then you have to ask yourself, who did Buddha pray to? Also we have all kinds of ritualistic rites by the Hindu worshippers; it's all in a form of prayer to the Gods.

"And some people never pray and still have everything and more, much more than people that pray. How do we explain that?" John said.

"They say that God showers gifts on the good and the wicked." Den hinted.

"That's a clever statement. It's one of the many ways to put you in a box. But ask them why then do they bother to pray." John replied.

"Then, why do people fight for a God that won't give them everything they ask for?" Den was lost and angry.

"Pretty much, man as man would fight and die for anything, anywhere and anytime. Remember the Kamikaze, when the young and manipulated minds of the Japanese were to do the honorable thing for their beloved country under a Man-God emperor.

"You've heard of man fighting to protect his ego, if bruised, even slightly. Man will die for a nickel and be happy!

"Don't forget we also have the almighty sport. The game of entertainment and man fails to remember it's for his pleasure; he fights and dies for his so-called distraction from everyday life. He doesn't even know the owners and they don't know him, either. He has latched his happiness on to the game, the team controls his moods. Team wins, he's happy, team loses, he's sad, and might even take his heartbreak out on his spouse and children or friends. And sometimes people who act this way blame the religious people for lack of tolerance. You should see them argue about their 'sportigion'. Gee, you will think they are talking about something they can control. They start exchanging verbal abuses; they push one another, screaming at the top of their voices to make a silly point about a player that is probably swimming in his or her oversized pool. And they wear their crosses too; their badge of honor in the form of a jersey, their saint's uniform.

"There was an incident in a bar somewhere in NYC, this poor immigrant just happened to be wearing a T-shirt of an opposing team. The long and short of the story is, the immigrant was beaten to a coma. You can imagine the chain effect of him being in that condition on his family. But some sports fans rationalized the incident, just like a religious man that straps a bomb on himself will. There are countless stories around the world that if we get into the subject, it will be sounding religious. Actually, sport is their religion. They win, they fight. They lose; they fight and, sometimes lose their lives.

"And when it comes to dying to make it to heaven, you'll do whatever your leader tells you to do without hesitation. Remember, people doing this are under a heavenly spell. And also aiming for martyrdom, which is the greatest evil in man's world. It's man reaching for immortality in the minds of his fellow men. Then what? They die fighting for Allah or not they are guaranteed heaven. Only in their minds! *(Surah 4: 75)*

"And forget the Christians disassociating themselves from the Muslims, the crusaders did the same thing, and like it or not, brought more people into Christianity with their swords of holiness than miracles.

"Even God, the father of Christ was a God of war in the Old Testament." John said.

Just as John finished explaining to Den, Jack joined them.

"This is where you guys are?" He said, looking up in the sky. Man would forever be captivated by the stars. Why the fascination? Maybe, man always desired to get out of the cage and be truly free.

Before Jack could say what was on his mind, Den asked another question.

"What about the atheists?" Den was thinking that these people were the lucky ones.

"I don't know about that." John began.

"These people are locked in the eternal debate with their counterparts, the believers in God. Back and forth arguments that would make God be rolling in laughter on his throne. Yet, each side is claiming victory. But the number is what matters and believers are winning.

"The line between the two camps is not clear; they switch camps sometimes, no matter how long they bark at each other.

"If a popular atheist converts, thousands of unbelievers tremble with fear and drift closer to the believers. On the other hand, if a popular believer turns atheist, few people follow his so-called falling from grace." John explained.

Jack was listening patiently to John's answer before getting something off his chest, too.

"I sure can sympathize with the atheist..." John continued, "not believing in something that's full of contradictions. But it's like fighting with a demented man, an outsider from another planet won't be able to tell them apart. And the fact of the matter is that the atheists, unbeknownst to them, are guilty of the same thing they accuse the believers of, 'show us proof'. But then, the atheists can't prove there is no God. There you have it, each side claiming absolute authority. The atheists' singular weapon is 'burden of proof is on your side'. They shout it just like the Christians shout the end of the world. But the burden of proof is just an excuse by man's logic. If the atheists can prove there is no God they would have done it. This is not CSI where you provide physical proof. This is the mother of all mysteries!!!

"Most of the people who call themselves atheists in this world are Westerners mainly because they have more freedom than the rest of the world in terms of expressing themselves; freedom of speech. And they are only responding to the God imposed on them by Constantine, so to speak. They are freeing themselves from mental slavery, too. Many others live in parts of the world where they will be severely punished if they speak their minds about their barbaric cultures or religions.

"But there are some areas that the atheists too falter, some atheists champion science and say there is nothing responsible for what we see and that's like taking the same position as their counterpart. There are so many mysteries about practically everything in life; even man himself is a mystery. To take a firm position on anything in this incomprehensible world is to be foolish and not know it.

"Even people who are claiming that science is tied to intelligence should be careful. Man has been made to believe that formal education will solve his problems. But to say that has failed is an understatement.

"One of the greatest scientists, Mr. Calculus, believed in a God of the Jews just as much as he worked on an apple falling from the tree. But all this is considered intelligence by man. Where is the intelligence of such a man, or should I say, morality, in a Jewish God snuffing out a poor baby's life? Isaac Newton had more than thirty bibles to consult before going with the Jewish God. That showed how diligent he researched God, using one specimen. How scientific?

"The Jewish experience shouldn't be used to explain life here. That will be myopic of man, thinking his father's land is the biggest land ever, until someone showed him another land. Or we might as well thank the two Mayan brothers that turned themselves into the sun and the moon for us to have romantic moonlight dinners.

"Things do happen in this world that man's puny brain can't decipher, but he arrogantly claims that's the way things must be. He doesn't even question the fact that he might not have the slightest notion about what really constitutes life here. Yet things happen that will make even his 'Science-god' fail him. The number one claim by science is that we are all one lump of molecules; DNA married together in a particular way or another and man or all kinds of species would emerge, then, is there a gene that knows good or bad, compassion or hatred, love gene… self control? Then how does one chemical in one person makes some good? 'Judge, I didn't steal the money. My stealing gene did it. Take it out.' Who has the control…me or the gene or collections of genes? Then what am I? Mind over matter? Now where does that come from? From science-god or from the massive energy of light that exploded… the big bang. Then what or who started that…and how could the 'bang' explode in a space, who or what made the space?

"You have to tip your hat to science, though. Scientists can dissect things, manipulate them and even produce something incredible…but? Here too, we have commercial scientists exploiting the vulnerable. More than 90% of science is not exact. Don't think for a moment that they are not exploiting the public by selling, 'it's science' slogan to take your money, promising to make you happy and many more guarantees.

"The atheists have their own prophets too, Descartes and Sigmund

Freud to name a couple. And Graham Bell who revolutionized the way man talks would be seen also as intelligent by man's standard, but it was the handling of the deaf society of America that intelligence, can we say, failed him. Then, again, what is intelligence?

"Why man unwittingly places his own understanding of this world in another man's experience is beyond me, bad example. So my advice to man is to start understanding love, nothing but pure love in mind if he can. And where there's pure love, there's no hatred. But in a man's world hatred is perceived as love. I think we are here just to learn about love or what love really is. So our family is not really what we think it is, but an avenue for us to learn love, and that applies to practically everything in life; love affairs, work place, pretty much everywhere is school for us to learn love. Even If we die without any faith, we would have lived a life worth living." John preached and then turned to Jack, gesturing to him to say what he wanted.

"Why is it that we dread the afterlife? Even knowing that choosing one religion or the other is a gamble, no guarantee." Jack asked.

"Let's for once forget there's God or no God, or life after we die. Man will still scare himself. Take superstition." John commenced. "All around the world there are countless things that scare the pants off man. And sometimes these superstitious people don't belong to any particular religion, yet they pride themselves to be better than the religious ones. What they fail to see is that their paranoia is from their society, too. And they believe it completely.

"They can't prove their superstitious beliefs whether they prevent some evil or not from happening. They too are paralyzed with fear. Say one sees a black cat in the morning and he's scared of having bad luck, who knows whether the cat seeing him too will bring bad luck to the cat. Then how do you explain people who live with black cats?"

Jack smiled at John's explanation.

Then John decided to go deeper into the issue.

"In parts of Africa, putting your hands on your head is asking for something bad to happen. In North America, if you talk about what you'd like to accomplish in the near future and you want it to come true, you knock on wood. If someone suggests to them to knock on rough surface, they will and won't even question it. And if you ask why, they will see you as odd. And besides, they are knocking on the symbolical cross of Jesus. The unbelievers don't know they hold Jesus dear, too. Just like everyone says bless you when we sneeze. I hear the soul or the spirit jumps in or out...and you defeat the devil and win back your soul, and we say bless you. What about the dogs? What's jumping in and out of them? They sneeze, too. That should mean they have souls. Sometimes someone will send a silly phrase to others, urging them to do the same or else something will or won't happen.

"And it's fear of whatever that makes people adhere strictly to one superstition or another. It's hard for man as man to live fear free. And it varies from the simple to the absurd. Some will pick up pennies, claiming an angel is watching over them. Some are scared stiff when it's Friday the 13th. Some will walk backward to enter a particular door in their house. Some will throw salt over their shoulders. Be careful you might throw salt in someone's eyes; it could be a law suit. And sometimes, it varies from one person to another, even with the same object of superstition. We have the broken mirror scare, and the one that says you can't see the bride in her wedding dress before the actual day...is this why marriages don't last around the world? And we should stop demonizing Hollywood marriages. Marriages generally don't last. It's just that we have turned the spotlight on them.

"We just scare one another in this world. And the scariest of all will get most people to tremble and that's the lake of fire in hell." John said.

"And we are as blind as a bat to it, hmm." Jack summed it up.

"Don't think it's easy to break someone's superstition, either. It's hard as hell. But the hypocritical nature of it is that some superstitious people see other superstitions feared by other people, say, in another country or culture or group, as stupid or uneducated or unsophisticated." John added.

"So it's like...it's sounding like religion to me." Den said.

"Yes, you're right. If there's nothing to put fear in man in his world, man being man will create something to scare himself. He is afraid of his shadow. What a nature." John said.

"Coming back to your question, Jack, man only celebrates life and forgets the other part that's equally important, hey, should you voice it out, you will hear, you don't want to enjoy life; you're looking at the ugly side of it. And we run away from it, though it seems, from talking about death. Why rock the boat. It's our fear of dying that makes us prone to preachers of heaven and hell. It's inevitable. It's something not to be feared, but embraced. Dying is living. Even Jesus raising the dead was a wasteful miracle. Are they still alive physically?

"Things die around man every time, the animals, the trees, the fish and the flies, yet, he's scared to go. Some even want to freeze themselves for later, in order to come back to this physical life. Cryogenic is the way not to go...like taking out a frozen meat in order to prepare dinner later.

"Man, you see, is paralyzed by the fear of afterlife that in order for him to remain sane, really that's debatable, he comes up with all these ideas to console his mind.

"Take Tao religion for instance. They are so scared of hell, with them there isn't just one hell, but ten or more. Can you imagine that? This is even tougher than the Allah or God's hell. But in order for quick release from hells, they make paper money, houses, cars and whatever they think the hell keepers might need and burn them, symbolically. In a way they are offering a bribe for a quick release from hell. Then after ten years a feng-shui expert tells the family where to rebury the dead." John said.

"What if the family dies before the ten years?" Jack asked.

Both Den and Jack were just shaking their heads. Incredible, yet believed and lived by man.

"Then we have the church of Mormon, the Latter Days, trying to baptize all the dead in the world (we all become Mormon when we die) in order for them to go to paradise, whether the dead wants it or not. I bet they won't forget the Mountain Meadows massacre, where women and children and their men were senselessly murdered by the followers. They should get the first baptism of the dead, I would say. Somebody's got to fight for their rights.

There is nothing to fear about dying. It's just our attachment to this world that makes it difficult and sorrowful when it comes to it. Good luck on the other side, whatever happens, happens." John concluded.

"Man uses another man's eyes
to see what he can, by
himself, see."
Stan

Man as Man

Seemed every question was answered. But as they were about to depart John remembered what he wanted to tell Jack. This was as good a time as any.

"Oh, I wanted to tell you something, Jack, before the episode with Fred."

"What is it?"

John began.

"It's about man. I don't want you to lose your cool or, at least, try not to let it get out of hand when it concerns life as we know it here. I told Den the witch's story to help him see man for who he is, and with the two of you I'll share my objective experience. Please don't be alarmed or try to stop me. I will answer all your questions at the end or maybe my talk will leave you with no more questions."

Both men looked at each other with a little concern. John stretched out his arms and brought them back together, and then shut his eyes. He went into a semi-trance. He opened his mouth and the words tumbled down like manna from heaven.

"When man as man stops being one, he's perceived as a self-hating Jew, a self-hating white, a self-hating Arab, a self-hating black or simply a self-hating man. He has ceased speaking for millions of his so-called people, which is the most ridiculous thing in the first place. (Yes, man as man is lost if he can't identify himself with this or that. He has to belong in his mind to a group; a group that is further divided into a group and still divided some more…God wants me to maintain my purity!) He has just stopped drinking from the well; a unit of cloud floating away from the collective consciousness. He has taken himself out of the same game played over and over with different reasons by the human consciousness. He's MAD.

"Man as man wants to be begged to see his bad, uninformed way. He doesn't want to be called ignorant, yet calls others not in his circle ignorant. Tell him openly and you are the bad one, the insensitive one. Yet the cloak that he wraps around himself for salvation or pride is not only stained but meshed in the blood of the innocent. But the only effect on him will be that his feeling is hurt by telling him to look at himself in the mirror of life.

"Amazingly, man as man proudly builds magnificent houses for his gods only to bomb them, either by the opposing faith or by believers themselves for godly reasons or not. He would rather build houses for god than for people who are homeless i.e. the biggest church is in a third world country-Ivory Coast. They compete to construct the most glorious one ever, to show god's might…and blessings. It makes them feel useful to their gods, building everywhere. After all, god is going to house them, too, in his mansions in heaven without collecting rent from them.

"Man as man's vision is crystal clear. So I take a look. In the play ground I see children of all races; creeds and classes come to play. Having pure, honest fun without fear or favor, without biases…until I see parents come to the park, they put on their superficial smiles. Meanwhile, hatred, ignorance, fear, superiority complex and biases fill their minds. Then they take their children away and fill them with their ill-advised fears, close-minded faiths of separation and hatred, archaic cultures and traditions, turning loving hearts into…You know, just look at your society.

"Man as man says his creator gives freedom of will to all his creations, yet man, himself, now makes that will worthless. How ironic. In his effort to build a good, loving society, he creates fear and intimidation, totally missing the mark. But the truth is man as man, himself, wants to rule others without giving them freedom. He's just using all the tricks and excuses to carry out the task.

"Man as man promises to be able to beg and pray to his God for healing. The Muslims use a special board they write the prayers on and tell the believers to drink it; the Christians lay hands on the sick, and many others with their special ways to persuade the Maker to grant long life, success, happiness, prosperity and the list is endless. Yes, that is the scam that puts all in bondage. Because when the blessings happen, they praise their God, but when they fail, they still praise their God. Any fool could do this. It's a win-win situation for God! Human fear is used to manipulate man.

"Man as man cries to his Gods saying, why God, why, why do you create people that don't look like me. Now, see how they have ruined my life and the lives of your highly compassionate and civilized people.

"Man as man will mutilate himself, blood oozing from every part of his body. He's full of excruciating pains yet believes strongly that it will endear him to his given God.

He wakes up the next day, puts on his modern clothes, goes to head a successful business or teach in one of those so-called higher learning universities that you need an IQ of far above average to get into. And the most popular of them all, his father nailed him to the cross as a sacrificial lamb.

"Man as man thinks there is something special in his blood: Jesus' blood cleanses all sins; in Islam you can't be blood brothers if you join the faith; animal's blood is used for sacrifice to the Gods to cleanse us of our own sins, how sad. Poor animals, not only do we eat them. The Muslims won't take the blood of Jesus but that of a ram will do the cleansing trick; vampires even suck your blood for healthy drink; racists and tribalists want to maintain the purity of their blood, no contamination here. Yet when rational people get sick and need blood, we give blood to them in order to live a healthy life. Humans even drink animal's blood. So, what's the importance of blood, again? Man is ritualistic. Pretty much man still dances around the fire!

"Man as man cries how man treats man, but how deep is the cry? Trying to figure this out I became confused. But, really, is our outer display of emotion truly that tangible in this world as we know it? During the reconstruction in South Africa after the end of apartheid, people came forward, especially the whites, to bare all about the killings, the torture, the frying of victims, the disappearance of people who were leading the resistance against the evil regime, especially the outspoken university students. And the head of the reconciliation was none other than the Bishop, the Nobel Prize winner for peace. Several times he broke down in genuine tears hearing man's inhumanity to man. But will this man shed the same tears in heaven? I hear no tears in heaven!

"Man as man would only find whatever is good about his so-called religion and dismisses the not so good aspects of it - this is a contradiction in terms, how can everything not be good coming from God almighty! He tries to console himself by explaining it away or turning a deaf ear and blind eye to it. The mainstream believers are the worst hypocrites of them all. Either they are ignorant of their holy books or...They can all put in an appropriate name that fits them. I'm running out of names to call them. To annoy a Christian, tell him he doesn't understand love, just like telling a Muslim that Muhammad couldn't have been the last prophet.

"Man as man's method of persuasion is really a piece of work. They might as well be talking to a brick wall. The Muslims will say to a Christian, 'use your head; this is what your holy bible says about Muhammad. Think...look at it. You will see what we are telling you.' Of course, the good Christians use the same lame means for the Muslims and others. Somewhere there you are allowed to use your head, and then, you are stopped to continue using it. Did you see it? It's like magic! The amazing thing is that they think they are better than the other group. Other group is always evil.

"Man as man thinks that his god has made him powerful, successful and given him all that he desires in his society. Well, if he looks into history he will find that the Mayan gods provided fantastic civilization for the worshippers, the Aztec gods also did the same. And numerous other gods provided well for man in all cultures. Jesus is now praised day and night for making the USA a mighty country. (Forget that the numbers of Indians were reduced by the persecuted Christians from Christian Europe. Wonder whether the Indians would go to heaven?) First, there are other Christian countries that don't have enough to eat. How can I explain this? Jesus is picking and choosing like poor people going through used clothes in a bargain store. I get it, he wants to provide for you so that you can give them. You must have prayed the hardest!

"Man as man, the charitable organizations (churches and mosques), collect money tainted with fear from all converts (10%) and sympathetic ones and distribute the funds to the less fortunate ones and claim it has something to do with their Gods. How does one arrive at this conclusion? Yet, they steal the glory of man's kindness and glorify their God that will burn the givers who stop believing or giving later in hell. This holy work is also done by one agency…called government. Just like government can't honestly use the money for the good of all, the so-called religious organizations can't, either. What is the difference?

"Man as man will fight and die for a God given him by another man. (With the religion comes the culture and language of the imposer) He forgets in a hurry that he claims that his God is all powerful and should be able to defend himself. Well, it's like having Michael Jackson as Mike Tyson's bodyguard during a fist fight.

"Man as man will find a linkage; any means to assure himself that God or Allah or any popular God of his time hasn't forgotten him. He will make sense out of insensibility. Join the God of the day, the popular God, like going after the latest fashion.

"Man as man, and this concerns the ones that see through their religions and don't follow everything they say sheepishly without their logical inputs. Bravo…but what part of the Koran or the bible are they not following religiously, (seen obviously as, maybe, evil or wrong) the part that will burn the unbelievers and usher them to paradise? These true believers really can see through a soiled looking glass.

"Man as man has always been putting a human face on the punishment that awaits the infidels. This is in the area of Christianity. Islam is not compromising yet. Anyway, some good hearted Christians now say that God will just burn people once in hell. But if they really want to be good, they should tell their merciful God or Jesus not to wake the dead in the first place. What is the point? We all know they are guilty, why double kill them.

"Man as man, especially those who are literates - with their PhDs in everything, and the illiterates of course, still not devoid of sound reasoning, will use what they believe is logic and good thinking to come to their wonderful conclusion that Allah or God put this world together. For the record, they are all deluded. And this is absolutely sad because the society respects their misguided views. Only in this world can people like this be listened to and paid generously.

"Man as man is so proud of his God's nature that he brags about his unchanging character day and night. Here is another teaser. A pastor says that God can never repent; after all, he is God.

> *Numbers; chapter 23 verse 19*
> *God is not a man, that he should lie; neither the son of man, that he should repent: hath he said, and shall he not do it? Or hath he spoken, and shall he not make it good?*

"Am I supposed to read this upside down?

> *Exodus; chapter 32 verse 14*
> *And God repented of the evil which he thought to do unto his people.*

"Man as man will incite other men to destruction by his so-called holy revelations. Any man that tells us we are better than other men in this world is leading us to the path of anarchy and chaos, either in terms of religion or nationalism. Sometimes I can't tell which is worse.

It's like choosing between a manipulative wife and an abusive husband. Superiority in any form is vanity.

"Man as man uses parables to convey his divine meanings. Here is my parable. If a Muslim feeds a hungry child and a Christian also feeds a child lacking food, then an atheist buys food to feed a child dying of hunger. Who's really doing the will of Love without any condemnation, whatsoever? Also, they credit themselves of saving man from his addictions. News flash! Man is known to reform himself, by himself and also, within a group, whether religious or not. But the big question is whether the reform will be lasting.

"Man as man, especially the dominant group in any society, tells the subdued but liberated how to argue, what to remember and what to forget, what is childish and many more, just like you tell someone that can't fight you head on where to hit you and the degree of the intensity. Sometimes they throw a bone to the minority and pad themselves on the back for growing. 'Don't tell us when to change and how, let us grow at our own pace.' Their pace is always at the expense of the minority. Wonder whether the minority can tell them the same. (Then, again, one in a million makes it to the top in the minority group and says the system works.) They don't lay the proper foundation for genuine development for the minority, proper developments that they have enjoyed for centuries, but always ready to bash them when failing, or to catch up with them, which they don't want in the first place. Case in point, the Ijaw people in Nigeria, where the bulk of the oil that runs the economy comes from, don't have a say in what feeds the entire country. I'm sure you can see hundreds of examples everywhere. Doesn't even matter whether minority has something or nothing, the majority will still treat them bad, another case in point, the Yagua villagers in Peru fighting to hold on to their land. The majority has the moral compass and sound logic for their actions and inactions. The simple logic here is that there is power in numbers.

"Man as man will showcase what he calls piety before the assumed Almighty in front of the rest of the people like a peacock. 'Look at me, I'm investing in eternal life of bliss and you…I'm sorry for you, you've only got life insurance.'

"Man as man's religion is another form of dictatorship. He will burn books again. He will censor opposing opinions by force and all the tricks of the trade; age, position, relationships, tears, emotional blackmail, silent treatment, banishing and torture and killing and many more are the tools he uses. Actually, he's scared and that's how man at that level of thinking reacts. This is man's darkest side, but misunderstanding it as love; religion doesn't give freedom of worship in any other way. This is like saying my 2+2=22, and that's it for everybody; you can't know more than me and my prophets. They will always have one complaint after another to carry out their god's rule or law. They can't be satisfied, even when you are in your grave! Remember, they claim to be in constant communication with the Maker. Who can quench the thirst of a dictator?

"Man as man speaks in tongue, not of other languages as clearly stated in his holy book, but in gibberish that can't be understood by anyone. According to man he is trying to bypass Satan to get his prayer delivered to God safely, like the US Poster Service. Really, we have to redefine what constitutes madness. To compound this singular mess that man has put himself, some have come out to interpret the gibberish. Now that is scary.

"Man as man thinks he's special. Actually he's suffering from SPS (special people's syndrome). This is the greatest deceit in the world, because from it stems how he sees everyone. My forefathers were great, loving and good; my tradition can't be compared to any others', my religion is the only way, my civilization…okay, if all our forefathers were great then we wouldn't have this kind of world. No enslavement, no taking of other people's land either by one God or the founding fathers, and no stealing of other people's mineral resources, too.

"Man as man will never sit down for a moment and reflect on this simple question. In the face of everyone claiming this and that to be the truth, what if in my deluded mind I'm actually misleading people? Can I really carry the burden? The fact is man can't think for himself. If he can, he would have considered this amongst hundreds of loopholes in his defense of his given God. Why would Jesus say he didn't come for the righteous, but for sinners, and at the end of his life damned every non believer to hell? Is righteousness no longer rewarded?

"Man as man doesn't really bother to examine the story told him about his God. This reminds me about the boastfulness of the Muslims knocking the crucifixion of Jesus off the minds of believers. I can agree with them, but I have one question regarding fairness since Allah is fair. The man that his face was miraculously replaced by Jesus' face by all accounts was innocent. So, who was this guy and why should he (John Doe) die? This is what I would do if I had the power like that... miraculously beam Jesus up to heaven, because he begged for his life. And also miraculously hail on them so everyone runs home. But that didn't happen according to the story. So, that means this unknown man took Jesus' blame. He died for the sins or accusation of the prophet. Does that still sound fair?

"Man as man continues to rationalize his forever unchanging God. This is where the gays in this triangular religion come in. 'Judge not... 'they cry quoting the holy book. Well, no one is judging because God actually killed people who were gay in the bible. One gay pastor was beaming with pride about his sexuality that he said the bible should be seen as a progressive book and not static; conveniently said. 'Hey God, you know...why don't you let everybody in paradise...people that don't believe in your son that you killed for the redemption of sins. I think that will be cool. That will be progressive thinking.' Actually, Jesus did the same thing with the Sabbath day. God stoned people to death, but Jesus changed it. Good news for the unbelievers, God will soon be so progressive we will all end up in heaven! By the way, homosexuality doesn't mean you're a nice human being.

"Man as man, a Nigerian Muslim is so blown away by the Saudis that he is of the mind that they have been blessed by Allah, providing them with oil. Unbeknownst to this devout Muslim (actually drinking from the well), he fails to see that his country also sits on oil. Forty percent of the world oil sits at the bottom of the oceans. The Saudis must own it too. How can we make him see! Pretty soon he will be giving them his hard earn money and maybe serve them, too. If you ask him why he does that, he will tell you because of them he's going to heaven. Ask him what about the Jews being the light of the world? He will say, 'do you think I am a fool?' By the way, this same guy agreed that Fela Kuti was a prophet. Hey, don't crucify him. He has freedom of opinion, but it would be interesting to hear what Muhammad would say to that. Also, they feel proud when people give them tough times about their faith, they feel 'persecuted'. They have been brainwashed to feel this way. It shows they are loyal to lies!

"Oh, man as man! The (whites) Christians are beginning to love the Jews now, but there is a catch. The aim is to convert them, to make them accept Jesus as their messiah. If my memory serves me right, wasn't this the aim of Constantine...mmm, hypocrisy making a full circle, taking on a gentler face or approach because they have no more political clout.

"Man as man from time immemorial has been ignorant of love; that is to not enslave one another. So, slavery has always been part of his history in one form or another; someone to do your dirty work and serve you, while you bask in sunshine enjoying your god-given life. (And the irony is that when their slaves died they buried them with the symbols of their gods on the graves. Like the Whites did, putting the cross of Jesus on them.) Even the Gods are guilty of the same offence and their prophets. After all, prophets get the right and true instructions from all merciful, fair and loving Gods. So, who do I blame here? Man or the prophets and Gods. I will blame God (and his holy prophets), who is supposed to know right from wrong from the get-go, because man has stopped the trade openly and now prosecutes anyone that engages in it.

"Also, man as man brings up the Intelligent Design. This is actually by the Christian scientists. After all they have all their colorful Ph Ds in logic. They now weave the God in the bible to what they call empirical signs that everybody can see and understand. First, they conveniently left behind the fact that science says the world is older than 6,000 years. Second, they excluded all the other Gods known to man. How scientific?

"Man as man would further deepen his ignorance and hypocrisy by wrapping big words like allegory or figurative expression around words that are simple. So I guess when God in the bible told Moses, I'd kill all the first sons of Egyptians before they let you go wasn't literal, but figurative. He actually didn't do it.

And when Mohammed said, well, that's according to Allah (the most merciful), after all, Mohammed just recited Allah's words that you should beat your wife, the prophet didn't mean that. The translation of the word 'beat' could mean something else in the original language of Allah, like cuddle. But what does the tone of the passage tell us? I forgot we don't have the divine knowledge to comprehend that. They pride themselves in understanding a language of intolerance and hatred and go about the society with their cosmetic compassion for all. 'How is my foundation? You like it, not too thick. How is my eye-shadow? Nice…what about my lip gloss?'

"Man as man will come up with the most senseless argument to defend his position, pretending he doesn't know what's right or wrong when it comes to his God's actions. So here is a thought. The so-called lesser animals know what's love and hate. It's a shame, according to you they don't have souls, just continuously kick a dog everyday and see whether it will keep coming to you. On the other hand, do the opposite, pet the dog and play with it and see the result. If they know love and hate, how much more the self-titled higher intelligent beings, upholding that a God and prophets that killed babies, suckling and pregnant women, even healthy males and females for whatever reason in their holy books is not tantamount to evil or murder. This God or Allah and his worshippers have taken away the work of Satan and his angels. Ignorance is praised, celebrated and encouraged from generation to generation with slight modifications!

"Man as man has the propensity to worship anything and everything. Look at all the public figures; the sportsmen and women; the so-called movie stars and so on, that we stay in line for hours to see and cry, and get their autographs and shower praises on them as if their jobs are far different from ours. And we pass this cool social salute to our children. I tell you it's nothing short of religion. Don't tell the secular people that or they will call you a hater or a wet blanket. The stars posters are bigger than our pictures in our own homes. This is man showing his potential to worship pretty much anything or anyone. He keeps going round and round in circles until he wakes up. Man has attached his fun and happiness to them. Take them away from the socialites and you will have a 'religious' fight on your hands. No difference.

"Man as man is not raising children, but recruits. We create monsters that we have to deal with later in the four corners of our world. When we teach hatred, ('they are going to hell, they don't obey God the way we do...they don't eat what we eat...they are gays...) subtle or overt of any kind to our children and they carry it out to others outside our environment, we rejoice. But sooner or later, since hatred like everything else is like a boomerang, it comes back to us, and we start scratching our heads; asking what went wrong. Imagine if it's love, there won't be anything to fear. Which finger are we using to point at them—the ones that carry out what our God/Allah wants or acts like Him in the holy books? Love doesn't condemn, love doesn't exclude and yet man is trying to find it with the religion of hatred- no matter how he sugar-coats it. We cannot tell how far our children will take the religion or idea given them. So, we are responsible for their actions.

"Man as man either fools himself or doesn't know what he is saying. You hear, I am just a Christian or...just a Muslim - I don't practice. But why call yourself either one if it doesn't mean anything to you? They might want to consider calling themselves something else; after all, they don't mean it. Just like they mean well for all the dead not in their religion with their tears and grief. Maybe beneath their 'I'm just this or that' is the allure of heaven - just in case they are right and the fear of hell, also - hey, you never know, stealing the New York lotto slogan.

"Man as man, in this case, the civilized man beats his chest that the primitive societies of old were always waiting for a god to save them. I look into the cyber-age and I still see the same expectation. Jesus is coming down from the cloud to claim his kingdom and save the faithful! Who is primitive now? I get it, those backward thinking people used spears and you use laser beam.

"Man as man unwittingly sells himself short by allowing another man to tell him that his God is the GOD OF ALL and he should be cared for, loved, respected, protected and blessed by the rest of mankind. This is worse than selling your soul to the devil. You have deprived yourself of any shred of your humanity; selling it to another mere man like you. It's a shame. Reclaim yourself. Remember the story of someone selling his birthright? How ironic! Are we learning from these stories?

"Man as man gives others a bogus story that should be hard to swallow but man's throat makes room to gulp down the tale just like the whale swallowing that man…let's reason please. Say I'm a God of fairness as everyone would like to believe. I'm using one tribe or race or nation or a gender as an example to millions of people that I have created, all my creations don't know right from wrong, and the unit I'm using in my lab keeps messing up just like the unassisted, Godless groups. So, what should I do? Because there's a big problem…both nurtured and the unassisted are dying before my chosen group learns to enlighten the whole world, and I'm sending them to heaven and hell. Well, I have reached an impasse, OMG; maybe one of those 10-year-old kids will someday resolve my crisis like those mathematical problems that baffle scientists for decades.

"Man as man and this concerns all the conquered people that their land produce, people, natural resources were siphoned to the conquerors' lands that now believe that the same conqueror's religions and God/Allah will take them to paradise? I get it. Their forefathers and mothers were their sacrificial lambs. Sorry, I am the one that doesn't get it. What do I KNOW!!! But they cry and feel sad for all the slaves that were taken to the rest of the world. How genuine! Buffalo soldiers don't know what to fight for anymore.

"Man as man for some reason never bothers to examine why someone will tell him he has to believe…to just believe, because if he doesn't he will burn in hell forever. What does it mean, really, to believe? What does believing in God do? No proof, no reasonable proof! I have a good one, if 6,000,000,000 people don't believe that I am sent to save them; they will eat a whole cow and won't be fed. They will always be hungry, and the animals, I don't know how I will deal with them yet, suggestions? With all the confusion and scams that have saturated humanity from day one, it's ridiculous for anyone to just say believe me or…, and like a dunce go along. This is the biggest joke.

"Man as man can be compared to a herd of hippos, the beach master raises his head, the rest of the hippos do likewise, he faces north, they follow suit, he thinks one way, and they do the same. And humans say they are better than animals.

"Man as man really is a funny creature. He can steal other people's land, jewelry, food, money, but to steal other people's God. Where is the shame? Man leaves one pit and jumps right into another. Way back then, man used to combine Gods. What happened? 'How many Gods do you have?' 'Oh, I have many; one for rain, one to get the girls, one for work and one to forever look young and sexy.'

"Man as man living under pretentious love with his neighbors was exposed in Iraqi.
Yes, the invasion was one of the stupidest wars in history, just like all the fought and yet to be fought holy wars, but it only lasted 21 days. It wasn't the invasion that prolonged the war for years. It was the Iraqis themselves killing each other, turning around to blame the invaders rather than blaming themselves. And to make matters worse, Muslims don't like Muslims to stop being Muslims. They are afraid of each other, and that is the truth. You can't quit publicly if you are known. Forget the sectarian killings.

"Man as man has varying degrees of fundamentalism. You want to pray for the lesser degree amongst your dear friends, brothers, sisters, wife, husband, lover, father, mother and bunch of relatives because they won't take you out now, they are civilized about it. They will wait for their God to do just that. The others you want to run away from. But be careful, the state of being brainwashed can shift from mild to strong in a twinkle of an eye. Kaboom, you are gone!

"Man as man has been given countless reasons why God is not answering his heartfelt prayers; you haven't truly forgiven others, you are not giving enough to the house of God, you are just paying lip-service to God's words, you are not praying hard enough, you are not believing hard enough, your nose is not pointing north enough, your grandmother didn't pray for you well enough, your food is not holy enough...your country is cursed by God. A day is a thousand years in God's eyes. That means Jesus died two days ago! Wait 200 years to get your prayers answered. But who has been answering some Christians' prayers?

"Man as man says in the afterlife he will enjoy endlessly in paradise (pretty much the things he does on earth) but debars other people not in his religion from enjoying themselves here. No more festivals and secular thinking for you all.

"Man as man hides behind these words...'I'm not perfect.' Then I flipped through their holy book and found this. 'You must be as perfect as your heavenly Father in heaven,' Jesus' words. Now, where is the excuse for the sexual abuses, corruptions, killings...please, someone help me fill in the rest of the sins! Really, going by their god's nature, they are acting real perfect in my view.

"Man as man, especially the Muslims now, will turn blind eyes and ears to Muslims killing Muslims but will cry to the world that other faiths and atheists are mocking their Allah. They don't even respect their own Noble truth. This is like a man that his 'holy' house is in chaos but wants to sanitize the whole world! They always complain that outsiders are quoting the Koran out of context. Really, they are the ones not seeing the whole paragraph or book for what it is. Here is a quest they should embark on. They should start fighting the Muslims that are killing Muslims just as they are ready to fight Christians and others.

"Man as man...and this is for the Muslims also for having a language that can be so flexible any word could be used to mean anything. With that in mind I look at this surah.

> *Surah 70;1*
> *They think the Day of Judgment is far off:*
> *but We see it near at hand*

The day in the verse must be 100 years...200 or a 1000? In my view it should have happened. Unless we have another easy way out that is devoid of logic and says NEAR means forever. And by the way, THEY, in the surah means the people living at that time. He sure didn't know me, let alone to address me. For the uninformed, many languages have words that could stand for many meanings. You just have to give it to the Muslims for trying.

"The last question for people who love this God so much to answer is, which God's character do they like - the Old or the New Testament one? Or would they have loved so much to live in the Old Testament era? Don't lie now, God is watching. How did I know you would not choose to come from the people that God of Israel chose to destroy or the ones their lands were taken over by the Israelites just because...oh, you don't want your papa and mama and brothers and sisters to starve to death? Oh, how considerate! However, if you faithfully chose the Old Testament time, it would be like the blacks in the land of the free wanting to live in the 1800s USA.

"Now from my understanding which is unholy I share with you.

Allah is not the most merciful, if he is, he won't burn people in hell over and over just because...and that goes for Jesus, too. Christ won't threaten people with a lake of fire for eternity. He didn't even turn the other cheek in the house of his father, he whipped them. Remember the money changers? Hey, I just committed blasphemy. They could put the whip in his hand but never say he used it. On the other hand, he's father who is the holiest could be said to have ordered massacre.

Why can't we have a cool swimming pool after this hard, unpredictable life? It's so absurd that man keeps holding on to an archaic idea of what's God, but then hops on a jet plane to carry him from place to place. Where are your camels and donkeys for transportation forever?

"And to the billion supporters of God, I say, this is not an assault on God, rather, an assault on mental slavery and the pressure to keep people within the flock. I'm not saying there is God or no God, but to lord one Jewish idea of what is God on the rest of mankind, either through so-called persuasion or trickery is religious colonization. Whereas it is okay to condemn the Gods of other people and uphold the notion of a God of a family, the so-called twelve tribes of Israel is ludicrous. And we complain that the white race is not the superior race of all races.

Here is a teaser from the very beginning of the bible - there's confusion on what's moral or not. Reading the story of Onan, you start wondering what kind of God this is.

> *Genesis 38, Verses 8-10*
> *"And Judah said unto Onan. Go in unto thy brother's*
> *wife, and marry her and raise up seed to thy brother.*
> *And Onan knew that the seed should not be his; and*
> *it came to pass, when he went in unto his brother's*
> *wife, that he spilled it unto the ground, lest that he*
> *should give seed unto his brother. And the thing which*
> *he did displeased the Lord wherefore he slew him also."*

"I'm sure all the properly educated Christians would laugh out loud if a pagan God did what God in the bible did to Onan. The only reason Christians won't see anything wrong with Onan's story is simple; they have drenched themselves in the water of the well after drinking it. If good Christians that will condemn mere man for being bad don't see anything wrong with this, then what about this? God punished Achan for stealing gold and silver from the captive with his entire family (sons, daughters, oxen, asses and sheep) by being stoned to death and their bodies burnt. Prophet Joshua would attest to that.

"You might think you have heard it all, but the hypocrisy deepens.

One of the heavenly comical things is when a Christian interviews a Muslim, so-called moderate on public TV.

First, what can a really rational person take away from this meeting of the 'holy minds'? Nothing, Zero, Nada!

'You're bad'

'I'm not bad.' (Sounding like Michael Jackson)

'Do you condemn extremists?'

'I do.'

'Islam doesn't teach that.' They continue to chat about light weight stuff, like usury...why do you take interest? You are not to do that. It's against God's law. Therefore I'm better than you, I obey

God's…Meanwhile tough questions are avoided. Important topics are conveniently left out like killing, fighting, having slaves, taking other people's land and imposing by force a religion mandated by their God or Allah, and breaking up into sects. Like, why didn't Muhammad stay in Medina where he was chased to but had to fight back to let everyone know how great Allah was? Listen, man is not that much of a fool. If they saw the beauty of Allah and how he provided well for the faithful, they would join willingly without bloodshed. I guess that advice would be evil; they had to kill people in order to save people from going to hell. Whoa!

And they both go on blah, blah, blah, but in their minds, each wants the other to come to his senses. Based on what?

Oh, I get it.

What's in my book and my personal experience, so therefore, I have the truth.

"Man lives in a world of hypocrisy, but some hypocrisies are potential bombs. So, as the hypocrisy deepens, I hear the cry of the moderates.

Has any good Muslim thought of what would happen to those 9-11 victims in front of Allah, who were even prayed for at the ground zero by some Imams!!! Soon they will build a mosque there.

That was a real life show of hypocrisy; that was reality TV at its best. What would Allah say to the true Muslims that carried out the plot? 'Thank you for killing those infidels. You did a good job. I was watching it and I sanctioned it', after all, what does *Insha Allah'* mean? 'Now, enter paradise and enjoy for all eternity'.

Then one hijacker would ask Allah, 'what are you going to do with those infidels?' And Allah would reply, 'I will burn them again and again because they didn't convert to Islam or believed in my last prophet and that makes me sad, real sad that I can't sleep.' Do I need to say more, even in the so-called Muslim world they were cheering the deaths of the 9-11 victims; it's on tape. These cheerful Muslims must have forgotten that Muslims too died in the senseless crash. Oh…I forgot, Allah would send the Muslims to heaven?

This is where all the moderates and the metaphysical-Sufis should search their hearts that's full of compassion and check their hypocrisy at the door, if they can. Yet the moderates will cry that their prophet is not respected by the radical Muslims when they cut off the hands of people that steal, sanctioned by the Prophet. Why are the moderates' children still going around with ten fingers? Don't tell me their kids don't steal?

And before anyone starts pitying the Christians too, here is a question that needs answering. Where would the forgiving Jesus send the victims of the crusaders to or the ones the Popes roasted or the Christians themselves killed?

Remember you can't enter paradise without accepting Jesus as your savior. No matter how good you are. Donate all your blood, your money and be as clean as a whistle. Care very much for the sick; belong to countless charities for all kinds of diseases or what have you. You still will end up in hell. So when you see those finely dressed and inspirational pastors on TV you now know how they see the rest of mankind in their hearts, since they always preach about listening to the voice inside. And it's such a sad thing when you see modern Christians (civilized) trying to distant themselves from the Old Testament laws. One million irrational excuses have been given. But the question that won't go away is, could any of them have told God - the father of Jesus, that those laws of old were ridiculous and evil if they were living at that time. And if not ridiculous, why not continue to practice them. Well, they find it difficult to say it even now with their excuses. Even when God himself said he used evil to carry out his holy work.

"Still hypocrisy takes a nosedive.

They continue to blame themselves for not understanding the words of Allah or God; you don't want to delve into this holy brainstorming. A whole generation will die and you're just scratching the surface of the argument.

Your heart can only go out to the sheep that has been lied to over and over, who doesn't even know it. He will fight you for trying to free his mind.

They have turned him into a vegetable. They have made him scared of his shadow, he's afraid of doing certain things on certain days. You don't need a monitoring bracelet for someone like this, fear is enough.

"And to all who pray in faith and in truth and in spirit, here is my prayer since the triangular religions agree on the Psalms.

Thank you God for allowing me to perform these good deeds in your holy name, the one that takes other people's land and gives it to his chosen, that kills babies and suckling.

And the one that opened my heart, my mind, my soul to accept your only son, Jesus, and the one that will eventually burn the infidels in hell forever. And lest I forget, the one that says Israelites should have my kind as slaves also. You are a God that keeps his promises and never fails or changes.

Thank you for all these blessings, my family, my job, my friends, my cars, and I can go on and on. And before anybody crucifies me for being creative about my prayer, here is the original version, psalms 135.

> *Praise ye the Lord. Praise ye the name of the Lord; Praise*
> *him, O ye servants of the Lord. For I know that the Lord is*
> *great and that our lord is above all gods.*
> *He causeth the vapors to ascend from the ends of the earth;*
> *he maketh lightenings for the rain; he bringeth the wind out*
> *of his treasures.*
> *Who smote the first born of Egypt, both man and beast*
> *Who sent tokens and wonders into the midst of thee, O*
> *Egypt, upon Pharaoh, and upon all his servants.*
> *Who smote great nations and slew kings*
> *And gave their land for an heritage, an heritage unto Israel*
> *his people.*

"How deep is the hypocrisy?

Can I close my eyes and ears to this?

Can I really as a true Christian go to the funeral ceremony of my best friend's parent and truly offer my condolences? Shouldn't I feel guilty, like a hypocrite, knowing my best friend's parent died a non-believer?

And when my co-worker gives birth to a baby boy or girl, can I truly share their joy, knowing they are of a different faith, and mine condemns them to hell.

And the poor baby, I already condemned him or her. There's no need for the baby to steal my bread or pick my pocket or steal my identity.

"As the hypocrisy deepens further I see missionaries rush to war torn and disaster areas with food and shelter in one hand and their holy books in another. I guess there are strings attached to their unconditional services and compassion, just like they bribed people with goods and food at the initial meetings with the so-called unbelievers around the world. You can't win people over with just stories.

"Yet the hypocrisy crisscrosses the oceans of why's. 'I can't understand how the Muslims would hate the Westerners. These people are backward in their thinking. How can a man in this day and age hold that view?'

Well, if they look around themselves, they should see the KKK and the covert racism against other people in their midst. Why point the finger? All are in the same boat of hatred and all hold a conviction like this based on foolishness for lack of a better word.

"As the hypocrisy deepens I hear something. It's the famous thinking-at-the-time argument. For starters, this view is only used by the defenders of the oppressors in any society. It's used to placate their ignorance. But is it truly stark ignorance in this case alone? Ignorance is when a man prays to his urine. This is convenient ignorance!

With this in mind, I look at the Pope's apology for all those poor victims that died horrific death at the hands of those who professed to break bread with the highest intelligence (God or Jesus). They were roasted and sometimes cooked, yes, cooked. Families were scattered; children abandoned and countless ills befell the oppressed. So the heartfelt apologies reek of the worst hypocrisy ever.

Look, unless the people who were oppressed were of the same mind. 'Please take our land, please torture us to death, please rape my mother and sister, and don't forget to take my children and sell them to the highest bidder, and my father, please continue to subdue him physically and mentally, and of course, economically, so he can forever be dependent on the crumbs that fall from the master's table.' So the master's head swells as he says to himself proudly, 'any other place and this man won't even see what I am giving him, he should be happy.'

How about 'please come and catch us, we are not hiding, we are not crying and begging your evilness, and not at all defiant and certainly we don't bleed the same blood that runs through your veins and your savior's.'

The same argument, thinking-at-the-time, is used for slavery and sitting at the back of the bus. When will man wake up? Man has always had choices. A white boy, way deluded about his honesty said he wouldn't know which side to take during the slavery and segregation eras in the US. This guy grew up in church. One of those altar boys turned nationalist. 'At least I'm honest.' he boasted. He has turned into some academician with some silly theories about man. Head full of jargons passing it as knowledge. There have always been opposite opinions, but man stubbornly defends one and then claims ignorance. How fitting!

Maybe we should put the guns and the land in the hands of the oppressed and really argue it's-the-thinking-at-the-time bullshit.

"As the hypocrisy deepens, I hear you have to have divine knowledge to interpret the Koran, Bible, Torah and other so-called holy books. The question is how do we get divine knowledge? Why so many countless divine knowledge and in fighting? They haul insults, hatred, and eternal condemnation at one another; from the Mosque to the church to the synagogue. A three-way-missile is sent on Friday, Saturday and Sunday; so much for days of prayers!

The so-called intellectuals on all sides continue to delude themselves based on their self-acclaimed enlightenment, and they're leading the ever so gullible to listen to one or the other. There's no need for divine inspiration. You only need love, not a sugar coated one, to see plainly that all these triangular religions for instance are full of hatred for one another and then for the rest of the world. And if those so-called words are the true words of the true creator, God, Yahweh, Allah, then we are in trouble, and any kindness based on kindness sake is not worth it in this world.

I don't need a PhD in theology or to be filled with spirit to arrive at this conclusion. And until we stop teaching our children hatred and passing it as love, the world will continue to be a pain for all of us.

"As man slides further into the abyss of hypocrisy, I see modern day

Christians and Muslims, well according to Islam, Muslims shouldn't kill Muslims and others…well, and the Jews cry on national television and radio that they care so much about the war torn Africa, Kosovo, and many other places and yet won't bat an eye for the destruction of entire kingdoms by their God or Allah. I guess one blood is better than the other or maybe the past is the past, why cry over spilt milk, let's deal with the present. Well, only if their creator won't judge those people on the so-called, much awaited, and much delayed judgment day. 'Don't worry; just turn the other cheek for now. I'll burn them later.'

"As the hypocrisy deepens, no one can see through its thick smoke anymore. Most of us don't want people to see us as being racist or tribalist. Nevertheless, we still find ways to condemn one another in the area of what we erroneously consider is God, the creator. We probably think we are better than the racist bastards as we like to refer to them. But in this religious superiority the line is distorted; it's interracial, intertribal, interclass, and interfamily and all are blind to it. Man doesn't know that hate is hate and love is love.

And man thinks he has finally come of age. We unfortunately continue to cherish our arrogance, embrace our prejudice and reward our ignorance.

Man must outgrow his family, tribe, color, class, tradition of hatred, religion, gender, nationalism before he can begin to see clearly.

"These are questions you ask yourself in the quiet time in your heart.

"If your book says you should fight for the cause of your God, you're far from love and compassion, my friend. You need another God.

"If your holy book tells you you're better than everyone not in your group and you shouldn't associate with them, but you benefit from the hell-bound people one way or another. Then you should carry this sign on your forehead, HYPOCRITE.

"If in your good book, some of your prophets of God killed or were told to kill by your chosen God, then you don't understand love. Or will you like God or Allah to kill you and your husband and children by his godly prophets and take your daughters as slave booties to be systematically raped? You boast of selling the most books. Yes, it's true. Books bought out of fear, suppression and ignorance and not the substance in them.

"Tell me if you would want God or Allah and his prophets (faithful of course) to take your house, land, salary, insurance, vacation money, savings, college fund, pensions, your surgery money for your face lift and breast implant, and give them to his chosen just because...(Father that created everyone, please fight my fellow creations on my behalf and kill them just for me; give me thy properties, too. Thanks). Or you'd prefer God and his prophets (army of prophets) to destroy your race, tribe, town, village or family because you believe in nothing, like I seek and believe in nothing.

"I'm sure you'd want God to test your faith, sure your faith is strong, and in the process he kills your wife and children. Don't worry or shed a tear because at the end of the trial, God will replace them with new ones like broken down toasters or punctured tires. Are all Mr. Jobs and Mrs. Jobs listening? Children ought to pray their dad shouldn't be tested. You would be surprised that a devout Christian defended this awful wrong. So, here is my desire. God please test me and let Satan kill all my family, including the newborn and my wife and you know I will pass, so that I can get new and better wife and brilliant children, I hate going through divorce. Change them as I change my wardrobe. This is the ultimate selfishness of man as man!!!

"I'm certain you'd want another man's finding of whatever paradise is to be a nightmare for you, your family and the rest of the world. Waking you up early morning with their call to prayer is done without consideration for the unbelievers. You have to know when I'm praying to my gods. How come you are sleeping?...and many more that I can't count here!

"Now I enter the phase of confusion galore.
In order for some to make sense out of the insensibility of Allah or God they create their own confusion. Rather than hand off completely, they try in their heads to rationalize the holy books. I guess they can't

see any further than these books. It's like putting a square peg in a round hole.

"They say Islam doesn't contradict Christianity. There is no name for minds like this, but they call themselves Christlam. This thinking is like marrying fire and water just like some hold on to science to find the answer to life and at the same time believe that humans have souls. Maybe we all don't know that there is no half-way in Christianity; you are either in or out. You can't think outside the box. You are just deluding yourself the more.

Still they hold on to the confusion by claiming that these books are full of sound morals. If we can't read, then we won't know better. But anyone that can put a, b, c, together and still maintains this falsity should see a real shrink.

"Yet they hold on tighter, you can't wrestle it from their tight holy grip. They so badly want to anchor their faith in these books that they now think the books were tampered with. Who told them? Never mind asking, though. And if they do know, why can't they print the right one? I am sure God will finally be pleased with the correct version. Actually Queen Elisabeth commissioned the Bishops to do just that, called the Bishop Bible as against the Geneva Bible.

I think the problem is they find it hard to swallow that a supposed loving God or Allah would commit all those atrocities, and they had better not contemplate it or hell will be their home for eternity.

"Here is an example of their feeble attempts at whitewashing the holy book. The Christian scholars are now giving the holy book a gentle expression. They call it 'Clear Word' or some new-Interpretation fancy title. Remember this is from English to English. So I flipped through to see whether 'my bad' would be there. No. But instead of them to use words like, 'God kills', they now use, 'God takes the life of that wicked man.'

Another interesting one is that Peter and the Holy Spirit didn't kill the couple that sold the land and lied about the price. They just fell down and died. The most ridiculous one is the burnt offering of the daughter of Jephthah because of the father's silly vow. Here they write that if it's an animal that comes running to meet him after his victory, he will sacrifice it to the lord. (I saw an American soldier coming home from Iraq and at the airport an elephant ran to welcome him, shouting sacrifice me please, please.) The second part is even more irrational. And if it's someone from my household that comes running to meet me, I will dedicate him or her to serve you, God. First, how do you force someone to serve God for life on your promise? (God, if I win the Olympic gold medal, I will dedicate all New Yorkers to serve you as Muslims.) This is deception employed by God fearing scholars, propaganda 101.

But the one that tops it all is that of Job. In this interpretation Satan only has charge of the earth. (If you live on Mars or in space capsule, Satan can't corrupt you) Other planets now have representatives and they all meet once in a while to confer with God. This must be why Pluto got demoted from a planet status because the representative didn't come to a meeting? There is more. Now it was Satan who came to God regarding faithful Job and not the other way round. Still nothing can make this clean or nice sounding. God now goes with the 'theory' of Satan. (God in the lab to see whether plutonium and nitrogen wouldn't result in combustion) But God passionately commands Bad Satan not to take Job's life but everything else…well. His initial family still died in the new version. They couldn't whitewash that. Man is trying to make God good. Shouldn't it be the other way round? There are many more in the white-washing book. It's a treasure trove for comics.

"I take a look into the near distance but the fog of confusion covers my sight. These holier than thou are told not to enjoy this world, it was preached by Muhammad, but to expect a better and lasting one in the afterlife. He would rank as one of the top ten people that really enjoyed this world; women and power. Well, this is the question they should ask themselves. Why did Allah create me in the first place? Where shall we put Solomon's enjoyment? Hefner, the Playboy magazine owner, can't hold a candle to Solomon in this area, even with an overdose of Viagra. Tell me how you rival a thousand sexy women? And all the bling-bling worn today by the rappers can't compare either to Solomon's bling. And besides, do these people have sex for the purpose of procreation only or 99.9% for pleasure? I hear women are like my fields, I can plough them anytime I please. Isn't that pleasure? Isn't that enjoying this life?

"As the confusion deepens, the intellectuals and the deep thinkers tell us the stories in the Old Testament are meant as fables to help people learn the true purpose of life, and that they didn't happen. Well, these Christian apologists deserve an award for making Jesus appear as a fool; their Lord and Savior referred to the stories of Jonas, Solomon and many Old Testament stories as true, not fables. Who is right and who is wrong?

"I am further confused about good and evil, angels and demons, right and wrong because anyone that is familiar with the Jewish God turned everybody's God now knows that this God kills indiscriminately. You sin, he kills, you don't sin, and he still kills. Just like the Holy Spirit that is supposed to minister to the Christians killed them, too. Remember Ananias…

Really, I won't want to take my case to this God during judgment day. He can change anytime. His past records are not encouraging. He can toss you in hell and the hardened criminal or should I say sinner, who is not a believer, can end up at the right hand side of Jesus. A black man would have a better chance in an all white jury in the land of the free and the brave in the 1800s.

"Am I wrong to think this way? How do people come to choose one belief over another? Am I very lost and confused? So I flipped through the noble Koran and came upon this verse given by Allah.

Surah 3: 164
The misfortune which befell you when the two
armies was ordained by God, so that He might know the
true believers and know the hypocrites.

"Now, the question is, why didn't Allah take out the untrue believers before going to war? And surely we can't forget that Mohammed himself ran to Medina in the heat of a battle. All the same, now it implies that a Muslim army should always win, unless they are false believers.

Then I flipped open the bible and read about Gideon's army. And in this case God actually told Gideon to test the soldiers for readiness before the battle and, the number of men considered ready was reduced from 2,000 to 300 men or so. The mission was successful.

Who did Napoleon, Alexandra the Great and Gengha Khan consult?

"Now, here is where the confusion about man, himself, comes in. It's impossible for man to cooperate or react to any rule or promise 100%. It's like the unwritten law of gravity. It's just what it is. But what we know is that when a holy book gives sanction to kill in the name of Allah and we pretend that we as a society shouldn't talk about it, then, we are failing as one. So when we say logically that not all Muslims engage in this barbaric act, that doesn't means we should disregard the source (holy book)? If we do, then we are fooling ourselves. Not all nationalists kill or discriminate, either, and surely not all soccer fans fight the opponent! So...?

"The Christians in the western world condemn the Jews for lack of divine understanding that the messiah had already come, but will only come again to kind of draw the curtain on the world. Christians all over follow their former colonial masters in condemning the Jews as well. This is really not hard to figure out. Just follow the leader. They can't see this in a million years. However, there goes the love-hate relationship between these two opposing views about God. Forget their third cousin for now.

And if this is what they call true or divine love, then I'm sure I'll never find it. I won't be allowed to join the coalition of the Jews and Christians. They won't even take my donation to move the Jews to one spot or plant olive trees in Israel. How come they are only moving the less fortunate Jews back to Israel? Why not the ones in the Western countries and the good old USA? Because according to some Christians all Jews must return to Israel before Jesus comes.

It's no longer Jews and dogs not allowed here, but you, John. You can't come in with your thoughts. For a country that doesn't really believe in Christ, (Seen as a fake messiah by 95% of the Jews) it's amazing how they enjoy the benefits of Christ from Christians all over the world! They openly take their money but fight to keep the Christian Jesus away from their children. 'We only use your Dollars here but can't sacrifice heaven for that.' Who says hypocrisy is limited to some?

"Sometimes when man as man loses his faith, he asks his unfair God 'why didn't you hear my prayers for my dying this and dying that...'. You have to wonder why this important person should be let down by a God that takes the lives of babies and children for no good reason. We should all pity this wonderful soul. Sorry!

"In order for man as man to understand his world, he comes up with the word, destiny, which invariably clashes with the free will concept. Anyway, they say whatever happens is from his God, good or bad. Primarily, people who hold this view are those that believe in judgment day. So the question is why would God destine me to kill unbelievers, for instance, and then would send them to hell? Or why would he kill some himself and still be okay for him to sit and judge them? Hitler must have been destined. Look, if a mountain falls on a baby or on a pregnant woman that I can understand, but to have a God and prophets take people's lives and have you tell me it's destiny is just like you pissing in my backyard and telling me it's rain. Unless these discerning minds don't complain about anything in life, but they do, maybe the one destining people tell them which is which.

"This confusion is just as pathetic as it is sympathetic, a true story. The wife is a 7ᵗʰ Day Adventist and goes to church on Saturdays. The husband believes in nothing. One day she came back from church unhappy or rather angry that some church members said the husband would be burnt in hell and other heartless tongue-lashing he got from them. Rather than the husband to be angry too he asked the wife, 'so what is wrong with what they said.' She replied, 'how could they say something that terrible about the man I love dearly.' The husband thought about it carefully and said, 'they are right according to the bible. It's you, honey...that's confused.' You would think she wouldn't go next saturday, but you'd be wrong. That means you've not understood the power of fear and confusion. She woke up briefly and then went back to slumber...went back to being a robot. One 'day' she will wake up fully. (She must have forgotten herself, when she wanted the husband to convert, that she pointed to their 'manifesto', I think #7 on the list or so that unbelievers/hubby would be burnt once in hell.)

"Can someone help me see through the window of confusion?

Some Buddhists bought some livestock in order to free them so they can quickly climb the ladder of evolution to the level of humans. 'Please, don't eat them, set them free, its bad karma. Eat fruits and vegetables instead, as if the veggies are not living things, and also the fact that some plants eat meat for nourishment.

Well, they have to write a letter of petition to the heads of the jungle, lion and tiger. Eat grass so you can evolve faster to our level. Maybe they should meditate themselves to Nirvana quickly. By the way who created the non-existence? I will leave this for the Dalai Lamas (Lamas are numerous—I like the one in China) to answer. Have they stopped setting themselves on fire for non Nirvana issues or trying to imagine the sound of a one-handed clap?

"Sometimes you just have to laugh at man's logic in order not to go crazy with their holy argument. So I take a look at the much awaited rapture.

> *Thessalonians chapter 4: verse 17*
> *Then we which are alive and remain shall be caught up*
> *Together with them in the clouds to meet the Lord*
> *In the air: and so shall we ever be with the Lord.*

Now the 'we' in the verse is a holy we that stands for generation after generation. And the guy that actually made this statement, was either raptured or still living now in the 21st century waiting to be raptured! It's an elongated WE. Come to think of this piece of harmless info about the coming of Jesus by an Holy-Spirit-inspired writer, you wonder why Jesus didn't come in his days…well, probably because the Holy Spirit didn't tell him that Israelites must come back to their land in 1948, that all the nations of the world must be preached to, that all the Jews must take Jesus as their Lord, that computer must be invented, that there must be global warming, that Soviet Union must crumble, that communist China must compromise and tango with capitalism and love it, that US must win the world cup, real soccer world cup, and that…yeah, China must be a democracy, that I must be a Christian, too. I'm running out of things to come before the coming…

Suddenly John stopped. "What did you see and what did you

hear?" Before they could give him a reply, he started laughing and they joined in the laughter that echoed around the entire world, reaching up to the heavens.

As they were laughing, going back to the building John decided to let them in on a secret; the ultimate open secret.

"When I was giving the stories of how other people thought the world came about, I deliberately left out one important aspect and it's probably the most vital to the triangular-religion." John said.

"Tell me," Jack wanted to know.

"It's about Egypt. People have given Egyptian Gods a bad rap due to the deliberate suppression of their religion. But thanks in part to Napoleon for his insatiable urge of conquering the world. After he conquered the country, looted the treasures, there was one thing that fascinated him about Egypt and that was its civilization. This brought the curious minds all over to solve the mystery of the ancient writings; the hieroglyphics. They are known as Egyptologists and their findings make every hero in the Bible and the Koran a double." John alluded.

"What do you mean?" Den asked.

"Moses mirrored Akhenaton of the Egyptian religion. Everything about them was similar; their age and position in power, likewise, Solomon and Jacob. If you read the ancient scripts you are bound to come to the conclusion that these guys were living simultaneously in Egypt and in what we know as Israel." John answered.

"That's impossible." Jack said looking serious, trying to connect the dots. Magic secrets finally revealed.

"Here is the real story recorded by man..." John started. "Moses, whose real name was Akhenaton, was following in the footsteps of his Father, Amenhotep the 3rd, who introduced the concept of monotheism in Egypt, which infuriated many would be jobless priests. In the great upheaval that followed, Moses was expelled; he ran away only to return to persuade 'Israelites' to follow him to worship as he pleased. That started the idea of 'promised land' to this day. He could have led any group that would follow him to start another empire elsewhere. The great Moses was an Egyptian not an Israelite!"

"There is another mirror image here." Jack informed.

"Where?" Den asked.

"The sun god and the God that about 3 billion people now bow down to, pray to, praise night and day." Jack replied.

"You mean the Christians and the Muslims and the Jews, alike." Den agreed.

"Isn't it ironic? Man has gone to space, studied the moon (the moon landing I hold my breath), the sun, the other planets and we still pray to the sun; fighting for the sun." Jack summed it up.

"No, it's not like the Egyptians were worshipping the sun. The sun just represented the power and glory of The God to them." John clarified the issue. "There is more."

"Say no more." Jack said.

"The Easter Holiday is just like the Breath of life celebrated 5000 years ago in Egypt. And the famous story of David and Goliath, please, another plagiarism of Twthomosis' story, including some of the so much loved praises in the books of psalms and proverbs. The alabaster ointment was stolen from the Egyptian culture, just like the very Ark of the lord that Israelites used to go to battles with in the Old Testament, and similar to a time in Europe too, way back, when they used to carry the image of Mary, mother of Christ to battles---so much for the 'mother of God' being full of divine love. Anyway, the Book of the Dead, The Book of the Gates and many books by the Egyptians found their way into the Holy Bible.

"Even baptism, the art of dipping people in water for purification was stolen by the Christians. It was practiced way before Jesus came to earth by other religions, and the story of the great flood accredited to Noah, stolen as well. You see, the bible is a mixture of stolen materials, fiction and some recorded history." John demystified.

"Be very scared of the unknown, but please don't die foolish." Jack begged.

"There's this last thing, though." John continued.

"What can top all this?" Jack asked.

"You know how the Bible is so meticulous about details, describing the creeks, the water falls, the history of many tribes, the sharing of the lands and the millions of names and much more. But nowhere in the bible will you find the names of the reigning Pharaohs. I'm sure James Bond should be able to figure this out." John informed.

"Even all knowing Allah, Gabriel and Mohammed didn't remember the names of the Pharaohs in the Koran?" Jack was beside himself.

"Of course, we know the names of all the Egyptian kings or Pharaohs, but to further compound their lies we are told Prophet Moses wrote the five famous books of Moses…or I should respect the guy by calling him his real name, it's impossible for Akhenaton to have written his death in the book of 'Moses'." John added.

"We have been fooled. Even most Egyptians now are Muslims or Christians, and they probably started Judaism. They carry their treasure loosely in their hands and hold dear in their hearts the fake gems." Den sighed.

"Also in Tanzania where they have found 4 million-year-old human fossil, the country is divided mostly into Christianity and Islam." John added.

"How sad is the mind of man. Man has made such incredible innovation in terms of science and technology, yet his gods are still in the prehistoric era!" Jack exclaimed.

They all went back to the room to relax. Soon they would all assemble to hear what would be the latest news concerning the project.

"If it takes a man to defend God in any kind of abuse; then, maybe, man should find another God that can fight his own battle without the help of a mere mortal."
Stan

"We are fighting for freedom when we haven't freed ourselves yet."
Unknown.

Reflection

They sat in the conference room waiting for Bob. Everyone seemed to be in a good spirit. The door finally opened and he stepped in.

"Hi guys. Sorry it took all day to give you this news. This is going to be brief, really, there's nothing to say other than field work starts tomorrow." Bob said.

"Finally, we can get our hands dirty." Jack was ready.

They all got up and instead of going out through the front door took the back one that was obvious to all led nowhere. But one after the other all of them went through the door except Bob who sat there thinking; maybe these guys had found a way out.

John was the last person to leave and there was a mysterious smile on his face as he looked intently at Bob. Then the door closed behind him. Bob was curious. He got up and opened the door. There was no exit. The only thing that he saw written on a big banner was 'Still searching'. That didn't make sense to him.

Where did all the guys disappear to? He shut the door and went the opposite way.

'What's happening? Are they playing tricks on me?' He couldn't figure it out. But really this wasn't the time to play practical jokes on your boss. Not good. But more urgent matter was Ruth. He hadn't been able to get in touch with her. He would call Frank to re-assemble his heavenly team tomorrow.

He got into his car and zoomed off. He couldn't wait to share his experience with his wife. But that wouldn't be any time soon, there was traffic.

Suddenly his thoughts went back to all the discussions he had with those guys. He couldn't even picture their faces clearly anymore. But their arguments stayed in his head, to the last detail.

'It does seem we are of different stars willed by an unknown knowledge and in the affairs of men conflicts and compromise ensue like a pledge. Mmm, life is like a maze. Yet in all these complexities, we tirelessly search for the ultimate truth, but the journey is like heading into a black hole; the abyss. Because the unrelenting hold of culture guides your views and the uncanny grip of religion caresses the innermost part of you, and they tear you apart in a world overflowing with countless opinions. You try to swing to the left or to the right looking for a balance that seems elusive, just to survive.

'So when we're born into this world according to some people, we know nothing. But can that be true? How do you explain some people knowing something without really been taught? Where do they get that from? But we do get some attachments from our society; our names, language, culture and religion. Sometimes they even give us our likes and dislikes without our ever knowing it. How do we explain the spread of tribalism and racism for so long? Hatred without basis!

'I'd be very suspicious when I'm old enough to think for myself and my parents tell me we are the chosen people of The God. That we are special and given certain privileges because out of the abundance and mercy of the creator we are to be the light of the world or universe. Or it could be my group or race or tribe that makes such a heavenly claim. Shouldn't I ask myself whether those not chosen have eyes like me, nose like me, and heart like me? Simple things like that; the a, b, c and 1,2,3 of being a human? But I'll continue to delude myself 'cause it feels good inside and when I get to paradise I'll tell G-d to look after the non-chosen for the good work they do for people like me on earth. You can give them bread. Hey, are we still doing the unleavened thing. I will like mine with steak and the purest wine. Wait a minute, am I mixing this chosen thing up. Am I an Aztec or a Jew?

'But then, most of us just take it as the gospel truth and we walk amongst the rest of mankind with pride, that unbeknownst to us is shallow. It's not my fault that these people aren't special, and wear something that won't confuse God about his chosen. You know them, every group has one. As if it's that cut and dried. The irony of it is that a larger percentage of people do have this notion in their heads. How do you migrate to another man's land and be a racist to anybody?

'On the other hand, we are quick to see the shallowness or pride of a beautiful person that flaunts it in front of everyone or the bragging of a rich man. Yet, in the most important issue to man; the afterlife, he claims the creator's mercy for himself alone. This is the most egotistical of them all. Nothing comes close to it. But we all reward this behavior. Shouldn't this delusion stop with me? What did I do to deserve such blessings, dwelling in paradise with the creator? Because, if we truly take a look at ourselves, the way this world is right now, we'll see another human being in ourselves. So what will be the criteria that God will use to select me and discard others like a used syringe? Once you start thinking like this, I guess that's what they call waking up.

'Looking at the major religions contesting with one another about knowing the unknown, it's interesting to see how everyone sees everyone. But it's hard to digest the fact that everyone's hypocrisy is so apparent, yet they are not ashamed of it. To man, it's not a matter of shame, rather one of victory in the conviction that Satan or devil or whatever you call it is holding them back, "thank God, I am not one of them."

'So, to the Christians and this depends on your type of Christianity, after all, the holy spirit helps all different denominations to understand the holy bible, well, you can only wonder when each claims this supernatural understanding while a Christian of another denomination is claiming the opposite concerning the same story. So it's better not to delve into the bottomless pit on this one.

'Nevertheless, to a good Christian, all those who don't believe in Christ as their personal savior will perish in everlasting fire. No exceptions, even teenagers that die in the wrong religion.

> *Matthew Chapter 11 Verse 22*
> *But I say unto you, It shall be more tolerable for Tyre*
> *and Sidon at the day of judgment, than you.*

But believers have put a human face on the no exception issue by including babies and people with mental problems in paradise. I wish I'd prayed to this God to die within months of breathing air.

'The Christians have now stolen the history of the dinosaurs and put it in their six-day-creation tale. Really I don't know how they could steal gigantic creatures like that and put them in that tiny black book. In order to maintain their illusory tale of creation, everything and anything must be in their story. People who accept this injustice regarding the 'dinos' are beyond understanding. I'm sure when the green men from outer space start appearing they will move some chapters around and fit them in, too. "They are from the tribe of...?

'At least the Neanderthals didn't get any recognition in the bible regardless of mountains of evidence. Let's leave that for now. Maybe, Muhammad would know? I wonder whether the blood of Jesus would cover them, too.

'Anyway these Christians should first focus on other Christians that are not in their denomination to convert them before preaching to the rest of the world. Because only one kind of the Christian-faith will make it to heaven!

'How did Noah fit dinosaurs in the ark? Maybe I'm reading this literally. Pardon me. Even so, did they just die off after the flood? But seriously God or Allah never destroyed the world, the whole world. Give me a break. Did the sea creatures die because of too much water? Because I can swear to you that the turtle said to Noah, "Don't save me. I can live on land and in water. I will see you after the great flood in 41 days".

To the Jews, well, they pride themselves of being the chosen just like any other tribe that claims they know their own God, nothing strange here. Every tribe is of the same divine opinion.

'Whatever their idea is about God and this world, the intriguing thing is that they hardly ever go out to convert people of other races. So many times God warned them not to mingle with his after-thought-creations, but you can only do business with them or have them as slaves.

'It's an exclusive club. But if you are a Jewish woman and marries outside your God-chosen-people, that lucky man becomes a Jew, halleluiah. But in their minds, you're not a full-fledged Jew because the orthodox Jews are still trying to keep the converted ones out. Stories abound in the newspapers.

'But through them the rest of mankind will somewhat get something, whatever that something is. And also you'd better bless them. If not…God will crush you like a bug; you don't want any plagues now, do you? You'd better not hate Muhammad too or…

'So, they really look at the rest of mankind not as equal in the sight of God. This view becomes a dangerous way to teach your children in this world as we know it. And they complain about the Saudi's syllabus that's packed with the hatred of the Jews and the infidels. If they ever have political power in this world they would use it the way they see the rest of us as instructed by their God.

'And then the Muslims, this is an interesting group. They claim to share the same fatherhood in Abraham because he slept with the Egyptian slave and, she turned into the mother of the Arabs. How could she be their mother? Was she the first of her kind who eventually gave birth to all Egyptians? But Muslims can't claim blood brothers or sisters unless they are of the same family, in a way preserving their Allah given lineage. You can however; claim brotherhood of Islam. Now I'm confused.

With all this confusion, we don't even know which son was offered for sacrifice, Ishmael or Isaac?

'But, somehow you build a nation of Islam from all races. This is an all inclusive club. And the reason is not far-fetched. It was a matter of life and death during the formative year of Islam. People were needed, of all kinds, to fight for the goal of the religion. The more the merrier.

'In a way God has now opened the exclusive club of the Jews, because they went astray according to Mohammed. But there is a catch, you must be a Muslim and accept Mohammed as the last prophet of God to all mankind, otherwise you're playing with fire forever. Just as the choices expand on one hand, they shrink on the other.

'As a Muslim I go out into the world seeing others who are not Muslims as infidels. Not worthy of Allah's blessings and yet I beg from them. And I'm told or rather instructed by Allah to stay away from them. But in reality Muslims can't live in isolation from the rest of the world, whether they believe it or not. (But the moment they are a considerable size in a multi-community they carve out their state, as if they will live in harmony with other Muslims!) They are doing it as I'm thinking right now. They trade with infidels, marry infidels and kill infidels, after all, Muslims shouldn't kill Muslims according to Mohammed, but others are…hey, they don't matter. Just like black on black violence should stop. Why not, don't kill anybody, and don't perpetuate violence against another human being, period. We should be very careful where we get our holy advice from.

'I can even migrate to the land of the infidels. They migrate in large numbers to green pasture before the heavenly one promised by Mohammed and start demanding infidel's laws changed. They take infidel's help, money and sympathy; use the inventions of devil's people. But you can't go to their countries and dress the way you want. Hey, democracy is about numbers, at least for now. (If I'm a true Muslim I won't use their devices in the name of Allah, like cell phone, computers, car, plane, missiles, TV, radio, and this and that…gee, I won't have anything until I get to paradise, good…)

'And they must not say anything against my Koran or my prophet or else, its war. On the other hand, I can say anything against their so-called God and pagan rituals and condemn them outright. It makes you wonder. The be-header does not want the sword near his head.

'This is the group that's fighting so hard for acceptance and reaching all out for proof, even in science. They are even claiming that Mohammed's name can be found in Hindu bible. There is no need to go into this because believing in reincarnation kills this argument in its tracks by Hindu worshippers.

'But looking at the so-called "why Islam" is interesting. They are claiming that man originated from the ocean; water. So if man was created from the sea that would mean Adam and Eve evolved, following the theory of Darwin. That also would mean Allah didn't create Adam, he evolved. Then how did Eve and Adam evolve at the same time and not many more humans scattered around the Atlantic Ocean or the Pacific or the pond near my house? That also would mean that apes or gorillas could be our forefathers, they share like 99% of our DNA. (Then how come the animals don't have souls?) Or did Adam walk out of the sea like the Atlantic man? I am sorry again. I am a man that lacks understanding of the 'Noble truth' or, the noble interpretations by the apologists trying to further delude themselves about a faith that was borrowed and manipulated by a man in order to achieve his ambitious goal.

'And in their mad rush to show Muhammad that they are fighting their own jihad in the intellectual arena, in order to be counted among the ones that would make it to paradise, they run into self-conflicting theories that further compound the already contradictory Koran.

These self-acclaimed scholars think because they can read and write; therefore, they can be logical. The answer is a fat no. Thank goodness they fight with the pen and not with the sword like Muhammad. I've got a good point for them to ponder. Beast in the Arabic word could also mean dinosaur. "See, see, even the Koran mentioned it. How could this information not come from the Creator HIMSELF? How could an unlettered man be aware of this?"

'Let me piece together their threads of sound evidence. But first, did Adam and Eve's children marry one another? How does the Koran explain this in-breeding, the book that contains all knowledge?

'Here are the self-contradictions of Muhammad's words regarding who will eventually make it to paradise.

> *Believers, Jews, Christians and sabaeans- whoever believes*
> *in God and the last day and does what is right- shall be*
> *rewarded by their lord; Surah:2:61*

'For clarity there's no mention of believing in the last prophet. What do I make of the second statement? That if you choose any other religion other than Islam you will be amongst the losers.
surah---3:83

'And this is their favorite answer when asked why is Islam forcing everyone (that is if they can) to join the only true faith?

> *There shall be no compulsion in religion. Surah--2:255*

'But if you read the complete paragraph you will discover that it says once anyone understands Islam, you will just know not to worship idols, nothing about not forcing, really. The fact that man says a word doesn't mean he carries out the true meaning of the word in question as the next quotes will tell us. He was actually making wars, not defending himself in wars.

> *'Fight against them until idolatry is no more and God's*
> *religion reigns supreme'---surah-2:193*

Prophet, make war on the unbelievers and the hypocrites, and dealSternly with them.. Surah--66:7

Believers, make war on the infidels who dwell around you. Deal firmly With them. Surah--9:121

'When all these religious people use words like hypocrite, fear, peace and love and compassion, you will think they actually know what they are saying. No, they don't. Looking at Muhammad that was always talking about justice and being fair to the orphans and then he, himself, kept slave-girls. And the way they shy away from talking about the girls issue is laughable. After all, that was the practice of old. Black and Arab Muslims would argue like that. But asked whether people were worshipping different Gods then, amidst of hundreds of other things people used to do, like stealing. Why fight for old-new God and not against slavery? And why can't we do it now? I need a slave girl, no, girls.

'Even Mary, the mother of Jesus, was barely a teenager before the holy spirit decided she was matured enough for the Savior to come through her, why blame the Prophet and many religious-cult leaders now? Nine-year-old Aisha's marriage to the prophet was in order as one of the benefits that holy men enjoyed. Some Muslims say that the marriage was for creating an alliance. What alliance, alliance with an infidel kingdom? Wouldn't that be like dining with the devil that they throw stone at? Or was it an alliance with another Islamic kingdom? Then I don't know what to say to that.

'Yet another half truth, the truth we are made to believe coming from irrefutable source claims that all communities, and that means, all. Every part of the world, no part left untouched because Allah is fair and just and gives everyone a chance to hear the truth before punishment is given. It's not like human rule that says ignorance of the law is not an excuse.

An apostle is sent to each community--surah 10:47

'Now consider this truth which is actually true judging by the history of the religion. Yes, finally, I agree. This scripture categorically said two communities before the last one, the Arabs'.

*'The scriptures were revealed only to two communities
before us; 'Had the scriptures been revealed to us
we would have been better guided than they.'--surah 6:157*

'Guess no more, I am sure your community didn't get theirs and the Egyptians didn't either. Sometimes their lame arguments are so annoying you wonder where the Egyptians got the knowledge to build a remarkable society from. Believe it or not, Islam claims without it man has no knowledge. Knowledge is the weapon of the believers, they secretly boast. This is really going too far. Hey, the Christians too say without the bible man won't know what's moral. Whoa!

'The pathetic comparison of the religion to science is comical. Muslims will interpret anything slightly close to what a poet will use in form of an analogy to mean God's words regarding physical creation.

*The sun hastens to its resting -place.. the sun is not allowed
to overtake the moon, nor does the night outpace the day.
Surah--36:37 & 40*

*Are the disbelievers unaware that the heavens and the earth
were but one solid mass which We tore asunder...surah
21:26*

*It was He that gave the sun his brightness and the moon her
light...surah 10:5*

'These above sayings are what constitute science 101 to them. To them, now that science says the sun moves and nobody knew this before means the prophet was God's mouth piece. The way the sun moves according to science is quite different from the way the quote is suggesting. This one appears like the sun and the moon are about to do a hundred-meter dash in the Olympics. And the second statement means to them that it's the big bang theory that the scientists are trying to explain. This is easy to understand. That means we can see the heavens. We can even get a better picture of it with the Hubble telescope. Where is Allah? And the third one can be explained by a fifth grade student. This also implies that the sun and the moon have separate light. It should read likewise, the sun gives the moon its light, not He, Allah. But how can anyone open the eyes of a true believer? Maybe this will and we can end the science baloney once and for all. Science is getting a bad name already, it doesn't need this one.

> *The heaven, how it was raised on high? The mountains,*
> *how they were set down? The earth, how it was made flat?*
> *surah---88:17*

'Well, science says the earth is not flat. Maybe this surah should be put under contradiction. Now that we are done with pseudoscience, let's move on to my favorite contradiction that needs no explanation.

> *Every misfortune that befalls the earth, or your own persons,*
> *is ordained before We bring it into being. --*
> *surah 57:22*

> *(Contradiction)*
> *whatever good befalls you, it is from God: and whatever ill*
> *from yourself. Surah---4:80*

'They so much want to distant themselves from the bible; after all, they have the correct version from Allah. Just like the Christians distance themselves from the Old Testament laws. So they now say the earth was not destroyed by the flood. Mohammed always referred to Noah's people and not the whole of mankind. That is true according to the Koran, until you read this also from the Koran.

> *And Noah said: lord, do not leave a single unbeliever on the*
> *earth. surah-71:27.*

'Just another contradiction, or maybe there were Muslims before Mohammed and, Buddha was the prophet Allah sent to his community.

Apart from all this clear evidence that the believers are blind to, what about these sayings that give little regard for a human life.

> *God has purchased from the faithful their lives and worldly*
> *goods, and in return has promised them the garden. They*

will fight for the cause of God, they will slay and be slain.
surah--9:111

Whether unarmed or well-equipped, march on and fight for
the cause of God... Surah---9:41

It was not you, but God, who slew them. Surah--8:17

'This is the saddest statement of them all, when a man is made
to believe that if he kills, he's not responsible, but its Allah that kills.
Talk of shifting blame to Allah. I thought Satan was always the
culprit.

Why would I want to listen to a prophet of God when he has this
to say about my parents; about my family that raised me and fed me,
took care of me and countless more...not to attend their burial? And
Allah would put a curse on those that hate Mohammed.

Believers, do not befriend your fathers or your brothers if
they choose unbelief in preference to faith. Surah--9:23

He that hates you (Muhammad) shall remain childless.
Surah---108:1&3

'How is this a wise statement in the first place? I will leave this to
the Imams to explain and lastly, because I can go on and on till the
messiah comes...

'We have predestined for hell numerous jinn and men's
surah---7:177

'This statement by itself needs no more explanation, but with
man you have to break it down. This simply means that no one can
change Allah's plan. Why bother preach the new religion to me. I can
go on and on talking about the wisdom of using sand to wash your
hands and face if you can't find water in the desert before praying. Or
saying stars rise and set. Or "believers, retaliation is decreed for you
in bloodshed: free man for a free man, a slave for a slave, and a female
for a female...or if you can't marry four women without loving one

more than the other, marry one or slave girls that you own because that is just." Gee, it's unjust to have a slave let alone marry your slaves in the first place.

'In conclusion, what I see here is that they hide the faults of their prophet and highlight the good works; no mention of slave girls or slaves and under age marriages. The treatment of women is not consistent. They now see things that their Allah-sent never saw, thinking for him and Allah. And please what has finding a lost city by the archeologists got to do with authenticity? The people who lived there knew it existed, why would God use this as an example of his might, to prove what? Besides, the travelers told Mohammed about the city in question. They now hate the Jews and the Christians because they have been brainwashed by the man. They see the faults the man saw and now carry the legacy of hate with them. Just like the African Christians now believe that the Jews should be converted if they want to be saved by Jesus; divine idea planted in their heads by the colonial masters; divine-colonial-masters.

'Then we have the moderates furiously pleading with any sympathetic ear that the extremists have hijacked Islam, a religion of peace, and only true path.

'To a layman or someone who is ignorant of the religion, their plea will seem honest. But the question is, can a so-called moderate look Mohammed, whose perfect life mankind should mirror, in the eyes and say no to him concerning fighting for the afterlife.

'Or say, Mohammed, I can't do this.

> *Surah 4:92*
> *God has exalted the men who fight with the*
> *persons above those who stay at home. God has promised all*
> *a good reward; but far richer is the recompense of those who*
> *fight for him.*

'(Why wonder then that the moderates are secretly sending money to people who fight for the cause of Allah. It's a 'fact' that a Muslim that physically fights gets a better heaven. So it's not that they are 'crazy'. They could be fighting to get a better part of Manhattan in paradise)
Or say to Prophet Mohammed, let's not pursue them anymore.

Surah 4:103
Seek out the enemy relentlessly.

Maybe, they will be able to add this to the pillars of Islam.

Surah 2:216
Fighting is obligatory for you, much as you dislike it. But
you may hate a thing although it is good for you, and love a
thing although it is bad for you.

'The other question that a rational person should ask is, what is the cause of Allah that is worth fighting and dying for? Recently, a so-called radical Muslim extended Islam to nations that were not Islamic and many people found this to be hilarious; Westerners and some Muslims who wanted peace. But this radical man was only following the footsteps of the Prophet Mohammed. It's a respectable way of saying, convert to Islam or we will deem it fit to take over your nation.

And before all peace seeking Christians and Jews alike condemn this barbaric behavior, they should talk to Moses and Joshua that were commanded by God in the Bible before they make a sound comment. That was the same way God instructed Moses. The way God, Allah, or Yahweh and his armies of prophets pursued their goal put dreaded Satan out of job; satanic jobs in recession.

'Fighting for the cause of Allah is clear. Convert everyone. They must want to go to heaven by force. Remember, no compulsion in religion? That statement is not worth the paper it's written on. Just like the 'separate but equal justice' law in America during the segregation era.

'The long and short of it is simple. Fighting for the cause of Allah is open ended. If they have the power, they will use it and will not lose any sleep because according to man, his good action is backed by his holy book. But then, after everyone becomes a Muslim, they will start to fight and kill each other on the grounds of "You're not Muslim enough." The people in paradise will be reduced drastically, hope you make it.

'I love the moderates because they sound so sincere. So, here is a thought for those moderates that secretly sanction suicide bombings. When they see a suicide bomber, a man heading for martyrdom in the crowd either in the western countries that they rush to for better living and tolerance or in the Islamic countries, rather than run away, should give him or her an embrace and shout "Allah is great" together.

'And if Allah can see the minds of men as proudly stated in the Koran, boy oh boy, he should have killed all the Hindus, Buddhists, Christians, Jews, non-believers, Pagans and Africans, for not covering their bodies due to their weather, and not forgetting the moderates in Islam, too.

'Even the tactic of strapping bomb on yourself becomes a strategy of choice because man can't face the enemy head on. The Tamil Tigers made it popular. So where do they go when the Tigers blow themselves up for their cause or nation? The Kamikaze did the same thing. Who would give them 72 virgins? It's a useless way man destroys himself in the name of a heroic or holy nonsense. And yes, there are virgins mentioned in the Koran ready for the faithful. How many women does a man need, anyway?

> *We created the houris and made them virgins, loving*
> *companions for those on the right hand: a multitude from*
> *the men of old, and a multitude from the*
> *latter generations. Surah--56:28*

'I still don't see virgins mentioned for the women. Only men need virgins? Women are indeed equal in Islam on earth and in heaven. And yet women are willing to blow themselves up to go to the promised paradise. But then, women are controlled and forced by men in this religion.

'Needless to say the Muslims around the world can't live in harmony; we already have the American Muslims condemning Saudi Islam, Nigerian Muslims condemning Iraqi Islam and these are the people advocating Islam as the religion for all mankind. Are they on this planet? Are they breathing the same oxygen? I can't understand their rationality. It is mind-boggling.

'If you take a deeper look at the whole quagmire that billions of people now find themselves in, you will see that this God of Abraham has caused man a lot of misery and bloodshed. And there are so many mistakes this all-knowing God made.

'One is restarting the world again. Why bother? It's back to square one. The second is rewriting the holy books several times. The confusion is unparallel. And third, the newly chosen people as claimed by Mohammed can't even see eye to eye. The conflict between the Sunnis and the Shiites is just the tip of the iceberg. There are many more unheard fights on the down low. Here is a theory. If you spread the religion to a new people; the groups within the religion will also spread their hatred to them. The chaos starts all over again. Sunnis in India hate Shiites in Iran.

'And before the so-called Islam for the world cry marches on, we know the Arabs discriminate against the blacks. And they probably put themselves at the top of the human race. "There is only one spot at the top of the ladder and we are it".

'And to show the selfishness of man, the Muslims are good examples here, too. I know it took Allah about 500 years to send Mohammed… the present ones don't even think of the people before the noble book; the in-between people.

'We are trying to avoid water boarding, but Allah in the gospel of Barnabas invited the honorable to witness the torture of people who didn't believe in the last prophet. Even the honorable had to cry. He showed compassion! Muslims will be able to see you in hell burning and burning and they will say to you, 'in your face, Bob, ha aha'. Just like John in Revelation told us of the same kind of heartless punishment by God for the unbelievers. (But there's a similarity between the Revelation of John and that of Daniel's. You be the judge. Who copied who?)

'And on earth the Muslims persecute the Baha'i faith for heresy, but fail to see the heresy the Jews and the Christians leveled against them. Who says there is no strength in numbers?

'The things that make us proud like race, tribe, name, success, beauty, heritage, country, culture and religion are the very things that make us inhuman to other humans: double-edged sword!!!

'I do pity the Muslims that now abbreviate 'peace be upon him' when referring to the prophet. Maybe it's a sin now. "What the hell are you doing that you can't find the time to write it out?"

'Their favorite argument against the Jews and the Christians is taking usury. (The Islamic banks don't charge interest.) A study of economics 101 will suffice here. The fluctuation of currency demands this. Even God in the bible told the chosen to charge outsiders usury but not within themselves.

'If there are certain passages in the bible that Mohammed in the Koran contended not to be right or true like Essa or Jesus didn't do one thing or the other, understandable. But why would the Koran switch the armies of Saul (Surah 2; 249) with that of Gideon (Judges chapter 7 verses 4,5,6) concerning readiness of the army by luring them to drink from the river to see who would bury his face in it or one who would drink from his hand. Something is fishy here. It has no significance, unless, stories were told, copied and forgotten how the original stories went. This guy, Gideon, is a thorn in the flesh of Christianity and Islam. Maybe, I will name my son, Gideon.

'And also you will never hear that Mohammed didn't write the Koran. Some people are of the opinion that it was written during his life time. This school-of-thought just wants to convey to the rest of the world that he monitored the Noble Truth. What is more realistic is that it was written during and after he died. Something like that leaves room for guess work and addition and subtraction from the original recitations. The same thing they blame the Torah and the Bible for is in their closet.

'Another group worth mentioning is the Nation of Islam. An argument could be made that this group came about because of the inhumane ways the whites treated the blacks in the US. It was part and parcel of the Civil Rights Movement.

'It gave rise to their famous Malcolm X and his blunt way of appraising the situation at the time. Obviously, all the blacks knew what was going on. He just gave the struggle a stronger voice. I don't see anything wrong about him strongly waking the rest of the blacks up and exposing the hypocrisy of the whites, but it's the claim I don't agree with, that the messiah of the Christians and the much awaited Mahdi of the Muslims already came in the person of Fard Muhammad, a black American in 1930.

'I need to know the importance of a Mahdi/ Messiah? Why didn't he beam the blacks to paradise or drown all the whites in the red sea?

'Next are the Nubians. They are closely related to the Nation of Islam in their hatred of the whites. Their leader who is going to take them away from this earth someday is in one of the numerous jails in the US for child molestation amongst other charges. His followers see conspiracy, of course.

'Their belief system is a little bit complicated. They have pictures of all the prophets of Judaism, Christianity and Islam as black. No mixture of races here, just like the Nation of Islam forbids interracial marriages. If you do, it means you have forfeited your right to be called a human being; you are lost, you have joined the soulless people; the whites, the Chinese and the Japanese.

'Jesus, Moses, Joseph and even Mohammed were all black. So if you want to see the picture of Mohammed, join them. The Arab Muslims would be furious to see these pictures; another Danish protest. To think that God would be any other color than black would be unthinkable. The only person that would disagree with them would be Joseph Smith of the Latter Days. The Father and The Son (God and Jesus) that appeared to him were as whites as snow with blue eyes. Go figure!

'But there's one question for the American Nubians and it's simple. Most of their members are of mixed blood, tracing that to the slavery days; when the master just took the girls and raped them while the wife was in the main house praying to God through Jesus before bed time. Now, how do they think they have pure black blood? They might as well invite their soulless white relatives into the group, making for one happy family.

'And then we have the Israelites. This group is actually different from the Jews that the world has come to know as the real Israelites. They claim to be the real Israelites and the ones in the present day Israel are impostors; fake! They stole their identity, like stealing their social security numbers.

'They hold the belief that they are the descendants of the lost tribes of Israel that were scattered around the world by God due to their disobedience of his laws. And the intriguing thing is that they believe that the Africans sold their forefathers to the whites during the slavery era.

'When members of this group talk to a non member, who is going to serve them in paradise, they make him accept his position as a second class citizen in a convincing way; "that is the best you can ever hope for in eternity, be happy."

'They don't agree with the documented history that the sub-Saharan Africans were the ones sold in the slave trade. To them, the whites and the Africans conspired to only sell the Jews amidst the Africans into slavery. How that was possible I need to know. They now see the whites and the Africans as the devils. But why would they complain about the harsh treatment their forefathers got as slaves from the Caucasians, calling them white-devils, when Moses, their prophet, sanctioned punishment like that in the bible. I guess they are not so deep anymore.

'Some in this religion now have their own twelve tribes reconstructed. They read from King James Bible with a twist of their own understanding. Reading from a white man's printed bible!

'When the transition from 1999 to 2000 came and all that scare about the computer crash; the end of the world cry, there was a split within them. One group was expecting their messiah, which would be Jesus, to come before 1st of January, 2000, but the other part refused to put a date on the return of their savior.

'These guys are well-groomed and eloquent that you will think they know what they are saying. But what they did not put into account was science; mere science would turn their truth upside down. DNA now could be used to trace them to their original root. There goes that theory in smoke. Somebody call the firefighters. Some popular African-Americans and not so known have already found their ancestral home in black Africa. Do I hear another conspiracy theory?

'Even if that's not proof enough, how come the native Americans, the Indians, (part of the 12 tribes) enslaved the black Americans? God won't be happy, brothers enslaving brothers. They were supposed to enslave outsiders, forever; yet they got the law wrong again.

'Way before this idea became popular on the street of New York, a group of blacks from Chicago decided to join their true relatives, not in Africa, but in Israel. I guess they actually put their faith in motion. They missed the mother land by thousands of miles.

'But if we only look at this type of thinking at face value then we will be missing a lot in understanding them. And we are likely to call them madmen. But looking at it a bit closer it becomes apparent that these people felt spiritually empty, and something else was at work, too. It's not only confusion or looking for identity that makes man do things like this, but rather it's an embedded arrogance that's mostly at play here. It's our pride that traps us and we can't see it.

'Most of us would like to believe we come from a heritage that history has praised or linked to important events. It makes us feel good, wanted, proud, important, and respected and all the nice sounding adjectives.

'These blacks for example didn't choose Africa mainly because they felt they couldn't have belonged to a conquered people. Nobody wants to hang out with losers. They headed to the land flowing with milk and honey, only to be seen as outcasts, but they endured. After all, it would be better this way on earth, you know what their eventual reward would be, the real children of God.

'Thank goodness for science. Their emotional and religious attachment to 'mother land' would be reversed. We don't need to wait for eternity to verify this one or wait for the messiah to separate the wheat from the chaff. We know, faith is very much irrelevant. Trash it. Be real. Go home.

'As a Buddhist, I look at everybody that believes in a creator judging mankind as, well, one day they would come to be like me, after a long series of reincarnations. The Hare-Krishnas also claim this lofty goal and many in the area of meditation-religion. But how do I know that Buddha himself has not come back again as a black man or a white woman, or he only comes back as the native of the Dalai Lama? How do you choose a Lama? Who chose Buddha? This aspect is a brain twister because there is really no yardstick to measure anything in this religion or philosophy, and every group has come up with its own unique way of reaching Nirvana.

'The question is how many Nirvanas are there? We may never know, but we do know that the Eastern religionists made their way to the rich Western world that is purely materialistic, why, when Buddha gave his own wealth away.

'So, if Buddha could just wake up one day, could he have done it without anybody's help or Spirits? Or is it because man has a built in system to wake up someday? But then, built in by whom, 'God'? I'm sorry, Buddha. That didn't sound right. So, it couldn't be only Buddha with this privilege. So, why do some Buddhists pray to Buddha for quick release from the cycle of rebirth? Who assisted Buddha?

'The eight principles are good ways to live in this crazy world, but why make claims that can't be verified? Because the leader of Jainism too claimed he broke the chain of reincarnation and reached Nirvana. At least for the record, Buddha and Mahavira made it out of billions of humans to go there. Not a very encouraging number for the rest of us.

'Even Buddha's reasoning of everything being in a state of impermanence was challenged by other Buddhists, proving that Buddha was wrong. Where does that leave anybody? Your guess is as good as mine. To compound the mess the religion has found itself, an 18 year-old boy is claiming to be Buddha, himself. At least, a sect of the faith agrees with him. Other sects are skeptical. Accordingly, Buddha shouldn't come back; that should be the last incarnation. Maybe, he got bored in Nirvana, nobody to chat with. The Hare-Krishna followers claim that the original Buddha was a reincarnate of Krishna. Now I have to go into mediation to figure that out.

'As a Hindu worshipper I pride myself to belonging to the ancient religion. That's a comforting thing. I am in the right place; the right time. (Disregard that it was introduced by an outsider. Just like the name, Yoruba, was given to the so-called Yoruba people by outsiders, too). The first must mean the right one to fully understand the mysteries of the world.

'But why is it that all the other religions of different tribes worship pretty much what I worship. Is the god of fire in my religion the same as other people's god of fire? Because fire is fire anywhere.

'It's a fact that some religions came after my faith. That can't be disputed. I don't need Vishnu to tell me this. The only thing that puzzles me is if my religion is fully complete and the mysteries of heaven and earth are solved, where did these religions get their ideas from? They complain about the caste system. So what? It's part of the design plan. But I wouldn't want to come back as a low caste, that life is hard. Okay, maybe they have a point. We'll sweep that under the carpet; after all, all religions are not perfect.

'I just can't wait to be reunited with God. Oh, how wonderful that would be? But if that's the case, why did God send me here in the first place? When I get there, I'll know.

'Who makes it the business of Jainism to complain about us having too many rituals? It's a beautiful thing to perform all these rituals to my many Gods and at the end of this month bathe in the river Ganga to cleanse (Though it's dirty. Science is trying to cleanse the water, not gods) me of my bad karma. Can low caste Hindu do the same; cleanse their bad karma in the river? Will their low caste status be washed away and they become like me, high caste? What if the river runs dry one day? How will I cleanse my karma? Will taking a shower do it?

'When other religionists like Sikhs, Muslims and Christians attack me, I must attack them back. You know why, they are always starting trouble. Then again, I know that I can't really kill their souls and they can't kill mine. But is it okay to play this deadly game? I'm confused.

'How do Westerners find solace in Hindu religion of a caste system and they are not complaining? Would they like to belong to such a class in their own society and accept it and continue to practice their meditation?'

Bob paused again. The traffic was inching forward, at least.

'Then what about fear.' He went back to thinking and sometimes soliloquizing.

'Wherever we come from it seems fear is packaged into our DNA. No matter how many times we are faced with fear, we still allow it to cripple us. The question is, fear of what? Dying? Fear of this, fear of that? Fear runs endless like the ocean.

'Sometimes this fear is made real by our constantly being in the circle of people drumming it loud and clear in our ears. And it has a contagious effect. Just like yawning in the face of your friend, it's hard not to succumb to it.

'With fear comes selfishness. It's every man for himself. We hardly care about anybody but ourselves. Come to think of it, the so-called lesser animals are killed and eaten by man, yet he cares less what happens to these animals when we eat them or when they die. Of course, the Muslims and the Christians just want to treat them right and eat them later and that is it for them. They don't have souls like us. So what is the purpose of having a soul, anyway? Does it make us not to steal, rape, kill each other, talk about others behind their backs, back stabbing one another? What does it do?

'Man just can't be bothered with the lives of animals. Some don't even think they have feelings. They have no heaven to go to. Which in a way, looking at life the way people who believe in heaven and hell do, a good thing. After all, the rest of us that don't share that view will for eternity burn in hell. If I had a chance, I wouldn't have come as a human being, but as a lesser animal. Like a goat. No, I think I would like to be a falcon. I can fly free without restrictions; maybe fly out of this world...

'Come to think of it, is it a victory to live long in this world? And what should the quality of that life be? Should it be materialistic? Comfort beyond some people's fantasy. We age whether we like it or not but celebrate it like there's no tomorrow. Or maybe we should measure life in love? Isn't life lived in a moment?

'Religion can even make your old friends and family members leave your company. You see, they are afraid that you'll lead them astray, if you don't believe the way they do, to hell or you might bring God's punishment on them. My friend, your friendship is worth losing in this case.

'And if they lose some members of their family to a non believer or another faith. It's a sad event in their lives. They'll pray to their chosen God to convert that outsider to their faith so that all can be in paradise promised by that religion. Of course, this is after they have tried to discourage the union. *What's love gotta do, gotta do with it*? But in all honesty, fear can paralyze him or her, stop man from functioning well. But it's just fear.

'What has anyone of us really got to lose in this world?

In the case of man, fear could come from any form in our world and not necessarily religious. To get rid of the fear is through gently exposing the person in question to the ways of other people around who don't share the same sentiment. Nothing is guaranteed. A good understanding of why man behaves this way is also helpful, showing man both sides of the coin in order for him not to go crazy in his world.

'But then, why do we believe that before we belong to any group, we would have exhausted all reasonable logic to come to that group, hmm? But we feel ashamed or angry or empty when someone or something clearly tells us the opposite; we just hold on to the belief no matter what. It becomes our security blanket, wrapped around like a man in a freezing cold weather.

'We always want our belief to be true so that others who do not believe as we do will look at us with a sense of accomplishment. It's like a victory for us, and well, you know what they will get; the unbelievers. Even though according to my religion its God that says I'm chosen. I can't even choose myself. There goes my dying as a baby or being an animal. Shit!

'But, why would God create people and departmentalize them into various religious groups to antagonize one another? Isn't that a God of confusion? Or is it man claiming falsehood, thinking he truly knows what God is when he can't even know the mind of his or her lover, not to talk of the God he can't see.

"You go to the Muslim family…

You go to the Christian one…

You go to the pagan family…"

"But God, the Muslims and the Christians will kill me."

"Don't worry; I know what I'm doing."

"Okay, if you say so, I will go…"

"You go to my chosen people. I'm confused now; anyway, choose between the Jews and the Aztecs when you get there…"

'So, if God really knows each individual before birth as the bible-believers claim, then the whole argument is upside-down. For example, why would God first allow Saul, turned Paul, to persecute and kill Christians and then would be the one to write more than half of the New Testament for the Christians. That's just one of many illogical points about this God knowing us.

'What about Israel, the chosen? Mmm, all throughout the history of the chosen people there had emerged a phenomenon undulating between sins and forgiveness. They did evil in the sight of God, God handed them over to other nations for punishment. But invariably God would end up punishing the people he used to punish his chosen! How does this make sense to anyone in this world is beyond me. Just like If God wanted an upright man to commit a sin he would send an evil spirit or harden the poor man's heart so he could punish him without guilt. That is like planting evidence in human world. We should consult the police for more information on that.

> *Judges ch. 4 verses 1,2,3*
> *And the children of Israel again did evil in the sight of the lord When Ehud was dead*
> *And the lord sold them unto the hand of Jabin king of Canaan that reigned in Hazor.*
> *And the children of Israel cried unto the lord.*
> *And Deborah, a prophetess, the wife of Lapidoth, she judged Israel at that time*

'Before Ehud died they were sold to the king of Moab for disobeying God due to intermarriage as one of the sins. And God raised Ehud up to save Israel.

> *Judge ch.3 verses 20,21*
> *And Ehud said, I have a message from God unto thee…*
> *And Ehud put forth his left hand and took the dagger from*
> *his right thigh, and thrust it into his belly.*

'A pastor preached this sermon and was delighted that the fat king got his reward, but when the audience felt that that was not funny, he quickly reminded them of the famous David and Goliath and Samson stories. He won them back. 'We are all in this butchery together; you can't accept one and deny the other. This is our God in action'.

But despite the documented stories of this God; the good, the bad, and the ugly in the triangular religions, the believers still go all out to sell this God as a good, fair and merciful one as the cornerstone of their argument, like a billion dollar drug to save man with more adverse effects than the original disease. It's so powerfully presented to man that he would leave his father, mother and sister to join the God that would save his 'behind' while the members of the same family would do just likewise. Why point the finger? Who says advertisement is bad.

> *Matthew Chapter 19 Verse 29*
> *And everyone that hath forsaken houses, or brethren,*
> *or sisters, or father, or mother, or wife, or children, or*
> *lands, for my name's sake, shall receive an hundredfold,*
> *and shall inherit everlasting life.*

'All you have to do is to accept this God, son, prophet and everything in your life will be fine. But when it's not fine, the reason is that Satan is trying to stop you from getting your inheritance. Then, many examples of endurance are cited in their holy books and you're hooked still.

Why do the religious people keep shouting family values when even the prince of peace, Jesus, had this to say? Why would Jesus allow his disciples to carry weapon, anyway? At least, one used it to cut off the ear of a Roman soldier. Earthly defense when you could say to the mountain…move.

Matthew Chapter 10 Verses 34& 35
Think not that I am come to send peace on earth: I came
not to send peace, but a sword.
For I am come to set a man at variance against his father
and the daughter against her mother, and daughter in law
against her mother in law.

'Is this why mother-in-laws are so evil, especially the ones from the family of the groom? I will leave this to all the newlyweds to figure it out. (Most in-laws don't accept outsiders, too. Mother-in-laws just lead the pack. In-laws have to be perfect!)

'But living in this world as we know it needs a lot of balancing within all the conflicting ideas. But looking at the notion of God; the almighty, the all knowing, the provider and the list of adjectives is endless. Why are Muslims in recent times migrating to the lands of the infidels in record numbers? Are they looking for economic and political freedom, why? When these are the people that never stop rubbing in man's face how glorious and wonderful Allah is. Why migrate? Why not stay in the Allah chosen land and Allah will provide?

'But before we start thinking that the Muslims are the only ones doing this kind of migration, we should look around us. Practically all have done it and are still in the process of embarking on a journey, not to a heavenly paradise, but to one of physical convenience. And if physical condition is better in Africa tomorrow, there, they will all migrate to.

'Why can't God in the bible snap his fingers and 'kaboom' land appears for his chosen people and save us all the headaches we have today between his sons and daughters. But no, that would be too much work. But let there be light was so easy!!!

But then again, in religion, throwing stones when you live in a glass house does apply. Hypocrisy is a man's disease. Because when it comes to God or what is God, you hear 'I pity you, you pity me…just because…' But shouldn't we just take a moment to just pity ourselves for pitying one another.

'For the uninformed, all cultures of the world teach about right behavior and wrong one. The indigenous stories are littered with good lessons and punishments for all the characters in the stories that don't adhere to ways that transcend personal gratifications. They tell stories of encouragement, of personal sacrifice and of rewards for the individuals. This is not an exclusive gift of 2000 or 6000-year-old religions. Period!

Every culture teaches hard work, positive thinking and patience, helping one another in good and bad times, having family and friends' support, living a productive life style and keeping your body well, enduring and praying to their respective Gods and believing that their God will answer in time. Really, these are ways humans try to cope in this changing world. They keep you grounded. All of a sudden a band of triangular religionists turned inspirational speakers now think they are giving mankind a valuable lesson. Actually, they all have an agenda!

'They keep trying to shock the rest of mankind with what's happening now. They parade the wickedness of man and the greed and preach about them. But the holier-than-thou conveniently don't mention in their wholesome arguments the atrocities in their holy books which were orchestrated not by man but by a so-called loving God. If a creator can't get it right, how do you expect mere humans to?

'They put us under a spell and make us do their biddings. They spin the stories in their unique ways. Even the stories we have heard before now come alive and take shape never imagined by us. The next time we're glued to our TV waiting for him or her to take us wherever. They sing, they dance, they laugh, they cry, they shout, they tell jokes, they flap their wings, they dramatize, they write books, they show us graphic movies about hell--hey, that's where you are going to go if…,they caution, they entertain us, and they bless us and feed us the words of God and most importantly, they tell us to sow seeds.

'There's no topic untouched now by these preachers. They even preach how not to get fat, competing with all those gym membership clubs. God wants you ripped.

'The charismatic pastors go to work on the congregation like a businessman trying to sell skis to an African. "Hey, the climate will change one day, better be the first to…" The knowledgeable pastors go into the history of a conflicting word in the bible. They articulate it in a way that the worshippers are full of awe regarding their preachers' know-how. "You see the word, evil, in Greek means to do wicked things, but it has two meanings; if Satan and man use it, it means real evil, but when God uses it, it means good punishment. And also the word, anger, if God is angry and kills your entire family for what one person does. That's good anger, but if you become angry and kill the one you are mad at. That's bad, very bad anger. There is a gulf of difference between the two. As a matter of fact, I want you to write it down, can I get an Amen." One of the ancient Egyptian gods is called Amen. What a coincidence. I'm sure an inexperienced, low grade detective can explain this little mystery.

'They eloquently tell them that their mother, father, sisters, brothers, friends, relatives, tribe and race and infants and suckling of their brothers, cousins, nephews that don't share their faith will burn continuously in hell and they quietly and humbly sit there and absorb the hate with 'peace, love and grace' in their best attire: their Sunday dress. And they further delude themselves that their families' cry in hell will not be heard by them in heaven. So, that makes it right.

'When a preacher tells them this in a beautiful and forceful manner, they accept without questions. Again, they fail to point to a passage about Lazarus' conversation in heaven and a rich man in hell, begging for holy water from heaven. Lazarus said, "no! die of thirst." The guy is already dead.

'Even the pastors of old, the whites, sing the praise of all people now. You have to wonder if the Holy Spirit was allowed to lead their forefathers then as they now proudly claim, maybe slavery wouldn't have lasted a day. Maybe, Holy Spirit wasn't that powerful, then... Maybe, those Christians were not born again, then... Maybe, there wasn't enough holy water, then. What do I know? I just can't wait to hear what they will preach in a 1000 years from now when the messiah doesn't show up. Another reason will be in order. I bet they are all restless now, waiting and praying for the end of the world.

'But Christ did promise that he would return to fight the anti-Christ, Satan, with chariots of fire and a thousand angels. But if the bible was written in the 20th century, he would be coming back to do battle with F-15s armed to the teeth with nuclear war heads, no, I think he would fly the stealth bomber and the angels would fly the B-52 bombers. He has to come back like a thief in the night. I truly lack understanding when it comes to the bible. Sorry, again!

'You will never hear a Christian preacher say that their beloved Samuel, one of the famous prophets of God, was conjured up by a witch after he was so-called taken to heaven to reside with God forever. A pagan ritual linking witches with the prophet of God in paradise!

1 Samuel ch 28 verse 15
And Samuel said to Saul why hast thou disquited me, to
bring me up? for the lord hath rent the kingdom out thine
hand, and given it to thy neighbor ,even to David. Because
thou obeyedst not the voice of the lord, nor excutedst his
fierce wrath upon Amalek...and tomorrow shalt thou and
thy sons be with me

'Whether they like it or not, the importance of him coming down can't be over-emphasized. This Samuel prophesied that Saul and his son would join him in heaven and it happened according to their story. Father and son died. But they don't want children reading or watching Harry Potter.

'Faith, they say can move mountains? But when God wanted to kill people in the bible, he didn't require their faith. But you need enormous faith now to get a loaf of bread. Yet they say they don't understand or can't imagine me coming back in another human form or an animal, but they can understand and justify a fair God taking other people's land and having them killed or massacred for his chosen. And they can also understand why a couple should be killed for lying to Peter. "How insulting to lie about the true amount they sold the land for." Good justice? But why aren't Christians dying in their millions now? They must be telling the truth every time in their lives. (That they actually 'died' could be explained) Ananias and Sapphira served to convey fear to the rest of the congregation.

Act chapter 5, verse 11
And great fear came upon all the church,
And upon as many as heard these things

'Here, there was no forgiveness and cleansing by the lamb's blood. I guess one of the many duties of the Holy Spirit is killing for the slightest offence. Would Jesus have killed this couple? Christians would jump over each other to say an emphatic NO. But who sent the Holy Spirit to care for the Christians?

"Hey, where are you going, H.S?"

"Peter wants me to punish these guys to death."

"Hmm, go quickly then because I want you to do something for me too...Okay"

"Jesus, I will be back in a few."

'A pastor was so glad God didn't kill on a whim like that anymore and the congregation clapped happily. I guess lying and killing then or any other sins are not the same now, but answering prayers remain the same. (So much for the accepted excuse of the Old Testament God being uncompromising when it comes to sin) How do I make sense of the famous statement that God is the same today, yesterday and tomorrow? Still, how many Christians read their daily horoscope? How many also practice Yoga? Some even call it Christian yoga. Maybe they don't know that's mixing of religions. A golden calf moment! Where's Moses?

'And just like the early white Christians justifying enslaving the blacks because they disobeyed God, so they were not guilty; God was punishing them that way. If you weigh this brainwashing phenomenon with how many times the entire Israelites disobeyed God, you will be floored. So the church with their holy interpretation engaged and supported slavery. "We have to help God punish these people." The irony is that some blacks bought this ridiculous divine nonsense as descendants of Ham, dark-skinned-man.

'The first enslavement of the Jews was not because they disobeyed God, it was the Pharaoh, meaning king, (Pharaohs then didn't have names, they had short phrases as names) that-didn't-know-Joseph, that turned them into second class citizens as we have been told to believe. Just like saying the president in the US that freed the slaves and automatically people will ask, which one? But when it comes to Pharaohs, the world is silent. Intelligent people question not, ha! They can't be a good contestant on a Jeopardy game show.

'Also, why would Abraham lie to poor Pharaoh about his wife, Sarah? He committed perjury! I'm sure when I do that in the US Court, Christian Nation; they will throw the book at me. Is thou shalt lie in the bible? Maybe, Abraham didn't read the bible—Ephesians Ch-4 verse 25. Saying that she was his sister and making Pharaoh desired her for a wife. Then, God of sound judgment turned around and punished Pharaoh for loving a married woman. I guess Pharaoh took the sin of Abraham. Just like Jesus took the sins of the world, later. There is a pattern here. By the way, which Pharaoh got the punishment? Oh I forgot, the Pharaoh-that-took-Abraham's wife. A preacher is so proud of never lying, always telling the truth to his wife, children and everybody. I guess he's more righteous than his father, Abraham.

'What about the f-word the preachers keep throwing around like a basket ball to all mankind. Mmm...I mean fornication. But studying the lineage of Jesus, we know David committed fornication with Beersheba. Who got punished, the man or the woman, or the descendants of David? Do we care what happened to the husband of Beersheba? Or the son that died, but seen as punishing David by God by devout Christians. Some people should remove the log in their eyes before seeing the splinter in man's eyes. Maybe Jesus should...!

'Believers claim to talk to Jesus every day, does that mean they can point to him in a police lineup. Maybe I should ask the next Christian I see. I know I will get an evasive answer or seen as crazy. Actually this is how to test their faith, apart from walking on water in their bathtub. Playing with poisonous snake belongs in the circus. Then we can know who is really talking to Jesus. I'm sure they all have the image of the Hollywood actor who played Jesus in their heads.

'How come Jesus didn't stop the crusaders before they killed non believers like he did Saul, but would forgive them afterwards as believers. A stitch in time didn't save nine in that case. I would have expected God to have allowed the coup plotters to succeed killing Adolf Hitler, knowing what this evil guy would do to his chosen. There I go again, thinking for God!

'What is this fascination about virgin birth, anyway? The idea has been borrowed, stolen and claimed by so many religions. It must be a determining factor of holiness. The sharks and the komodo lizards don't necessarily need male sperms to conceive. Are they holy, too?

Okay, would all these people actually do all these good deeds if not promised heaven? And they keep saying they do them in the name of love. Well, in the name of love doesn't put others in hell. Really they do them in the name of fear...

'They keep saying we should believe in the Koran and in the bible. It's not a matter of faith, but what to believe? How can I say God is fair and with the same breath say God favors and kills a group for another? I think all the so-called educated believers don't know what contradiction means. Still they say God is not a God of contradiction.

These people should reimburse the society for wasting our educational and tax payers' money.

'Even Muhammad's argument about pagan gods not being able to defend themselves is shallow. Mohammed and his faithful were the ones defending Allah. They should have posed the same question to him. Truthfully, Muslims are so drunk with Mohammed that in order for them to turn a deaf ear to him owning slave girls, rationalized it as a just act because Mohammed did not sin. I guess that's our reward for not sinning. These people would donate their girls to him and be happy; poor girls would die unhappy. Allah is great indeed. They also say that beating your wife like a slave is for her own good. Wow! A friend of mine couldn't believe that the father of the bride in her country, Ivory Coast (Sorry, it was changed to Cote d'ivoire, they had to change it to French words, they couldn't come up with their own unique name.) gave the groom a cane to beat his daughter should she misbehave in marriage, a true Muslim to the core. They also deny their women or wives sex as a form of punishment mandated by Mohammed, but the women had better not do the same! I'd think giving goat and chicken as gifts to the newly wed would be appropriate.

'Man beats his wife or wives whether Holy books tell him or not. It's termed a barbaric behavior. And how do you beat your lover or wife and in the night you want to cuddle up and make love to her? How? Once anyone is stronger than the other, doesn't matter the gender, the tough one should walk away. That is the real strength.

'They all claim to be defending God's honor. I don't think so… not really. Actually man is defending his own honor wrapped in his own ego. Whatever he deems as honor he defends with his life. Just like honor killing; it is the same thing, absolute irrationality for any human being to defend any God.'

He paused again and checked the rear view mirror. 'Every driver is having a panic attack, wishing they had a flying car. Maybe, we will have to wait a little bit longer for the mass production. But whatever the case, it has to be done before Jesus comes back.' He thought and smiled.

'So, if we agree that the earth is in trouble and Satan rules here, why is there a need for a new heaven? We obviously need a new earth with all these religious people fighting and killing one another. But a new heaven…,did another angel rebel against God? If I am a believer

I'll be very careful going to such a heaven. It doesn't look like there'll be peace in paradise after all these sects get there, even now. By the way, how does God handle collateral damage? We know how humans go about it; neglect, abandon and left to die.

'If a Muslim kills a Muslim, do they both go to paradise? Does that apply in Christianity, too? But the very sad thing is that they all do these terrible things to one another. How does one sympathize?

'What about all this talk about finding total bliss in religion? We tend to be overwhelmed by inexplicable feeling and in our rush to explain it; we attribute it to a heavenly blessing. Especially, when such an individual is in the midst of people who share that particular view or on the ground of what they have told him to be a mystical place.

'With this firmly fixed in his mind, he now champions whatever the cause he adheres to. He sets out to either start persuading people to follow suit or uses force to accomplish his heavenly view, believing to have been chosen or to be part of the chosen.

'For example, you go to a mosque or the holy land in Mecca and the worshippers will vow to have experienced bliss beyond this earth, similar to someone going to a Jewish Temple or the Wailing Wall. The Christians too have this awesome feeling when in church or visiting Jerusalem where Jesus walked on 2,000 years ago. They will swear about feeling the presence of Jesus in their body, mind and spirit. Though in this case there are two places in contention where he was buried, people go to both and still have the same feeling!

'And regardless of how they all confess to this heavenly sensation, you have to wonder, since each claims the other is on the wrong path, how then can they all have this same holy emotion from above?

'Actually, it's just like that whenever humans gather in a large number. Like going to a soccer game, you'll have the same sensation. A better example will be when you go to a place where a catastrophic event had taken place. Have you tried going to a charity concert? You will feel it too. But if no one tells you the land you are standing on is holy, you won't feel a thing.

'There are hundreds of feelings we humans have that we can't explain, but we attribute them to whatever they tell us or whatever we are inclined to attach them to. Under scrutiny though, we see clearly.'

His brain was doing overtime. Thoughts kept popping in and out.

'Grief...What about grief? This is one of the strongest emotional traits we animals have whether so-called higher or lower ones. To those who are still growing in this area of consciousness, yes, animals do grief. And one grief is not more sorrowful than the other. Grief is grief. But man will cry and hold on to a belief that condemns others, even those that come to console him, to hell for eternity, and yet wants the rest of humanity to understand him about the religion comforting him for a brief moment of grief in his time of need! And it does make you wonder how the tribes that lived before God or Allah created the world, dealt with grief? They probably didn't grief to death or they wouldn't have Jesus to save their descendants and Muhammad or Joseph Smith to reinforce the true words of God.

'How long is it going to take Jesus to come back? We've had the first and second world wars and many more mini wars and we still don't know how to count the dead. How many really died? How long can a loving person really stay aloof and watch. Or does he think things are going to get better? Or maybe we need a different understanding of life.

Even the Africans don't think about their slave history anymore, about the slaves that neither were Christians nor Muslims. That shows the power of fear coupled with selfishness. And when their colonial masters fight with their Islamic masters, fights that have been going on before they decided to spread the madness to...well, forgotten people by God or Allah, they fight too, killing each other, destroying each other's properties. And at the end of the day in their hearts think that they have defended their God as needed to be defended. How do you explain the Gulf war in Nigeria between Muslims and Christians? I will burst a brain nerve trying to figure this one out. Let it be, Bob.

'But how come they observe so much of the Yoruba culture and religion in South America? Did the God of the Yoruba send a prophet there too? They worship some of the Yoruba gods in Castro Cuba and Brazil, even Haiti, and pretty much the whole of South America, but mixed with Christianity, and no significant Islam. Why? Really, it was because of slavery that this religion spread to places like that. This is a reverse kind of conquering the natives and forcefully imposing your religion. The most popular is Iyemuja, goddess of the sea, in Brazil. They also worship Obatala in Cuba and Sango god in most Latino cultures.

'I'd better not tell the Africans this. But they would rather travel thousands of miles to now teach the colonial masters how to worship the imposed religion on them. Whoa! This is hypocrisy reversed. They go because of economic benefits. They should have headed to poor African countries or start adopting less fortunate babies within the continent.

'But to some, it is inconceivable that the universe could exist without something or someone being in charge of it. So the creator gets names from every language. But how and why he created what they can perceive or not is the big question. And there lies the greatest conflict amongst men.

'Then we have those who just disregard the whole thing as nonsense. Nothing is responsible for the mess we find ourselves in. We should be lucky we exist in the first place. So enjoy your life and once it's gone, it's gone. No afterlife. What I can't see, I don't believe. How do they know this for a fact, too? They too have put themselves at the top of the ladder in understanding this world, like the religious people.

'Then we also have the book. Once you put something in a book, you can't question it because the book says so. (So when I write a book they shouldn't question it, even the errors) I now must live my life according to the book, but they hardly follow the book. Forget the millions of interpretations. Thank goodness because if they do the world will be in chaos. I have to thank their God(s) for this. But we still have the effects of those who claim knowing God, and where there are claims, there are counter claims, leading to bloodshed and hatred. Yet everyone claims protection from this God. And when they fight, both sides die and lose the lives of the innocents. So, you wonder whether these people actually know what they are talking about. Yet they all want to be part of the solution, when they are part and parcel of the problem. No one wants to take a critical look at himself/herself, yet we blame others!

'Man cuts the infested branch of a tree and says he has fixed the problem. The branch grows again and he is shocked that the problem comes back, not knowing he has to uproot the tree. In other words, get to the core of the problem and solve it right there; the holy books or rather, the holy confusion. Man has always lied to himself that the three pointed religions are not violent. It's a big lie. Just read the record of their Gods and tell me how you want the worshippers to behave well.

'The dangerous thing is that Islam promises that if you die fighting, you go to heaven; if you don't die fighting you still go to heaven. But fighting actually holds a better position in Allah's sight. They are advised to confront a bullet without any protection. It's good for you. Maybe the greatest trick ever employed by man in this world is, "wait until you die and you will know what we have been telling you." That line alone has been used by various religions to intimidate their followers worldwide. It is the greatest scam. It's not comparable to credit card scam or the yogis claiming to levitate.

'On the other hand, what can be verified here sometimes viewed by the religious mind is muddled up. "I believe Jesus helped me to get this good job." You have to wonder whether it is Jesus or God that answers a nonbeliever in anything that makes life easy for him or her. Or was it Jesus that made Buddha very rich before he relinquished everything? Or it was Jesus or Allah that gave the Yoruba or Calabar people children before they met the Whites/Arabs. Those children must have come from the…I don't know! Maybe someday Jesus or Muhammad would tell us.

'And when there's no solution in sight to their problems, their explanation is that God is testing them. So it becomes a win-win situation for this type of mind. But if you ask whether these people see others who don't share their religious belief go through the same problems in life, like happiness and sadness. And sometimes pull through and sometimes don't. They become speechless, but stubbornly revert to eventually being sure of going to a promised paradise. You just have to throw in the towel, not only the white one, but every color of the rainbow.

'You don't even need a critical look at this world to know that the so-called lesser animals go through the same ups and downs in the jungle. Wonder whether some animals pray to God or Allah for food. Maybe we should all watch the documented story of Titus, the silverback, rise to power and do a comparison with any man's rise from rags to riches. And not forgetting Kusasi, the orangutan.

'But they will pound you with countless information till you join or they will term you evil, devil's son or daughter. And if you are not strong mentally, fear of hell sinks in. After all, this world is not easy; a reasonable man would want to rest his weary soul after this life, somewhere. Even I want to. By the way, other social animals are besieged too with pretty much everything we are struggling with. And they follow rules, but curiously without religion, hmm.

'And when asked how they become converted. They say through the grace of God or Allah. This shouldn't be argued. It's self-explanatory. But with man it's a different story.

"How do we get the grace?" From God, comes the answer. So, if the grace is independent of me, why am I being preached to in the first place? "We are told to spread the news so you won't perish." What if my understanding of this world doesn't tell me I'm going to perish? That's not acceptable to them. Their belief is golden. Yet within the, say, a religion like Christianity, there's no consensus on anything, not even afterlife. Some say you go to heaven, some say there's no hell, some say you just get burnt once, some say people are already in heaven and hell, some say dead people are still in the ground. These people that are bent on saving your soul as they call it don't know what they are talking about. I should be weary of people like this.

'But the thing that's fascinating about heaven and hell believers is the fact that they can be imperfect. That is to steal, rape, commit adultery, fornicate and what have you that they blame the secular people for, for not having the strength of their God or Allah to withstand temptations. They just beg for forgiveness and it's done. They are clean again. Then the circle continues, so what about the people who stop doing this kind of bad deeds forever, but not believing in any God. They still go straight to hell?

'All this bickering is really not needed. It doesn't have to be these many religions competing for the religion of God. If we only have one religion, it'll still be the same thing. Just like if we only have one tribe or race. Man will still find ways to hate and kill one another. That is why he has to outgrow being a man.

'Then again, man thinks defending his given God is the way to God's heart, but on closer examination we see that man is just stubborn in all cases accepting simple truth; facts that everyone can see but himself, regardless of the subject matter. There was this guy who believed that Africa was a name of a country in Africa. But when they told him no, he was hurt; his big ego was bruised. He lost face. His honor in the society was gone. They went further to provide solid evidence by goggling it for him. Still he accepted it not.

'Man is so ashamed of failure in any aspect of his life that he will rather commit suicide than to continue to face his fellow human beings in what he considers shameful. But then, man takes defending his shame way too far by taking another person's life to restore his humiliation. Like that is ever possible. Well, only in the mind of a sick man.

'When it takes your flesh and blood, as they proudly say, to kill you for being raped, and man thinks he's doing the right thing. Sad! And these are primarily the people who say Allah punishes the one that offends or are they saying that Allah will send these innocent victims to hell as well and they are only helping Allah to start the fire.

'The society accepts it, either because of lack of courage, or ignorance. Because once you become a victim, the entire society ostracizes you and your family; you have brought shame to them, they would turn their backs on you, for what, rape? Funny how these people come together, both government and defenders of the culture, and yet they fail to band together to really help the needy in their midst. They would rather kill because of shame. Honor killing is the most foolish of all crimes against humanity. Sad, I am sure a Muslim that engages in this barbaric slaughter of his own children sees the Popes as evil doers. Come to think of it Islam doesn't say what will happen to all babies of other faiths when they die. The all encompassing noble truth!

'We have to thank Mohammed though for stopping the killings of female babies by Arab men by putting the fear of hell in them or else they will still be doing it to this day. Just like some cultures still circumcise the females because according to their wise thinking, the girls won't be promiscuous, trying to make sex unpleasurable. Please we are meant to enjoy sex. They might as well cut off the tongue or remove the taste bud so we won't enjoy food. And if you ask them why they do this awful thing to their children, the ignorant minds will answer, "It's my culture", as if that makes sense and you shouldn't question it. "After all, they did it to me."

'Like the culture of burying the dead: Some people go into debt burying their dead, but wouldn't come together to help the poor guy stand on his own while alive; Some marriages cost an arm and a leg and last just a little longer than the time to prepare the ceremony; Yet, some will save all their lives, turning old and grey, just to pay the dowry, like a down payment on a car. Who says love is free? And in some cultures they dress the children according to their gender; pink and blue. You do the reverse in your children and the people will question you day and night. Man creates things, and then he allows the lifeless ideas to enslave him; they become slaves to culture and tradition— someone's once-upon-a-time-idea. Similar to what modern man will say concerning the law. "It's the law." As if it's written in stone.

'What is the role of a prophet, anyway? I hate to ruin the achievement of the last prophet in regards to saving female babies. To think it only takes a heavenly intervention to halt this barbaric, ignorant practice would be wrong again. Mary Slessor stopped the killings of twins in southern Nigeria, because the people there thought they were evil. And where there is evil there is religion. Just like the holy bible sanctions the killing of witches. (And I have to thank Saint Patrick for stopping the human sacrifice in Ireland. Ironic, though, but good all the same) This is where I think I might employ the Prophet's help by putting the fear of hell in the Chinese men, telling their wives to abort female babies because of a policy of having just one child, due to over population. The Japanese begged their gods to give the royal family a son. The country went into an intense ritual and prayer in order for a male child to be born. They dreaded the girl in pink to sit on the throne. You have to wonder whether science and technology really do touch people's mentality; male state of mind in this case. Man is still stuck in the past. And as unreasonable as it may sound, some women still cry that they have let their men down by giving birth to girls.

'So, before we say religious people are insane we should stop and look at man himself. Because the whole argument is about man, he's just using numerous excuses to carry out his negative and ignorant nature. How do we explain the people who were persecuted and when they got power persecuted others, too? The story of Australia comes to mind here. Treated badly by their kind in England and dumped in that part of the world, they gave the same medicine to the aborigines.

'Women, women, women. Why are women covering themselves from head to toe? We all know the idea came from the upper class women in Iran and Syria a long time ago. A fashion trend of the utmost superficial superiority to the lower class; "you can't afford me, I'm too good for your wrecked eyes to feast on." Now adopted by the Prophet and accepted by the Muslims, and given a moral, descent status; from bad to good. This is like the blacks now making the N-word which was used verbally to suppress their forefathers for hundreds of years sound cool. But other races can't use it...why? If it's cool, we all should use it! Maybe homie is the one not respecting his forefathers and mothers. He can't find another word to describe his situation?

'I guess the Koran did say guide your private parts as God has guided them. I don't quite understand this. First, that means the face and the hair are private parts. Second, are we born clothed in Baby Gap?

'Since we now know how this mode of dressing came about, why is it that man has turned it into a phenomenon? What if it is religious, given by God for some moral purpose? What is its function...to keep humans from lusting after one another...mmm? But in order to do that effectively we have to keep every woman at home, away from the eyes of men.

'First, man is attracted to woman whether you hide her in a sack of beans or not. It's natural. Second, the mere voice of a woman attracts a man and vice versa. How do we hide that? Third, even these women who are forced to conform now cover up in various degrees. By so doing they too are setting their own ways that all should follow their example. These women bitterly complain about being oppressed by their male counterparts but invariably will use the same holy book to judge others not in their group. This makes one's sympathy useless. And by the way, if a veiled woman sees a non Muslim in an infidel country, does that mean the man has committed a sin? Or the woman has sinned for looking at the man? Hey, you have to look where you are going...

'Some, especially in the Western world or in some parts of Africa where this kind of hide-and-seek clothing is carried on, wear scarf partially and some wrap it completely to cover every strand of hair on their heads. I've got news for them; they both make them adorable to men. In fact, it could be sexy. And now they even design their *abayas* with shining artistic pattern that catches the eyes, making them the center of attention (Humans always decorate themselves; whether you wear plastic bags or not. It's human nature). So, if attention is not the goal, then their aim is defeated. I even saw a beautiful woman in the subway wearing pants but wrapping her hair in a scarf. What can anyone make of that? In her mind she was doing the wish of Allah. I will let that go, too. I think she's trying to break free of the restrictions, layer by layer. Even the Nuns, their counterparts, show some legs. I bet they are not religious enough in Islam.

'The Africans dress according to the weather, which makes a lot of sense. Not forgetting the way the Eskimos too obey the environment. Even covering every part of your body in the sand dunes is sensible, but not in a modern city. Unless, the sole reason behind this madness is that you don't want another man to look at your woman. Shouldn't jealousy be a sin? Believers proudly say God is jealous. Also, Satan must be jealous of man, too. Who started the jealousy? How could God be jealous? Shouldn't jealousy be considered the real root of all evil now! By the way, women are jealous, too, but their jealousy is not put into consideration by men or God/Allah or Prophets. One or more is married to a religious man. They must have outgrown their jealousy!

Did Adam veil Eve? I guess there were no other males around feasting on beautiful and sexy Eve. (Some cultures have always used veil before Adam.) And who says all the veiled women are beautiful or sexy that men want to look at, anyway?

'What we are to make of it according to man is this. "Cover your head, hair and your ankle because, although I'm a self-disciplined man of God, I yield easily, ooh, so easily to temptations. Please don't let me go to hell. And by the way, when I see all those fine stuff people sell in the market, I want to have them, they too are giving me impure thoughts of materialism, please hide them. And when I pass through where they sell food, the aroma of the cuisine and the wine on the shelves…they make me want to eat and drink. Please hide them, do you want me to go to hell. I'm having impure thoughts. My mouth is watering…,hide them…in the name of…"

'These people's view about the world is unrealistic for crying out loud. Do we go to another man's house and there is food everywhere and because of that we lose our manners and want to eat everything in sight? No, we are meant to control our desire; put it in check. We don't burden another human being with our lack of self-discipline and tell the host to cover every food because it's making us sinful? We might as well say the world is made for us. "Hey, lecturer, can I see the answers to all the questions because I don't want to fail. Allah doesn't want me to fail." They are blind to that, though. Caging a woman in this manner is to deny her the full experience of life. Do we cry the tears of another person? If we stop the rain and the sun from getting to other humans (or animals), we would have denied them their rich experience in life. Man continues to enslave woman in the name of his god or culture for his illogical belief and childish control just for his selfish reason, but cherishes his mother. Someone should tell him that all girls are his mother. Call it whatever, but not love. Free the captives physically and mentally.

'But then, women have always been a punching bag for men. In China, way back then, it was suggested to women that having small feet made them attractive. So they crammed their feet into what could cut off blood circulation, calling them shoes. No wonder acupuncture came into being there a long time, just another way of drinking from the well.

'And the Westerners with their sophisticated outlook on life too are told to wear high heels to make them sexy. They bought it, too. If someone tells them now that the initial reason high heels were used was to avoid stepping on human waste, you will never get to the first base, don't even dream of third. As if men didn't find women sexy enough to jump into bed or barn with them without the six-inch-heel. They don't mind killing their feet to look glamorous, and, yes, they hurt like hell. Once, being pale-looking was the cool thing. They dreamed of it. Now sun-tanning is the way to go and we now have sun worshippers, literally. Forget cancer of the skin. Others, they have to lighten their skin and all their creams are geared toward toning, so much for black power.

'Christian women are to be silent in church, never saying a word according to the bible. But the Western women won't see that but will rather highlight the dilemma of the Muslim women, deliberately having a memory loss about the fact that the Christians in the past had killed more Christians than Christendom trying to wipe out the Muslims. Jesus must have been confused. "Who do I save, father? Both sides cry my name." Sorry, Muslims, Mohammed couldn't contemplate saving. He didn't have the power. Koran was his only miracle.

'I am not deceived by women's nature anymore. They are like men. It's because they don't have the power and that's why they pretend to succumb. Or maybe they have betrayed their nature. Really, being sympathetic is not a gender issue but rather a matter of consciousness. Women by their nature do a lot for mankind, though; the painful periods, the pregnancy and all its dangers and uncertainties. Maybe science will relieve them of this burden all together. Then we might start having supermarket or grocery babies…black babies on aisle ten, Japanese kids on eleven, mixed on six. If women are supposed to be women as we all would like to think; caring, thoughtful, understanding…then they should feel for all the pregnant women that the Allah or God they pray to for children killed. But they don't. They will rather fight for equality in church with their male counterpart, which is not sanctioned by God. The men are seen as not caring, but shouldn't the women understand the pain of motherhood?

'What about living once and not coming back? People who believe in rebirth probably think Muhammad has come back in another human form and now wonders why the Muslims are fighting over words of 1,500 years ago. And Jesus also is back, living in Las Vegas or one of the remote places in Africa waiting for the televangelists to preach to him about the kingdom of God that's at hand since 2,000 years.

'Still the endless debates rage on. Falsehood is debated over and over by intelligent and loving people, only in a world like this. Arguments and counter arguments abound like sands on the sea shore. Intelligent and well educated scholars, oh, sorry professor. I used educated and scholar in the same sentence, my bad. They go into the etymology of words to decipher the cogent meaning of the word in question. "There is a crisis here and it needs clarification or else the world will disintegrate into nothingness. You see, the Greek word blah, blah, blah means crap, crap, crap when used in this context." But interestingly, they all see and articulate the deficient points in the other equally educated Professors' arguments. Hey, Mr. Professor, most of these prophets didn't go to school. They couldn't read. Or maybe you are the one with lack of understanding…

'Also, the archeologists battle it out among themselves. Since carbon dating isn't exact, there leaves room for educated speculations. Religious people win again! Partial science is useless where faith is concerned. Even real science is having a tough time with the faithful.

'Man and God? Who is the God and who is the man? Man mirrors the kind of God he worships. In order words, he worships his own personal demon without knowing it. The bane of man is looking for God or so-called creator of this world. First, let's understand what love really means, and then we can start searching for the Maker or what put this mysterious place together. Really if there is a maker, he or it knows where we all are. Why search? Just love…true love.

'Can we really know the mystery of the beyond? I want to think we can, whatever it is. But the level of adventure and curiosity in man varies like any other thing in life. Some if confronted with a mystery of life, not the mundane kind, something beyond the physical, he will hesitate to venture beyond his comfort zone. Why, because of fear.

'The sheer wonder of the world overwhelms many minds and they crawl back into their shells, and at the same time will like to think that since they can't know, it's impossible for anyone in this world to, especially what would happen to us after we leave this one. People like this don't know that they have to get wet if they want to swim. You follow every mystery out there without bias and let the result speak for itself, without any preconceived notion.

'Even that will disappear in the face of what you experience. But these couch potatoes will rather wait for death before trying to know or have a little bit of understanding why we are here. They expend their energy on the impermanence. And to the people who think they have answers to all the mysteries of life from their religious guru's mouth, but fail to question the love and fairness of their God...mmm, well, it's like taking money for your health from the mafia; blood money. I strongly think the search should continue...!'

He paused from thinking about this and that. He was killing too many brain cells, time to listen to some radio. He loved the radio.

He turned it on and a commercial was on, talking about a magic pill to lose weight just like the magic pill to go to heaven. He changed the station and yet another commercial. Was he ever going to listen to some music? Maybe God was punishing him. As he tried to change the station again something stopped him and he increased the volume.

"To be a religious leader, these are the tools you need. Send $10,000 or use your Visa or MasterCard. No money back because our product works and no discount or coupon, either.

"First, take from existing religion and claim you get revelation from that God.

Or second, start your own. That might be difficult. So we advice you stick to the first method.

"Third, condemn other denominations in that religion. It's how you'll survive, and then claim that yours is the only way now.

"Fourth, have a bunch of rituals or prayer sessions different from the others, and you can even borrow. Nobody will be any the wiser, besides, it adds legitimacy.

"Fifth, claim to talk to The Maker on a regular basis.

"Sixth, put the fear of punishment (hell) into every one, every time you open your mouth.

"Seventh, remember to tell them they can't question or have doubts about anything you say, always to respect you.

"Eighth, chastise them severely if they disobey you. You'll need a scapegoat to show who is the boss. And remember to change some of the laws.

"Ninth, forever preach how wonderful heaven will be. That's where you're taking your followers. They don't need proof now.

"Tenth, tell them always to defend their faith till they die, the faith that you have planted in their heads.

"Remember, proof comes after death. You are home free.

My man, it's as easy as taking a Dollar bill from a baby.

Your clientele will grow and they will include philosophers, psychiatrists, doctors, lawyers, judges, scientists, old, young, inventors, students, presidents, criminals, politicians, military officers, prisoners, clowns, actors, writers, agents, publishers, inspirational speakers. Boy oh boy, the list goes on. They will argue amongst themselves forever; nevertheless, they will always donate. They won't even know when you die. Just send the money and we'll train you. Remember, the end is near."

He was laughing hard. Thank goodness he did not turn off the radio.

Bob was jolted back to reality when the driver coming behind him was honking his horn. The traffic was light now. He pressed the pedal and home was like five minutes away.

He ran upstairs.

"Ruth, Ruth." There was no answer.

Not knowing what to do next, he decided to take a nap. He hoped nothing bad had happened to his wife.

His wife gently woke him up.

"Bob, wake up, it's almost 6.30. Wake up honey, your big project is today, rise and shine."

He turned around to look at her with eyelids trying to open like flowers in the spring.

"Thanks."

"You're welcome."

As he struggled to get out of bed a paper fell. But he didn't notice it.

Ruth picked it up to see what was written on it. Before she could make sense of it, Bob recalled that he had a wonderful dream.

"Honey, I had the most amazing dream, ever." He said.

He sat his wife down and told her in brief; the crux of the matter.

"Whoa!"

"You can say that again." He replied.

"So, what do you think now about everything?" She asked curiously.

"I don't know...I think man is growing in consciousness to know good, real good, not superficial. I mean love...real love."

He was excited about the whole dream and didn't know how to respond calmly.

"I hope you're right." Ruth said.

"I hope so, too."

"So, what's this paper that fell from you?" She asked.

He suddenly stopped paying any attention to her. He was trying to figure out what was with the door that led nowhere but suddenly opened.

"Look, this fell from you." She gently hit him with the piece of paper to get his attention.

"What is it? Can I see it?"

She straightened out the sheet and read it to him. But her words seemed to have no sound.

As he sat there it dawned on him.

'Man has always wanted to pierce the unknown with his instrument or with his mind or spirit, and yet no one has a road map; is it outside us or right within, can it be seen or touched? Yet no matter what we do the quest of the unknown beckons us whether we belong to a sect or not. The fearless and the adventurous dare to search amidst the chaos of the mind, and yet there is no promise of ever finding it; no assurance. And all over the bones and flesh of seekers liter the grounds that lead to the unknown. But one thing is certain; that's discarding the half-truth, the no-truth, the man made truth, the lies, the fears, the empty promises, the comfort zone and, the only instrument with which I will seek the unknown, whether knowable or not, is love, nothing but love as the search light. Life is really a solo voyage from the mysterious, back to the unknown.'

He sat on the bed transfixed like a statue, watching his wife's mouth moving but hearing nothing. Another thought that preoccupied his contemplation was whether he could have been all those people? Life to him became clear as a personal journey in a crowded road. A man of many parts indeed, until he shed all the impurities to arrive at his true self!

"That was on me?" He said after catching a word or two from his wife. He couldn't believe it.

"Yes, darling, it's your handwriting."

Then as he got up, getting ready to take a shower with his wife, he put on the radio. He stood there in his birthday suit waiting for her to do the same, and then his favorite song, *Fantasy*, by Earth, Wind and Fire came on. Needless to say, he knew the song by heart and couldn't wait to sing the last few words...*are you free...yes...I'm free...and I'm on my way...*

> *"The past is needed to be understood in order to comprehend why we think or believe the way we do in the present."*
> *Bob*

> *"The greatest man is he who chooses right with invincible determination."*
> *Seneca.*

The beginning...to a new end.

Acknowledgements

The HOLY BIBLE—Old and New Testaments in the King James Version. Published by Thomas Nelson Publishers.

The Koran by N.J. Dawood. Published by Penguingroup.

The Torah.

The Baha'I holy book.

The gospel according to Judas by Benjanmin Iscariot; Jeffrey Archer.